Development Policy in the Twenty-first Century

In the 1980s development policy and debate was dominated by the neo-liberal *Washington consensus*, heavily promoted in theory and practice by the World Bank and the IMF. Under mounting criticism of the Washington institutions, the mid-1990s witnessed a shift in stance of the World Bank to embrace what has become known as the *post-Washington consensus*. This book constitutes a critical assessment of the new position by comparison both with the old consensus and, more importantly, in the context of the broader development studies literature.

The old consensus set an agenda of market versus state and, in the ideological climate determined by Ronald Reagan and Margaret Thatcher, leaned exclusively on the side of the market. The new consensus, pioneered by the World Bank's then Chief Economist, Joseph Stiglitz, has claimed to be more state and people friendly, although the policy shifts have, in the view of the editors, been negligible. Across the issues addressed – finance, industry, privatisation, education and agriculture – the book argues that the attempt by the new consensus to broaden the scope and analytical content of development studies is a failure because it employs the same reductionist analytical framework as its neo-liberal predecessor.

Development Policy in the Twenty-first Century is unique in its depth and assesses the postures of the new consensus topic by topic, while posing strong alternatives. It will improve and stimulate the reader's understanding of this very important subject and is highly recommended to advanced students and professionals studying, or otherwise involved with, development economics, studies and policy.

Ben Fine is Professor of Economics, **Costas Lapavitsas** is Senior Lecturer in Economics and **Jonathan Pincus** is Lecturer in Economics. All three editors are based at the School of Oriental and African Studies (SOAS), University of London.

Routledge Studies in Development Economics

Development Policy in the Twenty-first Century

Beyond the post-Washington consensus

Edited by
Ben Fine, Costas Lapavitsas
and Jonathan Pincus

Routledge
Taylor & Francis Group

LONDON AND NEW YORK

First published in hardback 2001 by Routledge
11 New Fetter Lane, London EC4P 4EE

First published in paperback 2003

Simultaneously published in the USA and Canada
by Routledge
29 West 35th Street, New York, NY 10001

Routledge is an imprint of the Taylor & Francis Group

Typeset in Garamond by Taylor & Francis Books Ltd
Printed and bound in Great Britain by MPG Books Ltd, Bodmin,
Cornwall

British Library Cataloguing in Publication Data
A catalogue record for this book is available from the British Library

Library of Congress Cataloging in Publication Data
Development policy in the 21st century: beyond the post-
Washington consensus / edited by Ben Fine, Costas Lapavitsas,
Jonathan Pincus.
　　p.cm – (Routledge studies in development economics)
　　Includes bibliographical references and index.
　　1. Developing countries–Economics policy. 2. Economic
forecasting–Developing countries. 3. Development
economics–Developing countries. I. Title: Development policy in
the twenty-first century. II. Fine, Ben. III. Lapavitsas, Costas,
1961– IV. Pincus, Jonathan. V. Series.

ISBN 0–415–22822–0 (hbk)
ISBN 0–415–30618–3 (pbk)

Contents

Illustrations

Tables

Figures

Contributors

Sedat Aybar is currently undertaking PhD research at the School of Oriental and African Studies, University of London.

Kate Bayliss is Research Fellow, Public Services International Research Unit (PSIRU), University of Greenwich, London.

Christopher Cramer is Lecturer in Economics at the School of Oriental and African Studies, University of London.

Sonali Deraniyagala is Lecturer in Economics at the School of Oriental and African Studies, University of London.

Ben Fine is Professor of Economics at the School of Oriental and African Studies, University of London.

Mushtaq H. Khan is Lecturer in Economics at the School of Oriental and African Studies, University of London.

Costas Lapavitsas is Senior Lecturer in Economics at the School of Oriental and African Studies, University of London.

Dic Lo is Lecturer in Economics at the School of Oriental and African Studies, University of London.

Jonathan Pincus is Lecturer in Economics at the School of Oriental and African Studies, University of London.

Pauline Rose is a Research Officer at the Institute of Development Studies, Sussex.

Preface to the paperback edition

The appearance of this edition reflects the success of the hardback volume that sold out within a year. Growing dissatisfaction with the neo-liberal Washington consensus has promoted enormous interest in, and support for, the post Washington consensus, PWC. Any book that addresses it, critically or otherwise, is guaranteed a modicum of commercial success. In rhetoric and scholarship, it is increasingly difficult to find those who are prepared to admit to having been hard-line neo-liberals in the past let alone now to subscribe to the virtues of the unfettered market.

Of course, policy is a different matter and, as emphasised throughout the volume, whatever the path taken by, and the corresponding vices and virtues of, the PWC as rhetoric and scholarship, it only has a loose and shifting relationship to policy. In a nutshell, structural adjustment and stabilisation were always previously marked by extensive discretionary intervention under the perverse neo-liberal ideology of non-intervention. The PWC has, if anything, witnessed an extension and deepening of intervention, and otherwise of much the same type as under the Washington consensus. Plus ça change, toujours la même chose as far as policy is concerned. Not surprisingly, the instigator and leading exponent of the PWC, Joe Stiglitz, had to go from his position at the World Bank, once his analysis (and personal intellectual integrity) led him to proffer alternative policies in practice to those being put in place by his employer and its paymaster, the US Treasury.

But policy as such is not the main focus of the book. It is more about how development and development policy are (to be) understood. From an early stage, our concern was that the PWC was liable, on the wave of discontent with the Washington consensus, to establish itself as a new orthodoxy, more powerful and widespread in appeal than its predecessor, and absorbing or suffocating opposition and alternatives. This prognosis was based upon a broader understanding of the intellectual environment, going beyond the recognised fatigue with neo-liberalism in the development field. For the rise to prominence of concepts such as globalisation and social capital in the 1990s has signified a growing impatience with the extreme excesses of both neo-liberalism and postmodernism, a genuine concern to get to grips with the nature of contemporary capitalism and the systemic sources of uneven development. On the other hand, there has been the colonisation of the other social sciences by economics on the basis of the economic and the non-economic as the rational, collective, path-dependent evolved responses to market, especially informational, imperfections. This has been one, limited, response to the demands for a more worldly approach to political economy and development studies.

Even in the short time since the book first appeared, these perspectives have been borne out. There is no better way of illustrating this than through the bizarre trajectory taken by Joseph Stiglitz. Sacked by the World Bank, he is awarded the Nobel Prize for economics, for asymmetric information and his part in establishing modern development economics. In countries as far apart as China and South Africa, he is viewed as a heroic figure in the struggle against poverty. The World Bank continues to exploit his name and prestige to promote its own publications. And Stiglitz sees himself as engaging in a crusade to establish an alternative to neo-liberal dogma, of forging a new paradigm that is in opposition to mainstream economics. Indeed, despite having himself published hundreds of articles in main-stream, neoclassical journals, he asserts the need for a new journal, as well as for scholarships and tenured academic positions for those wedded to the (not so) new paradigm. Indeed, he argues, "the time for challenging the current reigning paradigm may be ripe, as dissatisfaction with globalization grows, and the spotlight placed on it has highlighted many of its deficiencies", Stiglitz (2001).

The reference to "globalization" is, however, purely rhetorical as it must be. The information-theoretic approach to globalisation is incapable of understanding it in holistic, systemic terms, of going beyond the dull incidence of market and institutional imperfections. Necessarily, for the PWC, globalisation is the piecemeal opening of national economies. Chang (ed) (2001) usefully collects together nine major papers delivered by Stiglitz, since his launching of the PWC. Although one chapter is devoted to the global development network, the volume's index has only one entry for globalisation. Without a hint of self-irony, Stiglitz observes, p. 192:

> It has become a cliché to refer to the new globalized economy. Yet the fact is, reductions in transport and communication costs have been accompanied by reductions in government-created impediments to the free flow of ideas, goods, and capital. We do live in a more integrated economic community.

He continues, p. 193:

> In approaching the challenges of globalization, we must eschew ideology and over-simplified models ... I believe that there are reforms to the international economic architecture that can bring the advantages

of globalization, including global capital markets, while mitigating their risks.

The point of these quotations is not so much to press the PWC for a fuller and more radical understanding of globalisation, not least because the notion has itself become chaotic and all-encompassing. Rather, it is to observe that, if pressed, globalisation proves an embarrassment to the PWC. Its doing so is indicative of the new paradigm's inability to address the common concerns and methodologies of much social science and political economy, those that deal in relations, powers, conflicts, structures and processes beyond the confines of the market and/or institutional coordination of individual interactions.

In this light, when the new orthodoxy or paradigm claims to be marginalised, it is time to worry about the fate of heterodoxy. Two concerns are of particular importance for development economics and studies. First is the extent to which much radical, oppositional scholarship, and the corresponding scholars themselves, are being reinvented in the image of the PWC. It is, for example, as if opposition to the Washington Consensus began with the PWC and is reducible to it. All that state versus market stuff, adjustment with a human face, the Asian miracle, etc, etc, is simply rerun through the filter of market imperfections. Second, over a longer time horizon, the history of development studies is itself being rediscovered and, equally, reinvented. The classics (rarely venturing back to classical political economy) from the immediate post-war period are perceived to have been inappropriately abandoned, Krugman (n.d.). They were unlucky for having been insufficiently mathematically precise and too radical to conform with the prejudices of mainstream economics – although the Keynesianism/ welfarism/modernisation with which they are often associated is far more radical than the tentative interventionism of the PWC. Now, the classics are to be rehabilitated. This merely serves to add the authority of the rediscovered past, rather than to draw upon genuine insights and add anything in substance to the new paradigm that is not already there.

In brief, the PWC seeks to command development studies in the same way and as part of the more general colonisation of the social sciences by the information-theoretic approach. As such it peddles an understanding of the economy, and of the relationship between the economic and the non-economic, that needs to be challenged by all social scientists genuinely concerned with the political economy of development and of development policy. This book is a small, initial step in posing alternatives to the newly emerging orthodoxy. Hopefully, it will inspire others to follow suit.

References

Chang, H-J. (ed) (2001) *Joseph Stiglitz and the World Bank: The Rebel Within*, London: Anthem Press.

Krugman, P. (n.d.) "The Fall and Rise of Development Economics", http://www/wws/edu/~pkrugman/dishpan.html

Stiglitz, J. (2001) "An Agenda for the New Development Economics", paper to UNRISD meeting on "The Need to Rethink Development Economics", Cape Town, September, http://www.unrisd.org/engindex/research/rethink.htm

Preface

For much of the 1980s and 1990s, the Washington consensus dominated development theory and policy. The term, coined in the late 1980s, denoted a series of measures that were presumed to lead developing countries to greater wealth and prosperity. The suggested measures were a natural outgrowth of the neo-liberal policy framework that already held sway in the developed world: fiscal and monetary austerity, elimination of government subsidies, moderate taxation, freeing of interest rates, lowering of exchange rates, liberalisation of foreign trade, privatisation, deregulation and encouragement of foreign direct investment. Free-market economics, with a strong US flavour, would take care of the problems of developing countries.

Two factors facilitated the global ascendancy of the Washington consensus. The first was the final demise of the development ideology and practice of the 1950s and 1960s. Import substitution, five-year plans, government ownership and control of strategic industries, regulation of the labour market and state controls over the flows of saving and investment seemed less effective at delivering growth in the 1970s and 1980s. This battery of policies – which drew inspiration, directly or indirectly, from the success of Soviet industrialisation in the inter-war years – had lost prestige and influence by the mid-1980s. The advancing crisis of the Eastern bloc, moreover, meant that resources for developing countries in Africa, Asia, the Middle East and Latin America were not going to come from 'actually existing socialist countries'. The final collapse of the bloc, especially that of the Soviet Union, appeared to signal the complete triumph of capitalism and the free market. Washington was the undisputed political, economic and ideological centre of the world.

The second factor was active advocacy of the prescriptive recommendations of the Washington consensus by the international Washington organisations, above all the IMF and the World Bank. By the late 1980s, the fundamental ideas of the consensus had become 'orthodox economics' for the thousands of economists employed by, and otherwise attached to, these organisations. What other view of the world could be 'rational', or should be taken seriously? Here was the cream of Western (mostly USA-trained) academe developing theory and formulating policy in full command of all economic knowledge that was worth knowing. To oppose the Washington consensus, as plenty did, both in theory and in practice, was to demonstrate plain ignorance or, worse, obtuseness. And in any case, if the effortless intellectual superiority of Western-trained economists were not enough to persuade developing countries to wear the hair shirt, a simple lever was available to force them to do so: conditionality. Loans by both the IMF and the World Bank came to be dependent on adopting policies consistent with the consensus. The debt crisis of the 1980s had severely limited the room of developing countries to manoeuvre in negotiations with international organisations. Pressure to comply was applied in the hundreds of polite and brutal ways so familiar to international bureaucrats.

The 1990s, however, have not been kind to the Washington consensus. Fiscal and monetary conservatism might be claimed to have achieved greater price stability in some developing countries, but that was just about the only possible success of consensus-inspired policies. Growth outcomes were deeply disappointing and, to add insult to injury, typically below the levels of the derided 1950s and 1960s. Poverty reduction made little headway, according to the calculations of the World Bank itself. Vast swathes of humanity have continued to survive on the equivalent of a dollar a day, or less. Worse, the elimination of restrictions on domestic finance and on international capital flows resulted in huge global crises but did not succeed in enhancing volume and efficiency of productive investment. Last but not least, the transformation of Eastern bloc countries into capitalist market economies on the basis of the prescriptions of the Washington consensus can only be described as an abject failure.

Until 1997, the only part of the world that appeared to have escaped from the blight afflicting developing countries was East and South East Asia, including China. For much of the 1970s, 1980s and 1990s, growth rates across the region approached double figures. However, here was an evident paradox: development success appeared to rest on conditions that contradicted several of the prescriptions at the heart of the Washington consensus. True, the states of the region were typically conservative in the fiscal sphere, but they also tightly controlled domestic finance, imposed restrictions on imports, often discouraged foreign direct investment, controlled international capital flows, regulated several domestic markets and owned significant parts of the national productive capacity. That is not to say that they did not participate in the world market – they did and avidly so, but on terms which they manipulated in their favour. The Asian tigers seemed to create their own comparative advantage in the world market.

Thus, the intellectual and policy pre-eminence of the Washington consensus was short-lived. Already by the second half of the 1990s, dissatisfaction with its dry certainties emerged even within the privileged circles of Washington. The failure of the consensus occurred at a time when information-theoretic and transactions-costs-theoretic analyses have become prominent within economic theory. This has important implications for the gradually emerging successor to the old consensus. It is now widely accepted among the neo-classical economists who populate universities and international organisations that, though markets are by far the most efficient social mechanisms for allocating resources and maximising social welfare, information asymmetries among market participants and inescapable transactions costs decisively limit market efficiency. Put differently, cost and information externalities result in market failure. Now, in itself, the recognition of market failure as a result of externalities is neither particularly radical nor particularly novel. Still, the conclusion that economists presently draw from it represents a sharp rupture within mainstream theory, namely that institutions are pivotal to the efficient functioning of markets.

Institutions (such as the government and the various branches of the civil service), and non-market factors more generally, are now thought to play a prime role in facilitating information flows and in lessening transactions costs. They make the difference between well-functioning markets and markets prone to disequilibrium. They could allow the private returns from economic activity to approximate more closely the social returns, which might be different as a result of externalities. Institutions could even create markets where none would have emerged spontaneously. It is now hard to come across an economist who does not pay at least lip service to the importance of institutions; though precious few of them have any notion of how to construct the various institutions that are supposed to be so vital to the efficient functioning of markets. Perhaps the most bizarre aspect of the rediscovery of institutions by the orthodoxy is that economic theory has remained characteristically blind to the fact that the market is itself an institution. It is still an article of faith among economists that commodity exchange is an inherent part of the interaction among human beings in a state of nature. The social conditions that make possible the emergence of the institution of generalised market exchange, such as class structure and access to the means of production, remain a closed book for the mainstream.

Be that as it may, market failure and institutions played no significant role in the Washington consensus. The emergent post-Washington consensus inevitably based itself on them. The new consensus, if such it can be called, is still an inchoate current of thought, possessing none of the prescriptive – and profoundly misleading – sharpness of the Washington consensus. However, acknowledgement of the importance of institutions in economic activity has led the mainstream to recognise that social factors are decisive for success in development. Once institutions are discovered, it is natural to enquire into the social junctures within which they operate, the articulation of interests they express and their interaction with each other. Development thus emerges as a complex social process that involves more than growth of per capita income or increases in consumption. It entails changes in the distribution of property rights over resources, alterations in the patterns of work, increasing urbanisation, as well as transformation of the family's productive and reproductive activities. In short, development represents profound social change and has to be analysed as such.

It is imperative to stress that the gradually forming post-Washington consensus remains deeply conservative in fiscal and monetary matters; it does not in principle oppose liberalisation and deregulation, and it is broadly in favour of free trade and privatisation. The difference from the previous consensus lies perhaps in the following two elements. The first is advocacy of a 'milder' opening of the economy to the dictates of the market, drawing upon the analysis of market failure. Room is left for interventionist policy by the state, in so far as such policies deal with market imperfections, thus improving the performance of the market system as a whole. However, the areas and the limits of these interventions are not clearly specified. In the same vein, institutions are proclaimed vital for development success, particularly those relating to the financial sector, which is especially prone to market failure. Specific policy recommendations to developing countries on how to build the required institutions are not forthcoming. Note that these institutions in the sphere of finance alone could range from an exchange commission, which does little more than set and police clear rules of market participation, to a ministry of finance, which could intervene in the allocation of credits and in determination of interest rates. The demarcation lines among acceptable and non-acceptable activities by the institutions, which are presumably necessary for development success, are far from clear. Inevitably, the policy prescriptions of the new consensus are more vague and less explicit than those of the old.

The second element is an emphasis on the non-economic 'glue' that holds society together. The concept of social capital is of critical importance in this connection. This rather badly thought out notion is now used by social scientists as an envelope term for a vast array of social relations: membership of clubs, undertaking of communal activities, partaking of information networks, participation in civic organisations, fostering of ethnic rivalries and so on. Indeed, any social relation that does not directly fall within the purview of the market and the economy is included in social capital. In a broad and general way, social capital is thought to influence the development path of a country – not enough of it (or plenty but of bad quality, as, for instance, in crime-ridden countries) could jeopardise development prospects. It is apparent that, in this connection too, there are no clear policy prescriptions readily available to the post-Washington consensus, other than very long-term ones.

Nevertheless, the post-Washington consensus represents a welcome advance for social scientists concerned with development. The emphasis on market failure and the rediscovery of social relations, even in the unsatisfactory form of social capital, are far removed from the dogmatism and intellectual poverty of the Washington consensus. After a long period of treating development as a technical problem of growth in macro-economic aggregates, which could be tackled by the freeing of markets, social science seems to have awakened to the realisation that development is a process of profound social transformation. To analyse such social transformation, political economy is necessary, rather than plain economics. The post-Washington consensus implicitly recognises this, since it engages in political economy of institutions and seeks to employ the concept of social capital. However, the version of political economy deployed by the emerging consensus is lifeless and unconvincing. Information asymmetries and transactions costs are inadequate theoretical principles on which to base analysis of the process of development. The concept of social class is also necessary, as are those of generation of economic surplus, its division among classes and its utilisation for consumption and investment. More broadly, the concept of social reproduction is vital in analysis of the social relations to be found at the workplace, in agriculture, in the schools, within the family, in state organisations and between state institutions and enterprises. Development is reproduction of society on a different level and in a 'modern' way, implying radical transformations in all these social relations.

Put differently, development is a social process that calls for an analytical approach that would have been familiar to classical political economists, as well as their chief critic, Marx. After all, classical political economy emerged precisely on the cusp of transformation of Western Europe from an agrarian society into modern industrial capitalism. For Marxist political economy, in particular, issues such as the role of institutions, social relations, the methods of state intervention and the non-economic underpinnings of markets were never absent from its analytical framework. Furthermore, these issues are evidently contingent on historical events. By this token, development theory needs to recognise the specificity of the historical experience of each individual country. History, from this perspective, is not treated as simple accumulation of chance events, a register of accidental shocks or mere 'path dependency'. History is also a record of interaction among the various social classes, with all their inevitable conflicts, alliances and temporary truces. The development direction that a country is likely to follow depends on the balance of forces among its social classes, and that is an outcome of its history. The post-Washington consensus offers no analysis of this kind, but at least it promotes recognition of the importance of the social and historical context of development. Thus, it opens room for the required political economy of development.

This book is a collection of papers first presented at a recent seminar series on the post-Washington Consensus held at the School of Oriental and African Studies (SOAS) of the University of London. As Europe's leading centre for the study of Asia and Africa, SOAS is home to a diverse group of researchers specialising in the history, society and culture of the developing world. The Economics Department, which sponsored the post-Washington consensus series, is unique in the UK, and perhaps the world, in its emphasis on the importance of the specific historical and social context of individual countries to the development process. Nearly every member of staff is fluent in at least one African or Asian language, and all have extensive research experience in their regions of expertise. Members of the department, both students and staff, thus share an approach to the political economy of development based on a common appreciation of the embeddedness of social phenomena within the historically specific conditions of real people and places.

The nine chapters of the book tackle various aspects of the emerging post-Washington consensus and reflect the concern to build and criticise theory on the basis of strong empirical foundations. Ben Fine's introduction to the volume traces the intellectual roots of the post-Washington consensus and assesses its likely impact on development studies. One of the most disturbing features of the new consensus is that, although it attempts to broaden the theoretical agenda of development economics, it does so within the same narrow, reductionist framework of its neo-liberal predecessor. The result is therefore not a more heterodox economics, but rather a more aggressive *neo-classical* economics that now possesses the self-confidence (if not the analytical tools) to take its colonising mission to the other social sciences. Aybar and Lapavitsas reach similar conclusions in their chapter on financial system design: although the asymmetric information paradigm adds some subtlety to the dominant neo-classical approach to financial systems, it remains unwilling, and perhaps unable, to address the specific historical and structural factors that shape the relationship between finance and industrial development in individual countries. Cramer and Bayliss's analysis of the evolution of the World Bank's privatisation policy from the 1980s to the present raises parallel concerns. Neither the old nor the new consensus can provide a convincing theoretical justification for the 'blanket' approach pursued by the Bank: privatisation should not be treated as a synonym for increased efficiency and competitiveness. The authors argue instead for a case-specific approach that views privatisation as one policy tool among many within the broader context of the social, economic and political dimensions of industrial policy.

Industrial policy is also the subject of Chapters 4 and 5. Sonali Deraniyagala examines the relevant literature and searches in vain for significant differences between the Washington and post-Washington policy prescriptions. However, a consistent source of cognitive dissonance for orthodox theorists has been the countries of East and South East Asia: first as examples of successful state intervention in trade and industrial policy; and second, after 1997, as a graphic illustration of the hazards of financial-sector liberalisation. Dic Lo surveys the terrain and concludes that despite the fanfare surrounding the post-Washington consensus, the Washington institutions still adhere to a superficial view of economic institutions in the region based largely on a textbook notion of what constitutes the 'natural path' of development.

The assumption in the literature of the Washington institutions that liberalisation of one form or another is the natural cure for dysfunctional institutions reappears in Mushtaq Khan's chapter on the political economy of corruption. Khan points out that liberalisation is not only an insufficient response to endemic corruption but in some cases may actually exacerbate the problem depending on the distribution of political and class power. Mainstream approaches, both old and new, have failed because they seek uniform solutions to what is in fact a range of separate problems faced by specific countries.

For some, the World Bank's adoption of 'social capital' as a necessary complement to physical and human capital signalled a new willingness on the part of the Washington institutions to take the social and political dimensions of development seriously. Ben Fine is not convinced. In his chapter on 'The social capital of the World Bank' he argues that this incursion of orthodox economics into the realm of social theory is an offensive, rather than defensive, move. As long as the orthodoxy is unwilling to revisit its core assumptions, the incorporation of the social will not yield a more progressive analytical or policy agenda.

Similarly, in their chapter on the World Bank's approach to education, Fine and Rose examine the implications of what they term the Bank's 'obsessive attachment to human capital theory'. The obsession has grown more compulsive under Stiglitz's tutelage owing to the real or imagined linkages between his economics of information and investment in education. The main appeal of human capital theory – like the concept of social capital – is that it allows orthodox economics to handle complex social phenomena using the familiar tools of micro-economics. However, as Fine and Rose explain, these metaphors quickly become overloaded, and eventually collapse under the weight of their own contradictions. For human capital theory the moment of absurdity arrives when education systems, abstracted from their specific social and historical contexts, are called upon to explain social and economic phenomena ranging from savings behaviour to fertility rates.

The final chapter of the book turns from economic theory to the implications of theory for the World Bank as a public-sector lending institution. Pincus reviews the evolution of the World Bank's approach to rural development, and finds that change is easier to effect in the virtual world of development rhetoric than in the concrete world of lending operations.

It is a sombre, although perhaps apt, note on which to conclude that, whatever its development theory and rhetoric, the post-Washington consensus remains remarkably remote as far as policy stances in Africa, Eastern Europe and elsewhere are concerned. The dissonance between policy rhetoric and practice has already been felt within the World Bank with the resignations of Joseph Stiglitz, Chief Economist at the World Bank and pioneer of the post-Washington consensus, and Ravi Kanbur, lead author of the figurehead 2000 *World Development Report on Poverty*. This draws a postscript commentary to Chapter 1.

Ben Fine
Costas Lapavitsas
Jonathan Pincus
SOAS, November 2000

1 Neither the Washington nor the post-Washington consensus

An introduction[1]

Ben Fine

In 1994 the World Bank and the IMF marked the fiftieth anniversary of their founding meeting at Bretton Woods. The occasion was hardly one of celebration for the two Washington institutions with which official post-war international financial arrangements are most closely identified. This was because, paradoxically, in the lengthy wake of the Uruguay round of the GATT, the World Trade Organization was looming on the horizon, signifying the long delayed but culminating success in creating the trade counterpart to the financial institutions. In contrast, the prospects and standing of the IMF and the World Bank were at their lowest ever ebb. The institutions' own activity around their anniversary was muted, introspective and defensive.[2] To some extent, this was a consequence of what has been termed an 'identity crisis'.[3] It was made up of a number of elements. The neo-liberal Washington consensus, in favour of the market and antagonistic to the state, was at its height. However, the institutions were clearly failing to deliver in terms of economic development and stabilisation. As de Vries (1996, p. 65) reported:

> After more than fifty years of operations, the Bank still faces a world where over 1 billion people live in deep poverty, with per capita income of less than a dollar per day. Many countries suffer poverty rates between 25 and 50 per cent of their population. These conditions persist despite important improvements in critical social indicators such as life expectancy, infant mortality, access to safe water, primary school enrollment and immunization.

Criticisms were mounting around the environment and women, quite apart from poverty, and the more general efficacy and impact of the adjustment policies being advocated, even imposed, by the Bank and the IMF.

From the right, the ideology of *laissez-faire* was inevitably being pushed to its logical conclusion – the negative impact and futility of the interventions of the Washington institutions themselves. Far more telling, however, was the growing weight of criticism emanating from development academics and practitioners, evidenced by the titles of their work – such as

Beyond Bretton Woods: Alternatives to the Global Economic Order, Fifty Years is Enough: The Case against the World Bank and the International Monetary Fund, A Case for Reform: Fifty Years of the IMF and World Bank and *The Globalisation of Poverty: Impacts of IMF and World Bank Reforms.*[4]

The fiftieth anniversary coincided with the convergence of an increasingly dogmatic neo-liberal posture, the stubborn failure of adjustment policies and mounting criticism to which response was at best limited in scope. The situation was in one sense suitably symbolised by the World Bank's report, *The East Asian Miracle* (1993). In the report, the success of the Asian tigers was reduced to the Bank's extensive interventions being equivalent, where successful, to what the market would have done if working properly; it drew the conclusion of non-replicability in other countries. The 'developmental state', associated so closely with East Asian success outside the World Bank and IMF, was not so much dead as undead – from the neo-liberal perspective only ever having been alive as a parasite on the market.

However, the unadulterated market had passed its sell-by date. Even looking back today, after the passage of only a few years, both the status and the stance of the Washington institutions look completely different, albeit with the World Bank leaping ahead of the IMF, which continues to drag its feet. The World Bank's renewed commitment to poverty alleviation, its more favourable attitude towards the state and its less dogmatic rhetoric have endeared it to the donor community. The report on the East Asian miracle can now be read in retrospect not so much as simply reaffirming the market but more as a renewal of a belief in the role of the state. In this light, if a single event can be pinpointed as having prompted the motivation for this sea change, it is that provided by the remarkable speech made by Joseph Stiglitz (1998) in early 1998. Here, even more than is suggested by the title of his talk, 'More instruments and broader goals: Moving toward the post-Washington consensus', Stiglitz was seeking to establish a new agenda for economic development. He deliberately perceived himself not only as broadening the scope of policy making in terms of goals and instruments but also as placing such policy making on a sounder understanding of how the economy, and especially markets, work or, equally importantly, do not work. Broadly, then, Stiglitz explicitly rejected the Washington consensus and offered a post-Washington consensus in its place. This proposed intellectual and policy watershed did not emanate from some disillusioned academic or NGO activist. Stiglitz was serving as Senior Vice President and Chief Economist to the World Bank as well as having previously chaired the US Council of Economic Advisors. In short, the Washington consensus was under assault from within. For Stiglitz (1998, p. 1):[5]

[The Washington consensus] held that good economic performance required liberalized trade, macroeconomic stability, and getting prices right. Once the government handled these issues – essentially once the government 'got out of the way' – private markets would produce efficient allocations and growth .... But the policies advanced by the Washington consensus are hardly complete and sometimes misguided. Making markets work requires more than just low inflation, it requires sound financial regulation, competition policy, and policies to facilitate the transfer of technology, to name some fundamental issues neglected by the Washington consensus.

The Washington consensus had emerged in the early 1980s as the neo-liberal counterpart for developing economies to the Reaganism and Thatcherism that had been prescribed for developed economies – an ideology of reliance upon market forces, and of the reduction of state intervention and expenditure to a minimum. It has had the effect of posing economic issues in terms of the state versus the market, leaning heavily, or falling over, in favour of the market. Opposition to the consensus (and it has been extensive) has, however, often been induced to accepting the terms of debate dictated by the consensus – to counterposing the state and the market, and to favouring state intervention whether in getting prices wrong, picking winners or guiding the private sector through public expenditure. In contrast, for Stiglitz (1998, p. 25):[6]

> Trying to get government better focused on the fundamentals – economic policies, basic education, health, roads, law and order, environmental protection – is a vital step. But focusing on the fundamentals is not a recipe for a minimalist government. The state has an important role to play in appropriate regulation, industrial policy, social protection and welfare. But the choice is not whether the state should or should not be involved. Instead, it is often a matter of how it gets involved. More importantly, we should not see the state and markets as substitutes ... the government should see itself as a complement to markets, undertaking those actions that make markets fulfil their functions better.

In this light, Stiglitz's proposal for a post-Washington consensus builds upon, accelerates and leaps ahead of the earlier, painfully slow, intellectual and ideological shifts that could already be detected as present within the World Bank over the last few years. The changing approach was barely discernible in the process leading to the production of the World Bank's *The East Asian Miracle* (1993)[7], and has subsequently gathered pace through successive versions of the World Bank's annual posture, as presented in its *World Development Report*.[8] From anti-market, through market-conforming, to market-friendly, the state has been seen more positively, if cautiously so. Stiglitz has emerged as the economist at the forefront of the charge, putatively sweeping aside the old consensus and underpinning the new with sound intellectual, policy and ideological credentials.

In short, even before the old consensus has been decently assessed and buried, the pretender to its throne is already grabbing at the crown in a palace revolution. However welcome the demise of the old consensus might be to those who have opposed it for almost two decades, the question of succession needs to be contested. It is not simply a matter of posing alternatives to the new consensus but whether the latter should be allowed to dominate the development agenda – as did its predecessor by posing state versus market. One of the key features of the old consensus has been its almost total neglect both of alternative approaches to the economy and to criticism of its theoretical, empirical and policy stances.[9] As will be seen, the proposed post-Washington consensus is based upon the need to acknowledge and address market imperfections. As such, it broadens the analytical and policy scope that it encompasses relative to the earlier consensus. However, by the same token, it does so by completely by-passing all criticism of its predecessor that is not based on an approach tied to its own understanding of market imperfections, and it precludes such approaches as alternatives for future perspectives. As will be seen, the new consensus deploys more variables on a wider scope and less dogmatically than the old. Nevertheless, its intellectual narrowness and reductionism remain striking, for it replaces an understanding of the economy as relying harmoniously on the market by an understanding of society as a whole based on (informational) market imperfections.

Intellectual foundations

The intellectual basis for the new consensus is readily identified, not least through the work of Stiglitz himself over the past two decades. Essentially, the motivating idea is very old – that market imperfections can justify state intervention to rectify them, although, in the wake of the Washington consensus, the state is no longer seen as the source of an all powerful and benevolent corrective. State failure must be no worse than the market failure it is designed to remedy. Traditionally, market imperfections have been seen in terms of the conditions under which a perfectly functioning market fails to prevail – as for the presence of externalities, increasing returns to scale or monopoly pricing. The new twist, however, is to broaden the scope of what goes into the making of market imperfections. These now include informational imperfections and asymmetries of various sorts, including the presence of transactions costs, so that market outcomes depend upon who has what information before, during and after the economy's passages in and out of exchange.

Stiglitz (1994) provides a typical example, drawn from the labour market. Employers might know the average productivity of all workers but not that of individual workers. If a less productive worker decides to join the labour market or to work for longer hours for whatever reason, the average productivity of all workers is reduced, thereby lowering the incentive of employers as a whole to take on workers. It is as if there is an externality, for employers behave as if the quality of all workers has been lowered even if this is not the case (p. 58):

> The unproductive worker, in deciding to work more hours, lowered the mean quality of those offering themselves in the labour market and thus exerted a negative externality on others.

Such an insight is far from novel, not least in the context of an industry, for example, that seeks self- or government regulation to sustain a reputation of quality for itself, thereby excluding 'cowboys' in the building trade or 'lemons' in the second-hand market for cars. The new microeconomics of information is remarkable for seizing upon such ideas, finding as many examples as possible and potentially generalising them across all markets. Market imperfections are pervasive and, when information is imperfect, markets may not operate at efficient levels, they may not clear and they may even fail to exist altogether. Indeed, Stiglitz and various collaborators draw upon formally proven theorems of the type which show that there should always be a mix between the private and public sector, and that the market always works imperfectly in the presence of market imperfections.

In this vein, Stiglitz (1994, p. 5) feels able to make two significant claims. First, he perceives that a new approach to economics has been established which enhances the understanding of how markets work, and which is applicable across a wide range of subject matter:

> During the past fifteen years, a new paradigm, sometimes referred to as the information-theoretic approach to economics ... has developed .... This paradigm has already provided us with insights into development economics and macroeconomics. It has provided us with a new welfare economics, a new theory of the firm, and a new understanding of the role and functioning of financial markets.

Second, Stiglitz counterposes the new paradigm to the old, or that of mainstream neo-classical economics, which is organised around perfectly working markets. This creates the impression of rejecting the old and breaking radically new ground.[10]

Further, the theory suggests imperfect markets in three different ways. As in the case above, the market may clear (supply equals demand) but in an inefficient way – with higher-productivity workers not prepared to work at the lowered average wage of all workers. In addition, the market might not clear (if, for example, employers offer higher wages to attract higher-productivity workers but do not employ all prepared to work at that or even lower wage). Finally, a market may not be formed at all (if employers do not consider that there is a wage at which average quality of, say, young workers coming forward is high enough).

While the example given is from the labour market, the new approach is general and can apply to any market, each of which is liable to have its own type of informational and other market imperfections. These are also presumed to be pervasive in developing countries, giving rise to inefficient, non-clearing or absent markets. While a whole range of new economic applications has been built up on these informational, and other, principles, it is the narrowness of their analytical scope that is breathtakingly presumptuous from the perspective of other approaches, both within economics and other social sciences. For example, many of the references above are drawn from Stiglitz's (1994) consideration of the viability of socialism. While modestly accepting that he is unable to claim to be an expert on the basis of a few visits to socialist economies, the question is reduced to how informational imperfections are handled. The only other work considered on the topic is that which, appropriately or not, can be forced into this analytical framework.[11]

By the same token, the break with mainstream neo-classical economics can only be exaggerated. In any case, the notion of a perfectly working market economy has long been seen by the orthodoxy as the standard against which the real world should be judged rather than as the real world itself – even if the Washington consensus has, in principle, with the triumph of neo-liberalism, sought to distort reality to fit its model.[12] As a matter of policy, it wishes to make the real world conform as far as possible to the fiction of a perfectly functioning market economy. It is hardly novel to have claimed that the market in practice does not and cannot work in an ideal way. Thus, while the introduction of informational imperfections is an innovation, even by Stiglitz's own account, they are equivalent in various ways to standard market imperfections. What is much more important to emphasise is not whether but *how* the model of perfect competition is rejected. What stands out is the extent to which the foundations for the new consensus continue to conform to the methodology of the old and even reinforce the rejection of alternatives. The latter are seen as unnecessary or obfuscating, relative to the analytical power provided by the new information-theoretic economics.

Central in this respect is the reliance upon methodological individualism of the type that is familiar to all students of economics. The economy is made up of an aggregation of individual agents, all of whom maximise utility, even if some do so indirectly through profit maximisation. The only departure from the mainstream is in allowing for imperfect information and, consequently, the result is a generalisation rather than a break with the orthodoxy's perfectly competitive economy. In effect, the latter can be seen as a special case in which information is perfectly known. Deviation from it can only be partially closed by state intervention, given the influences on the functioning of the state itself and the extent of imperfect information in practice.

The broader analytical context

In short, especially in formal modelling, the analytical basis for the post-

Washington consensus is extremely narrow and weak, especially from the perspective of anyone not wedded to mainstream economics. Indeed, it is best seen as resting upon two fundamental characteristics, which can both be understood as reductionist or the interpretation of economic and other social relations through the narrowest of explanatory prisms. On the one hand, there is the reductionism to individual behaviour. On the other hand, there is the reductionism to market imperfections based on informational imperfections. Essentially, the capitalist economy is seen as a construct of imperfectly informed individuals, imperfectly co-ordinated through the market place. It is far from parody to claim that because any outcome can more or less be explained in principle on this basis – the real world is after all an information-theoretic market imperfection – it is not necessary to incorporate any other analytical principles. Indeed, it is simply a matter of identifying in practice the wide variety of informational imperfections and how they are handled in particular contexts. Policy is concerned with handling them better than leaving them to the market.

Such an approach cuts a destructive swathe through the vast majority of social science, including radical political economy. Concepts such as class and power simply cease to have any purchase.[13] The significance of, and shifts in, economic and social structure can only be understood on the basis of microeconomic foundations. The idea of development itself, or the transition from one stage of development to another, is simply reduced to the alternative arrangements for dealing with informationally-based market imperfections (levels of per capita income or productive resources aside).

Now, for many, the remarks in the previous paragraph are surely little more than caricature. The writings of Stiglitz himself, and others in the same vein, are surely more sophisticated and less obsessively reductionist. This is undoubtedly true once moving outside the pure realms of abstract economic theory, but this tends to reflect divergence from the theory itself. This is because, by its very construction, the theory allows for considerable discretion in its application, even in ways that do not necessarily reflect its origins. More concrete or case-specific economic and social phenomena are interpreted informally in terms of better or worse use of information, but are also open to interpretation by incorporating a much wider range of factors. Here, the abstruse mathematical models of neo-classical economics and informational imperfections are unwittingly cunning; for, in view of the universal concepts they employ, like utility, production, inputs, outputs, etc., they are entirely ahistorical and asocial, without time or place. This, then, leaves an empty canvas of market imperfections upon which can be painted more informal and more concrete detail – bringing back in the social, historical, institutional, etc., for which notions like multiple equilibria and path dependence are highly useful.

To pick just one example that neatly mixes the formal and informal, leaps from informational problems to reductionist interpretation and policy making, and is full of criticism of the old consensus, for Stiglitz (1998, pp. 14–15):[14]

Incomplete information, incomplete markets, incomplete contracts are all inevitable features of the economy in general and the financial system in particular. In this circumstance the market outcome is not even constrained Pareto efficient; even a government faced with the same informational constraints as the market would be able to make Pareto improvements – a theorem Bruce Greenwald and I proved a decade ago. The finance system is focused on information problems. That is why it is so important that the government must play an essential role in the regulation of the financial system. For most countries, doing this correctly will entail a sustained regulatory reform over a number of years. In no country does overnight deregulation make sense. In the banking system, effective intermediation requires banking regulations to create incentives for bank owners, markets, and supervisors to all use their information efficiently. In securities markets, laws are required to protect the interests of shareholders, especially of minority shareholders.

Paradoxically, then, the post-Washington consensus is able to be unlimited in its grasp over subject matter precisely because of the narrow limits within which it is economic-reductionist. For example, it can deal with the regulation of the financial system, its efficiency and the protection of shareholders without once mentioning the economic and political power, and structures embodied in a financial system.

In this respect, it is worth setting such new theoretical developments within economics in the broader context of the role of the discipline as a whole. This is because, as argued elsewhere,[15] the relationship between economics and other social sciences is currently undergoing a change. Economics is aggressively seeking to colonise the other social sciences by extending its methods to them, treating non-economic or non-market relations as if they were economic.

This is most apparent in the work of Gary Becker and his followers, who proceed by simply universalising the so-called economic approach based on utility maximisation to all areas of life, including those that are traditionally perceived as lying outside the domain of economics.[16] Considerable advances have been achieved into some of the areas concerned, most notably in the general, and now uncritical, acceptance of the notion of human capital. It is also apparent in the new household economics and the new political economy, or any analysis incorporating simplistic notions of rent-seeking.

A moment's reflection suggests how successful such colonising efforts have been, not least within development economics. As discussed earlier, the informal appropriation of formal results conceals their reductionist content and origins so that concepts such as human capital and rent-seeking have become uncritically received as part of the lexicon of development discourse. It is surely no accident that Stiglitz's counterpart at the World Bank in the 1980s should have been Anne Krueger, who herself can be seen as the counterpart within the field of development economics to Becker. In Krueger's hands, Becker's methods were applied to the problems of development as a rent-seeking world, and policy readily followed as in the ideology of getting the prices right, the levying of user charges and privatisation. The world was to be interpreted as a benevolent market and reduced to it as far as possible, with the reverse for the malevolent non-market.

The colonising designs of economics through the Becker/Krueger universalising of its methodological individualism has, however, been constrained, at least in analytical principle, by two shortcomings. First, while the economic and non-economic are analysed on the basis of identical principles, this leaves unexplained the division between the economic and the non-economic. These divisions might be taken as given or an explanation can be proffered, for example, on the basis of transaction costs – with some types of business being more efficient when conducted through informal means rather than the market. None the less, the division between the economic and the non-economic, and the allocation of activity within and between them, is only poorly addressed, especially in the context of development and change in socioeconomic structures. Where does the market come from historically? Why does it march forward in some cases and not in others, when results are at best mixed – as in informal credit markets that can rely effectively on trust or be a source of corruption? Second, as a generalisation of the first point of the inability to explain the distinction between the economic and the non-economic, the social content of the theory based on the methodological individualism of neo-classical economics seems incapable of explaining the presence of social structures and institutions, let alone classes and the state, whose existence is glaringly obvious. Why and how do institutions and social structures arise and change? Why, for example, to use the vernacular, could the state be 'market-conforming' in some cases but not in others, when agents are supposed to be riddled with rent-seeking? How, indeed, could states arise on the basis of the atomised behaviour of individuals?

This is where the new microeconomics with which Stiglitz is associated has given rise to a most significant result, as far as shifting the boundaries of the scope of economic analysis and its capacity to address the social is concerned. In what appears to be a squaring of the circle, the new microeconomics allows for the explanation of *social* structures and institutions even on the basis of *individual* optimisation. Faced with imperfect information, individuals can decide to create or engage in socially structured activity both within and between market and non-market forms of organisation. These forms become endogenous on a microeconomic basis, where previously they were taken as exogenous.

In particular, especially for Stiglitz, it becomes imperative to study how informational imperfections that arise within, and are transmitted through, the market might be corrected by non-market institutions. As seen above for the regulation of financial systems, this entails a role for the regulatory state where other non-market mechanisms (such as culture, custom or business organisations, including trade unions) do not emerge spontaneously.

The broader policy context

In this light, then, there is a neat correspondence between the shift from Krueger to Stiglitz within the World Bank and the advance of a colonising economics from reliance upon Becker-type extrapolations to those attached to the new information-theoretic economics. The seemingly simple and limited device of incorporating informational imperfections has dramatic effects: the virtues of the market and its opposition to the state are replaced by a balance between the two; the perfection of the market gives way to emphasis on informationally led market imperfections that can be corrected; and the treatment of the non-economic as if economic gives way to a more rounded understanding of the formation of, and interaction between, market and non-market institutions. In case of privatisation, for example, it is accepted that creating private ownership is not enough, and even damaging, if not within the appropriate socio-political, legal and economic environment.

There is, then, a natural progression from the Washington to the post-Washington consensus from an analytical point of view. While their differences within neo-classical economics can be exaggerated and they have both gained influence through the informal application of their approaches, the new consensus generalises the old (a special case in which information is perfectly handled through the market), addresses issues that are proscribed by the old and opens the way for a wider portfolio of policy options. It would, however, be a mistake to explain the emergence of the post-Washington consensus in terms of its analytical superiority over the old consensus. A more fruitful way of comprehending the move towards the new consensus is in terms of the shifting policy stances being adopted by the World Bank and the IMF, and how they can be justified. While the neo-liberal Washington consensus might appear to be an inflexible monolith, it has been accompanied by considerable change in the role of the Washington institutions over the 1980s.[17]

First, the depth and breadth of economic interventions, never minimal despite neo-liberal ideology, have been extended both in the succession of repeated adjustment programmes to which individual countries have been subjected[18] and in the greater detail of policy advice that is proffered and imposed as conditionalities for the granting or renewal of loans. Effectively, the presence of the World Bank/IMF is pervasive if not always decisive. Toye (1994, pp. 29–30) lists the following nine chief elements of structural adjustment loans (with percentage of times imposed in brackets): remove import quotas (57 per cent), improve export incentives (76 per cent), reform the fiscal system (70 per cent), improve financial performance of public enterprises (73 per cent), revise agricultural pricing (73 per cent), shift public investment (59 per cent), revise industrial incentives (68 per cent), increase public enterprise efficiency (57 per cent) and improve marketing and other support for agriculture (57 per cent).[19]

Second, the interventions of the World Bank/IMF have been extended beyond economic policy, thereby straining the limits of the statutes precluding intervention in the political process. This is because, rationalised no doubt by the need to guarantee implementation, conditionality has increasingly been tied to issues of governance and democratisation, and support for those organs of 'civil society' that are most amenable to market-friendly policies – a far cry from the earlier presumption that authoritarian regimes are more suitable because of their greater powers of resistance to populist agitation against the impact of adjustment.[20] Not surprisingly, this has provoked an interest in crude calculations of the political economy of policy – what are the circumstances under which different conditionalities are negotiated and met, with the acknowledgement that outcomes are highly variable both between and within adjustment programmes.[21]

Third, there was supposed to have been a traditional division of responsibility between the Washington institutions, with the World Bank providing project funding as a contribution to long-run growth, and the IMF focusing upon bridging loans to cover short-run balance of payments deficits and restore macroeconomic balance. Thus, the World Bank has been attached to the long-run, microeconomic, supply-side factors underlying structural adjustment towards higher growth rates; the IMF has targeted short-run macroeconomic, demand-side factors underlying stabilisation of inflation, budget deficits and the balance of payments. There has also been an ideological divide between the World Bank, as interventionist and a source of expansionary soft loans, and the IMF, as monetarist and contractionary. Thus, Bird's (1995) assessment of the IMF is highly revealing. It has had unused lending capacity, its net lending to developing countries had become negative in the second half of the 1980s and it had even discouraged other forms of foreign aid and investment flows as a result of the stigma attached to the reduced credibility of countries adjudged to have adjusted inadequately.[22]

Over the 1980s, whatever their previous validity, these differences have been substantially eroded – both in policy stance and implementation, especially with structural-adjustment loans being offered by the World Bank from the early 1980s to finance balance of payments deficits. However, equally significant, both organisations offer policy advice and analysis that was previously the preserve of the other, and the substance of what is offered is indistinguishable between them and uniformly conservative in terms of reducing the role of the state, getting the prices right, promoting export orientation, higher interest rates, etc.[23] Partly to pacify its critics but, more fundamentally, to enhance its effectiveness, the IMF has presented itself as broadening its goals and as converging with the World Bank. In practice, this has entailed more extensive interventions to achieve primarily unchanged goals.[24]

Fourth, the World Bank/IMF have gone beyond extending the scope and depth of their interventions and have sought to incorporate governments into the formulation of adjustment policy in order to be able to present it as indigenously owned. While ideologically presented as a means of democratising and enhancing policy formulation by local participation, it is a moot point whether this is more accurately perceived as a form of repressive tolerance and a more sophisticated means of ensuring implementation. Helleiner (1994a, pp. 10–11) puts this most delicately:

> The World Bank now says that it is encouraging local programme ownership, 'insisting that the materials we use as the basis for ... lending decisions be the product of Africans', hiring local African consultants rather than foreigners wherever possible, and attempting ... to develop professional and analytical skills in public policy in Africa. These efforts are overdue, and they are probably biased in their orientations (toward orthodox Bank perspectives), but they have been welcomed in Africa.

A more blunt and honest assessment is given by Harberger (1992, p. 93). Having pointed to the trivial weight of the World Bank's loans, he observes:[25]

> The Bank must recognize that ultimately its role is that of a teaching institution. It teaches developing countries lessons they have to learn about economic policy. In part it does so by training young people from developing countries .... In part it does so through what people from developing countries learn when they occupy staff jobs. In part it does so through Bank missions going to developing countries and working with the ministers and their staffs.

Education, good governance, policy ownership and democracy are all about doing what the World Bank/IMF would do but also appearing to do it by yourself and willingly.[26]

Finally, as Wade (1996) has shown in detail and is now common knowledge, the most recent shifts in the position of the World Bank have had very little to do with consideration, let alone acceptance, of the overwhelming weight of research that has long been turned critically upon the old consensus. Nor is it a response to the emergence of the new microfoundations. This is because Stiglitz and others have been active in this area for two decades. Rather, as Wade argues, in part against a background of intellectual sclerosis within the Bank, the increasing significance of Japan as donor, foreign investor and self-reflective case study has rendered the old consensus increasingly unacceptable. Japan can hardly be expected to fund a set of policies, and an underlying ideology, which denies its own experience of having been heavily interventionist, and its own interests in promoting industrialisation and growth in the countries where it is directing foreign investment.

Indeed, the recently edited book by Ohno and Ohno (eds) (1998) reveals the extent to which there is a convergence between Japanese developmental thinking and the new consensus. Ohno (1998, p. 4) highlights the following differences with the old consensus. First, the need to attach priority to the real economy:

> Most Japanese aid officials find such obsessions with finance and the macroeconomy narrow and unbalanced. True, inflation must be dealt with but not *at all costs* to the society, especially when the country is distressed by collapsing output, joblessness, political instability, ethnic conflicts, lawlessness, and public discontent. Under such adverse circumstances, the highest priority for Japan would be the *real* economy and *not* the financial side: how to arrest the fall in output, how to secure jobs, how to initiate revival and industrial restructuring, etc. These real concerns take precedence over money, budget, and inflation.

Second, the orientation of long-term plans needs to be attached to annual targets; third, the positive impact of government needs to be emphasised in promoting the market and marketisation, especially 'important in the early stages of development and in economic crisis' (p. 7); fourth, the process of development is slow and not subject to quick fixes; and, finally, there is a need for specificity in dealing with particular countries, issues and sectors. Mainstream neo-classical economics is considered entirely unsuitable in contrast to the welcome insights offered by Stiglitz, a view supported by Hara (1998), who praises the new information-theoretic economics for its capacity to design institutions compatible with incentives. Only a mild note of caution emerges in the Afterword of Ohno and Ohno (1998, p. 310), who advise study of the different approaches to development economics prior to the emergence of the neo-classical orthodoxy.[27]

The increasing trickle-down of Japanese influence on the Bank's thinking has also to be set against longer-term changes in the functioning of the Bank and the IMF, and the relationship between them. Traditionally, as observed prior to the 1980s and the emergence of structural-adjustment programmes, there was a sharp division of labour, and corresponding analytical subject matter, between the two institutions – along the lines of macro and micro, with the IMF correcting balance of payments and the World Bank targeting infrastructural and other capital projects. Subsequently, given the severity and persistence of stabilisation and adjustment problems, both institutions experienced a creeping incorporation of more and more economic factors, not least with the IMF embracing microeconomic aspects (macro policy cannot succeed in the absence of appropriate supply-side policies), and the World Bank addressing macroeconomic policy (projects cannot succeed if there is, for example, low growth and no demand for output).[28]

This merging and overlapping of responsibilities has had the effect of consolidating the Washington consensus as long as the twin institutions were primarily committed to a neo-liberal ideology while remaining able to smooth over policy differences in practice.[29] However, paradoxically, the increasing scope of the analysis offered by both institutions, which proved a source of strength to the old consensus, leaves it totally vulnerable once questioned in any aspect. As the World Bank departs from the ideology of perfectly working markets, so its breach with the IMF is potentially devastating. As Stiglitz must be and has been made aware, the post-Washington consensus is nothing of the sort. It potentially signifies a fundamental breach between the two institutions, undermining much of the rationale for the IMF's stabilisation policies at the macro as well as at the micro level. Such divisions have been intensified by competing stances on explanations and policies for East Asia in the wake of its crisis.

It is precisely such a potential that renders the prospect of the post-Washington consensus so attractive to those who have previously rejected the old consensus. However, there are not only weaknesses in the new consensus, there are also considerable dangers, even for many of those adopting a critical perspective towards the old consensus. First of all, while the new consensus takes the new microeconomics and the old consensus as the basis for its critical points of departure, it does so through an almost total neglect of the heavy weight of critical literature that has built up against the old consensus. It is little exaggeration to suggest that reference is made to this critical literature simply as a means to support the new consensus, both pillaging and reducing it to the new consensus through its own single-minded information-theoretic framework.

In addition, given the broader scope of the new consensus, it has even greater claims and attraction than the old in setting the analytical agenda for development. The state *versus* the market gives way to state *and* market to overcome market imperfections. Indeed, the broad, alternative analytical thrust adopted here is that the relationship between market and state, or between market and non-market, should not be taken as an analytical starting point. Rather, the relationship between state and market, as well as their respective roles and interactions, is the consequence of underlying economic and political relations that condition and are, in turn, conditioned by socio-economic structures. These need to be identified both theoretically and in specific country or other contexts, and are not reducible to the optimising behaviour attached to market, state and informational imperfections.

Apart from the narrow analytical basis of the new consensus and its neglect of (and lack of engagement with) alternatives, it shares and builds upon a further feature of the old consensus. As indicated previously, paradoxically, the old consensus was consolidated by an increasingly interventionist stance, as micro and macro were integrated both analytically and through conditionality. Lending by the Washington institutions has been marked by a creeping, even a galloping, extent of intervention within the economic arena to impose *laissez-faire* policies. In a sense, the old consensus was caught in the trap of arguing for minimal state intervention and, hence, precluding itself from addressing what the state should do. In contrast, the new consensus can be understood as strengthening and extending the scope of permissible intervention in recipient countries. For not only is economic intervention justified on the basis of market imperfections but also the success of such interventions is attached to non-economic factors. In other words, the new consensus rationalises intervention by the donor agencies across as wide a remit as possible. While the old consensus claimed that there was nothing wrong with its policies other than that they were not implemented, the new consensus is able to push for command over what the state does and how it should do it.

This is all the more disturbing since the ideology of the old consensus, of non-intervention and of a minimal role for the state, has proven a convenient veil for extending the scope for discretionary intervention. This is whether in deference to the need to negotiate policy outcomes or to a more realistic assessment of what is economically and politically feasible and preferred.[30] What the new consensus does analytically is to strengthen and widen the scope for discretionary intervention under the guise of good governance and the imperative to moderate both market and non-market imperfections, and wrap it up in terms of local ownership.

It is important, however, not to exaggerate the interventionism that is underwritten by the new consensus. It is not providing a *carte blanche* for the state; nor is it even an ethos of being pro-state other than as a complement to the market. Apart from providing a general rationale for interventionism, the justification for it only arises out of a micro-level demonstration of the harmful effects of informational market imperfections for which state intervention is more beneficial than otherwise. To place this in perspective, it can be contrasted with the earlier Keynesian welfarism of the post-war boom, which has its counterpart for development in the notion of promoting modernisation. None of these concepts should be accepted uncritically, but each is based upon the idea that the state needs to intervene to guarantee economic and social progress in the light of macro-wide developments, whether in employment, growth and structural change or in the provision of health, education and welfare. The new consensus is much less audacious and does not even restore the policy commitment attached to modernisation that characterised official development policy prior to the emergence of the old neo-liberal consensus in the 1980s. Both analytically and in policy, the post-Washington consensus represents a regression relative to the McNamara era at the World Bank, despite its supposed rigour in specifying market imperfections and its claims to represent and reproduce its traditions.

Whither the post-Washington consensus?

Even in the short time since it was launched, the post-Washington consensus has already begun to run its own course. Stiglitz himself has released a volley of papers addressing everything from the East Asian crisis to the failed transition in Eastern Europe. These papers have done little to advance the analytical foundations of the new consensus as they are simply applications of its principles and framework. They do, however, share crucial features.

First, they are increasingly informal in content, departing from the formal techniques and mathematical modelling usually associated with Stiglitz's output. Second, they are increasingly accommodating to the old consensus even if market imperfections continue to be set against neo-liberalism. Third, they increasingly involve various lofty assessments with limited regard for detailed research and acknowledgement of the full range of existing literature. Fourth, the conclusions frequently amount to little more than the notion that account has to be taken of market imperfections – as in the conclusion, for example, that preconditions for market governance better be in place before proceeding with privatisation.

This is not meant to bemoan the passage of a leading economist into the role of figurehead for the World Bank. In any event, others can play the role of providing research and modelling. However, it does raise the more general issue of what impact the post-Washington consensus, and the Washington consensus previously, has on practice. Is it merely rhetorical gloss on unchanging or otherwise determined policies, or does it heavily influence outcomes? The truth is mixed and somewhere in between these two stylised extremes,[31] although it is worthy of remark that the post-Washington consensus might just as well not exist as far as adjustment in Africa and Eastern Europe is concerned. Stiglitz has, on the one hand, allowed for the World Bank to present itself as more user friendly and interventionist, and, on the other, allowed for genuine debate within the establishment over how to deal with the East Asian and Latin American crises of the late 1990s, and in whose interests these crises should be resolved.

While such issues can only be highlighted here, there is also the matter of the continuing evolution of development studies itself and the role of economics (and what sort of economics) within it. Whatever role the post-Washington consensus serves for the World Bank, it has a more general intellectual role in commanding a large slice of attention from those engaged in development. Previously, on considerably narrower analytical grounds and even less palatable policy perspectives, the Washington consensus was able to dominate the development agenda by posing it as market versus state. The post-Washington consensus on its own, marginally less narrow principles, is seeking not only to set the agenda but also to incorporate dissidence in its own reductionist form. In order to retain notions of class, power, conflict and development as a contradictory process involving major social and economic transformation, the information-theoretic approach must not be allowed to succeed in its colonising mission.

Postscript

World Bank Chief Economists tend to come and go, moving on and usually up, with little or no comment. However, Joe Stiglitz's resignation at the end of November 1999 caused something of a stir in the media, with accompanying speculation, as he had been due for renewal as soon as February 2000. As with all such departures, the main issue was whether he jumped or whether he was pushed. There were suggestions that he was told to keep silent or resign, especially over Russian privatisation and the handling of the East Asian crisis. It was observed that World Bank President, James Wolfensohn, had fully and openly supported him except for one public rebuke a month or so earlier (over Stiglitz's criticism of the IMF for its premature programme of Russian privatisation; not for being wrong but because of the unfair benefits of hindsight). Rumours were also rife that Wolfensohn's own renewal of post depended upon Stiglitz's departure, with Larry Summers, currently US Treasury Secretary, the source of the behind-the-scenes pressure.[32]

A second issue in the press was whether Stiglitz had been a good or a bad thing. Most delivered a favourable verdict, not least for his having opened up the policies of the World Bank and IMF to public scrutiny and debate. However, this tempered judgement on a third issue – was it right for him to go and, not quite the same thing, should he have resigned? Here the judgement has generally been that he can have his intellectual independence or his public position but not both. He should not have criticised his own colleagues in public.

Here, the perspective on offer is somewhat different and focuses upon the more lasting impact with which Stiglitz is liable to be associated – his launching of the post-Washington consensus. First and foremost is the claim that Stiglitz could go because his task had been completed, not halted or reversed. A remarkable feature of the vast majority of the press commentary, implicit in that reported above, is a complete absence of disagreement with Stiglitz's approach to economic theory and policy. Indeed, he is generally anticipated to be a future Nobel Prize-winner as long as he lives long enough to wait his turn. Informally, it is impossible in principle for most to disagree that there are market imperfections, that these might be due to informational asymmetries and that they can have important implications in practice. At an institutional level, Stiglitz's impact has even been fully incorporated into thinking around the IMF, with its now declaring itself to have been insufficiently focused on poverty alleviation in the past. In a speech just before Stiglitz's resignation, Andrew Crockett – General Manager of the Bank for International Settlements, and widely but wrongly tipped as likely successor to Michel Camdessus the then IMF's managing director – delivered a tract on economic principles that was unmistakably Stiglitz-speak.[33] Within the World Bank itself, in a private conversation reported to me, Stiglitz claimed a year ago that 80 per cent of the World Bank's economists had now come to support him. I take this to be a minority, given the old joke that if you put two economists together, you will get agreement on three differing opinions, each held with equally strong conviction. My own conversations with Bank economists suggest that the emphasis is more on the post than on the consensus, and that Stiglitz is merely a microeconomist.

Be this as it may, Stiglitz had already completed the intellectual programme of establishing the new development economics, first comprehensively broached over a decade earlier, with development analysis reduced to the incidence and impact of market imperfections (Stiglitz 1989). This has been refined and extended in scope over the intervening period, with the old neo-classical model of perfect competition taken as point of departure; from Stiglitz and Hoff (1999):

> In leaving out history, institutions, and distributional considerations, neoclassical economics was leaving out the heart of development economics. Modern economic theory argues that the fundamentals (resources, technology, and preferences) are not the only ... determinants of economic outcomes ... even without government failures, market failures are pervasive, especially in less developed countries.

Further, with casual reference to the Black Plague, as an illustrative accident of history, and multiple equilibria, an explanation is provided for the fundamental problem of why 'developed and less developed countries are on different production functions':

> We emphasize that accidents of history matter ... partly because of pervasive complementarities among agents ... and partly because even a set of dysfunctional institutions and behaviors in the past can constitute a Nash equilibrium from which an economy need not be inevitably dislodged.

Not surprisingly, on this basis, Yusuf and Stiglitz (1999) feel able to divide development issues into those that are resolved and those that are not. These seem unwittingly to fall into the theoretical as opposed to the policy, respectively, not least because the analysis is one of market imperfections but because the policy will depend upon their incidence in practice.

These academic considerations aside, it would be a mistake to see Stiglitz as having escaped unscathed from the World Bank, at worst being charged for being an uncut and impolitic diamond. *The Economist* delivers its judgement in its Christmas edition of 18 December 1999, and is unsparing in its criticism:[34] Stiglitz is nothing other than a lofty, ivory-tower academic, always ready to condemn others trying to make policy in the real world of free(ing) markets but is himself incapable of offering worthwhile suggestions of his own. Like much such commentary from *The Economist*, there is the merest semblance of truth dominated by a mountain of falsehood. They are correct, from the perspective of a *laissez-faire* stance for which you do not need to know anything to free the market, that Stiglitz requires detailed empirical knowledge for policy formulation. On the other hand, as Stiglitz has made abundantly clear in his speeches and publications, and, most recently, in articles in the latest issues of both the *Oxford Review of Economic Policy* and the *Economic Journal*, he and others have pressed explicitly and concretely for alternative policies, in advance, especially for East Asia, where raising real interest rates was advised correctly to be likely to have the effect of worsening recession.[35]

Thus, as *The Economist* clarifies, and is made even clearer (if more diplomatically) by Crockett, the market rules even if with market imperfections. For Crockett, free markets are the architecture, and market imperfections merely the plumbing necessary to the functioning of the system if not allowed to get out of hand.[36] Whatever the academic significance of the post-Washington consensus, its policy implications are to be subordinated to those attached to whatever is perceived to be sound, or, more exactly, globally free finance and reliance upon 'fundamentals'. This has been borne out by subsequent events as matters of resignation have gone from bad to worse for the ideologues of neo-liberalism. Every ten years the World Bank produces a report on poverty, as a special issue of its *World Development Report*. For the first time, the draft for 2000 has been publicly debated and, so, out in the open, before official sanction. Now, its lead author, Ravi Kanbur has resigned after more than a year's work and millions of dollars expenditure on the report. Why? – because of a firm belief in the connection between globalisation and poverty that senior World Bank management is determined to tone down. Moreover, reliable Washington sources indicate that, you guessed it, Larry Summers has himself been directly involved in rewriting the report!

Where does this leave the post-Washington consensus? Does it restore the *ex ante* Washington consensus? It is far from clear that either the IMF or the World Bank ever abandoned it in practice. However, its successor has fulfilled its mission for the IMF, endowing it with the same or even more discretion to intervene through stabilisation and structural adjustment, albeit with the benefits of a more user-friendly rhetoric. Within the World Bank, the extent of Stiglitz's continuing impact will depend in part upon the stance and role adopted by his successor as well as internal and external pressures. There will almost inevitably be some reaction against the post-Washington consensus, or at least some further debate around it before the self-styled knowledge bank resumes business as usual.

Nevertheless, whatever its impact within the Washington institutions, Stiglitz's departure, or its form, can only have strengthened the new consensus in the outside world. It is not so much that he has been freed to continue his crusade for the new information-theoretic economics from without; rather, while within, not only did he win the argument, he also displayed the courage of his convictions and suffered the penalty of conviction for his courage. For this reason, he is to be roundly praised and admired, but not at the expense of promoting the post-Washington consensus as the unofficial opposition to the Washington institutions, setting the agenda for development studies, as was its mission during his curtailed period of office.

Notes

1 This chapter was completed while in receipt of a Research Fellowship from the UK Economic and Social Research Council (ESRC), under award number R000271046, to study 'The New Revolution in Economics and Its Impact upon Social Sciences'. It draws in part on Fine and Stoneman (1996) and an earlier but longer seminar paper of the same title. Thanks to many for comments, especially Chris Cramer, John Weeks and Alex Wilks.

2 See Boughton and Lateef (eds) (1995). The more general lack of imagination demonstrated by the mainstream in assessing the fiftieth anniversary is heavily reflected in the Bretton Woods Commission (1994). For an exception, see the highly informative volumes of Kapur *et al.* (1997a) and Kapur *et al.* (eds) (1997).

3 See Pereira (1995), for example.

4 See Cavanagh *et al.* (eds) (1994), Danaher and Yunus (eds) (1994), Oxfam (1995) and Chossudovsky (1997), respectively. See also special sections in the Bulletin of Concerned Asian Scholars 26(4), and the Canadian Journal of African Studies 29(2).

5 Standing (1999) gives a succinct account of the various elements of the Washington consensus and an important sense of its having evolved to embrace further components:

> As the new thinking and policy action crystallised in the 1980s, the 'Washington consensus' evolved to offer a model consisting of eleven main elements, with more being added as its 'success' spread. Briefly, they are trade liberalisation, financial liberalisation, privatisation, 'deregulation', foreign capital liberalisation (elimination of barriers to FDI), secure property rights, unified and competitive exchange rates, diminished public spending (fiscal discipline), public expenditure switching (to health, schooling and infrastructure), tax reform (broadening the tax base, cutting marginal tax rates, less progressive tax), and a 'social safety net' (selective state transfers for the needy). A twelfth element, expressed in World Bank and IMF (and OECD) reports, is labour market flexibility, by which is meant decentralised labour relations coupled with cutbacks in protective and pro-collective regulations.

The term itself was coined by John Williamson (1990) in reviewing Latin American experience of policy reform in the 1980s. See also Williamson (1997).

6 See also Stiglitz (1997, p. 3), in view of the success of the East Asian economies:

> I have already referred to the intellectual impact that this has had: development is possible, and successful development requires, or at least is enhanced by, government undertaking appropriate policies *that go well beyond simply getting out of the way of the market*. While there remains an active debate about what are the precise lessons to be learned, and to what extent the experiences of East Asia are replicable elsewhere, there remains little doubt, at least in my mind, that government played a critical, catalytic role.

7 See Wade (1996) for an account of the conflicts around *The East Asian Miracle*. See also Gyohten (1997) and Ohno and Ohno (eds) (1998), but especially

Shiratori (1998, p. 81), for whom, in contrast to the neo-classical view taken within the World Bank's *The East Asian Miracle*:

> Competitive advantage should be understood in a dynamic context, not a static one as used in the neoclassical approach. It is theoretically justifiable to select a currently uncompetitive industry that is judged important for an economy's future and accelerate its development using policy instruments.

8 Assessing the World Development Report for 1997, in a special issue of the IDS Bulletin, in the wider context of a shift towards a new consensus, Cornia (1998) understands it as synthesising the old consensus with notions of the developmental state in the light of *The East Asian Miracle*. Moore (1998) sees it as replacing the new political economy by the new institutional economics. As will be apparent, this involves an understatement of the scope of the new consensus.

9 See Ranis (1997, p. 75) who, after reporting the $20 million budget for development research, also comments:

> Its dissemination efforts, especially in the Third World, are prodigious and overwhelming. At the same time the Bank has paid relatively little attention to the output of other national and international organizations .... Indeed even much relevant output by academia is largely ignored.

See also Stern and Ferreira (1997, p. 524).

10 For a leading post-Keynesian, see Harcourt (1997, p. 2): 'Stiglitz (1994) ... contains one of the most profound internal critiques of mainstream economics I have ever read'.

11 Harcourt (1997, p. 3) observes that Stiglitz (1994) makes reference to one hundred or so examples of his own (co-authored) work! Stiglitz (1999d) also provides an account on the same principles for the failure of the capitalist transition in Russia.

12 Dubbed 'economic virtualism' by Carrier and Miller (eds) (1998).

13 See Stiglitz's (1993, p. 111) response to the relatively mild suggestion from Bowles and Gintis (1993) that exchange is not only institutionally driven but also 'contested': 'There are good economic reasons, beyond the exercise of "power" (whatever that much-used term means) for the existence of hierarchical relationships.'

14 The passage here, however, is from the original draft of his speech, which is more explicit on the points being made.

15 See Fine (1997a, 1998, 1999a and 1999b).

16 See Becker (1996) and Tommasi and Ierulli (eds) (1995). A critical assessment of Becker's work in the light of some of the themes explored in this chapter is provided by Fine (1995, 1997b and 1999a).

17 It is beyond the goals of this chapter to explain the internal and external influences on intellectual developments within the World Bank and IMF. For an account, see Fine (1999d). Note that, to some extent, their role was transformed by the process of deregulating financial markets, which was partly a consequence of policies that they had promoted themselves!

18 For Bird (1995, p. 105): 'Evidence seems to confirm that the image of the Fund coming into a country, offering swift financial support, helping to turn the balance of payments around, and then getting out, is purely and simply wrong.'

19 See also Bird (1995, p. 116). Mosely (1994) argues that adjustment policies have to be disaggregated into their separate components. Obviously some of these percentages are effectively understatements since they are calculated over a

sequence of programmes in which some of the objectives might have been achieved at an earlier stage, rendering them no longer necessary.

20 As Lancaster (1997, p. 189) observes:

> The story of the World Bank in Africa is one of an institution seeking and achieving leadership, prominence, and influence on an important and controversial issue: the need for painful, complex, and often politically risky economic reforms. It achieved that goal during the 1980s only to find that economic reforms, to be successful, often needed to be supported by political reforms. As the Bank vice president and general counsel observed, 'The Bank's increasing concern with issues of governance in its borrowing members seems to have come as a logical last step in its gradually expanding involvement in policy reform through adjustment lending, which has been extended to social sectors.'

For Teriba (1996, p. 31), in a kind interpretation, there is a need that: 'the World Bank avoid the risk it now runs, albeit unwittingly, of incrementally taking on political functions that are both unnecessary and unrelated to its basic functions and general mandate'.

21 See Toye (1994), Mkandawire (1994), Morrisson *et al.* (1994) and Haggard and Webb (1993). Note that Jesperson (1993, p. 47) suggests 75 per cent compliance on average with conditionalities, and Bird (1995) concludes that there does not appear to be a 'moral hazard' problem for the IMF in negotiating with its clients.

22 See also Helleiner (1994b).

23 Hence the assessment of Mosely and Weeks (1993) that the World Bank's (1994) latest position 'transforms the Bank and the International Monetary Fund in Africa from fraternal to identical twins'. This process began with the infamous *Berg Report*, World Bank (1981). See also Shao *et al.* (1992, pp. 67–8):

> Henceforth, the WB changed its position and role from project aid, development loans and sectoral policy undertakings to structural lending. More importantly, the WB and IMF 'ganged' up in setting up structural lending policies and conditions for different countries and in the process convinced or induced other donors to adopt the same lending conditions towards African countries.

24 For Polak (1991, p. 20), the IMF has adopted growth and adjustment with 'equal fervor ... but does not insist with equal firmness on policies needed for growth and on policies needed for adjustment'. Further, it has embraced redistribution and protection of the environment as 'secondary objectives' along with, more informally, reduction in military expenditure. In short (p. 19): 'In other words, the growth objective is redefined to incorporate adjustment, income distribution, the environment and, in Eastern Europe, the transition to a market economy.'

25 See also Mwanza (1992, pp. 4–5) on the first half of the 1980s (though it should be borne in mind that the IMF's staff are also heavily deployed, particularly at the stage of policy formulation):

> The IMF usually adopts a more rigid position than the World Bank. It rarely deploys its staff in countries implementing its programmes .... The IMF approach to programming is, therefore, vulnerable to the criticism that it lacks a detailed appreciation of the local environment ... one IMF-designed policy framework paper could have sufficed for Malawi, Tanzania,

Zambia and Zimbabwe ... local expertise does not participate in programme design. The IMF will usually draw up a list of loyal IMF technocrats to be employed in key ministries or institutions for the purpose of implementing or overseeing the implementation of the SAP. In most cases these technocrats, most of whom are foreign, are paid from World Bank loans. This practice is more often than not accompanied by retrenchment of local experts made under the banner of making the civil service more efficient.

26 This has become transparent in the Bank's increasing reference to itself as a '"knowledge" bank' (Stiglitz 1997), a theme that is taken up remorselessly in the World Development Report for 1998. Stiglitz continues: 'We within the World Bank have a special responsibility not only to produce knowledge that will enable developing countries to grow more effectively, but also to ensure that knowledge gets implemented – including in our own lending practices.' This is followed by a discussion of fungibility, and the implication that those who do not learn their lessons the easy way have to be taught through loan policy. If it is a knowledge bank, is there not a case for applying Stiglitz's own market imperfections arguments to the knowledge that is created and used?

27 In case those wedded to the new consensus become too heartened by the support they gain from the Japanese, it should be noted that authoritarianism is the preferred form of government to ensure an appropriate development state in the early stages of industrialisation. See Murakami (1998) and Watanabe (1998).

28 For critical commentary on the record of adjustment and stabilisation, see Mosely and Weeks (1993) and Mosely *et al.* (1995).

29 Differences between the harder-line IMF and the World Bank came to a head in 1988 in a dispute over loans to Argentina. This effectively prompted an accommodation to be reached. See Kapur *et al.* (1997a and 1997b) and Polak (1994).

30 See Hildyard (1998) for a critique of the post-Washington consensus along these lines.

31 For a discussion of this issue, see Fine (1999d).

32 He is a former Chief Economist at the World Bank, attracting infamy for declaring that it was sound economics for developing countries to be the dumping ground for toxic waste.

33 There is no explicit reference to Stiglitz himself but there is to Akerlof's (1970) market for lemons, which is the classic starting point for the new information-theoretic economics.

34 Apart from *The Economist*, an article in the *Irish Times* of 17 December 1999, by Rudi Dornbusch, a former Chief Economic Adviser to both the World Bank and the IMF, is critical of Stiglitz along the lines that the IMF is not very good at predicting or preventing floods but is very good at clearing up after them (through sound finance etc.).

35 See also pre-resignation Stiglitz (1999c), arguing that world trade rules are unfair to developing countries, and post-resignation Stiglitz (2000) for the idea that real wages should not be cut in developing countries and workers involved in policymaking in adjusting countries. With rising public acrimony between Stiglitz and the defenders of his erstwhile employers, he was eventually removed from status of adviser to the World Bank in April 2000.

36 In closing, Crockett even refers to work advising of the inevitability of financial instability unless there is more intervention. He does so, however, only to display the prejudices of his palate while keeping his fingers crossed:

Studies of the history of financial instability, such as those of Kindleberger and Minsky do not offer much encouragement .... The choice would be an unpalatable one between damaging instability, and a far greater degree of administrative control over financial markets. Accepting instability would … be unsustainable. Public opinion would not accept such a price for a market system, whatever benefits it might have. Imposing wider ranging controls, while superficially attractive, would have just as damaging consequences. It would erode the efficiency of resource allocation, and condemn the international economy to a constant struggle between financial engineers trying to circumvent restrictions and regulators trying to plug loopholes. Neither is a pretty prospect. That is why it is so important that the plumbers succeed in making the architecture we have inherited a comfortable place to live, as well as a pleasing concept to contemplate.

Clearly, plumber Joe has had his tools stolen by those who are not prepared to set them to work as much as he would himself.

References

Akerlof, G. (1970) 'The market for "lemons": Quality uncertainty and the market mechanism', *Quarterly Journal of Economics* 84(3): 488–500.

Becker, G. (1996) *Accounting for Tastes*, Cambridge, MA: Harvard University Press.

Bird, G. (1995) *The IMF and Developing Countries: Issues and Evidence*, London: Routledge.

Boughton, J. and K. Lateef (eds) (1995) *Fifty Years after Bretton Woods: The Future of the IMF and the World Bank*, Washington: IMF and World Bank.

Bowles, S. and H. Gintis (1993) 'The revenge of homo economicus: Contested exchange and the revival of political economy', *Journal of Economic Perspectives* 7(1): 83–102.

Bretton Woods Commission (1994) *Bretton Woods: Looking to the Future*, Washington: Bretton Woods Commission.

Carrier, J. and D. Miller (eds) (1998) *Virtualism: The New Political Economy*, London: Berg.

Cavanagh, J., D. Wysham and M. Arruda (eds) (1994) *Beyond Bretton Woods: Alternatives to the Global Economic Order*, London: Pluto Press.

Chossudovsky, M. (1997) *The Globalisation of Poverty: Impacts of IMF and World Bank Reforms*, London: Zed Books.

Corbo, V., S. Fischer and S. B. Webb (eds) (1992) *Adjustment Lending Revisited: Policies to Restore Growth*, Washington: World Bank.

Cornia, G. (1998) 'Convergence on governance issues, dissent on economic policies', *IDS Bulletin* 29(2): 32–8.

Cornia, G. and G. Helleiner (eds) (1994) *From Adjustment to Development in Africa: Conflict, Controversy, Convergence, Consensus?*, London: Macmillan.

Cornia, G., R. van der Hoeven and T. Mkandawire (eds) (1993) *Africa's Recovery in the 1990s: From Stagnation and Adjustment to Human Development*, New York: St Martin's Press.

Crockett, A. (1999) 'International financial arrangements: Architecture and plumbing', David Finch Annual Lecture, University of Melbourne, 15 November.

Culpeper, R., A. Berry and F. Stewart (eds) (1997) *Global Development Fifty Years after Bretton Woods*, London: Macmillan.

Danaher, K. and M. Yunus (eds) (1994) *Fifty Years is Enough: The Case against the World Bank and the International Monetary Fund*, Boston: South End Press.

de Vries, B. (1996) 'The World Bank's focus on poverty', in Griesgraber and Gunter (eds) (1996).

Dornbusch, R. (1999) 'IMF's medicine beats all others', *Irish Times*, 17 December.

The Economist (1999) '"Resignation" of the World Bank's turbulent Chief Economist. Presumably, therefore, he was a good thing?', 18 December.

Emmerij, L. (ed.) (1997) *Economic and Social Development into the XXI Century*, Washington: Inter-American Development Bank.

Fine, B. (1995) 'From political economy to consumption', in Miller, D. (ed.) (1995) *Acknowledging Consumption*, London: Routledge.

—— (1997a) 'The new revolution in economics', *Capital and Class* 61, spring: 143–8.

—— (1997b) 'Playing the consumption game', *Consumption, Markets, Culture* 1(1): 7–29.

—— (1998a) 'The triumph of economics: Or "rationality" can be dangerous to your reasoning', in Carrier and Miller (eds) (1998).

—— (1999a) 'From Becker to Bourdieu: Economics confronts the social sciences', *International Papers in Political Economy* 5(3): 1–43.

—— (1999b) 'A question of economics: Is it colonising the social sciences?', *Economy and Society* 28(3): 403–25.

—— (1999c) 'The World Bank's speculation on social capital: Bursting the bubble', mimeo.

Fine, B. and C. Stoneman (1996) 'Introduction: State and development', *Journal of Southern African Studies* 22(1), March: 5–26.

Griesgraber, J. and B. Gunter (eds) (1996) *The World Bank: Lending on a Global Scale*, London: Pluto Press.

Gyohten, T. (1997) 'Japan and the World Bank', in Kapur *et al.* (eds) (1997).

Haggard, S. and S. Webb (1993) 'What do we know about the political economy of economic policy reform', *The World Bank Research Observer* 8(2) July: 143–68.

Hara, Y. (1998) 'A blueprint for Asian economics', in Ohno and Ohno (eds) (1998).

Harberger, A. (1992) 'Comment', in Corbo, V. *et al.* (eds) (1992).

Harcourt, G. (1997) 'Economic theory and economic policy: Two views', Discussion Paper, no. 369, Centre for Economic Policy Research, Australian National University.

Helleiner, G. (1994a) 'From adjustment to development in sub-Saharan Africa: Consensus and continuing conflict', in Cornia and Helleiner (eds) (1994).

—— (1994b) 'External resource flows, debt relief and economic development in sub-Saharan Africa', in Cornia and Helleiner (eds) (1994).

Hildyard, N. (1998) *The World Bank and the State: A Recipe for Change?*, London: Bretton Woods Project.

Jesperson, E. (1993) 'External shocks, adjustment policies and economic and social performance', in Cornia *et al.* (eds) (1993).

Kapur, D., J. P. Lewis and R. Webb (1997a) *The World Bank: Its First Half Century, Volume I: History*, Washington: Brookings.

——, J. P. Lewis and R. Webb (1997b) 'The World Bank as a development-promoting institution', in Kapur *et al*, (eds) (1997).

Kapur, D., J. P. Lewis and R. Webb (eds) (1997) *The World Bank: Its First Half Century, Volume II: Perspectives*, Washington: Brookings.

Lancaster, C. (1997) 'The World Bank in Africa since 1980: The politics of structural adjustment lending', in Kapur *et al.* (eds) (1997).

Mkandawire, T. (1994) 'Adjustment, political conditionality and democratisation in Africa', in Cornia, G. and G. Helleiner (eds) (1994).

Moore, M. (1998) 'Toward a useful consensus', *IDS Bulletin* 29(2): 39–48.

Morrisson, C., J.-D, Lafay and S. Dessus (1994) 'Adjustment programmes and politico-economic interactions in developing countries: Lessons from an empirical analysis of Africa in the 1980s', in Cornia and Helleiner (eds) (1994).

Mosely, P. (1994) 'Decomposing the effects of structural adjustment: The case of sub-Saharan Africa', in van der Hoeven and van der Kraaij (eds) (1994).

Mosely, P. and J. Weeks (1993) 'Has recovery begun? "Africa's adjustment in the 1980s" revisited', *World Development* 21(10): 1583–606.

Mosely, P., T. Subasat and J. Weeks (1995) 'Assessing "adjustment in Africa"', *World Development* 23(9): 1459–73.

Murakami, Y. (1998) 'Theory of developmentalism', in Ohno and Ohno (eds) (1998).

Mwanza, A. (1992) 'Theory and practice of structural adjustment programmes', in Mwanza (ed.) (1992).

Mwanza, A. (ed.) (1992) *Structural Adjustment Programmes in SADC: Experiences and Lessons from Malawi, Tanzania, Zambia and Zimbabwe*, Harare: SAPES Books.

Ohno, K. (1998) 'Overview: Creating the market economy', in Ohno and Ohno (eds) (1998).

Ohno, K. and I. Ohno (1998) 'Afterword', in Ohno and Ohno (eds) (1998).

Ohno, K. and I. Ohno (eds) (1998) *Japanese Views on Economic Development: Diverse Paths to the Market*, London: Routledge.

Oxfam (1995) *A Case for Reform: Fifty Years of the IMF and World Bank*, Oxford: Oxfam Publications.

Pereira, L. (1995) 'Development economics and the World Bank's identity crisis', *Review of International Political Economy* 2(2): 211–47.

Polak, J. (1991) *The Changing Nature of IMF Conditionality*, Essays in International Finance, no. 184, Princeton University.

—— (1994) *The World Bank and the International Monetary Fund: A Changing Relationship*, Washington: The Brookings Institution, reproduced in Kapur, D. *et al.* (eds) (1997).

Ranis, G. (1997) 'The World Bank near the turn of the century', in Culpeper *et al.* (eds) (1997).

Shao, I., A. Kiwari and G. Makusi (1992) 'Structural adjustment in a socialist country: The case of Tanzania', in Mwanza, A. (ed.) (1992).

Shiratori, M. (1998) 'Afterword to the Japanese translation of the World Bank report *The East Asian Miracle*', in Ohno and Ohno (eds) (1998).

Standing, G. (1999) 'New development paradigm or Third Wayism?: A critique of a World Bank rethink', mimeo.

Stern, N. and F. Ferreira (1997) 'The World Bank as "intellectual actor"', in Kapur *et al.* (eds) (1997).

Stiglitz, J. (1989) 'Markets, market failures and development', *American Economic Review* 79(2): 197–202.

—— (1993) 'Post Walrasian and post Marxian economics', *Journal of Economic Perspectives* 7(1): 109–14.

—— (1994) *Whither Socialism?*, Cambridge, MA: MIT Press.

—— (1997) 'An agenda for development for the twenty-first century', World Bank Ninth Annual Conference on Development Economics, 30 April and 1 May.

—— (1998) 'More instruments and broader goals: Moving toward the post Washington consensus', the 1998 WIDER Annual Lecture, Helsinki, 7 January.

—— (1999a) 'Interest rates, risk, and imperfect markets: Puzzles and policies', *Oxford Review of Economic Policy* 15(2): 59–76.

—— (1999b) 'The World Bank at the millennium', 109(459): F577–97.

—— (1999c) 'Two principles for the next round: Or, how to bring the developing countries in from the cold', mimeo, Geneva, 21 September.

—— (1999d) 'Whither reform? Ten years of the transition', World Bank Annual Bank Conference on Development Economics, 28–30 April.

—— (2000) 'Democratic development as the fruits of labour', Keynote Address, Industrial Relations Research Association, AEA Meetings, Boston, January.

Stiglitz, J. and K. Hoff (1999) 'Modern economic theory and development', Symposium on Future of Development Economics in Perspective, Dubrovnik, 13–14 May.

Tommasi, M. and K. Lerulli (eds) (1995) *The New Economics of Human Behaviour*, Cambridge: Cambridge University Press.

Teriba, O. (1996) 'The challenge of Africa's socioeconomic development', in Griesgraber and Gunter (eds) (1996).

Toye, J. (1994) 'Structural adjustment: Context, assumptions, origins and diversity', in van der Hoeven and van der Kraaij (eds) (1994).

van der Hoeven, R. and F. van der Kraaij (eds) (1994) *Structural Adjustment and Beyond in Sub-Saharan Africa*, London: James Currey.

Wade, R. (1996) 'Japan, the World Bank, and the art of paradigm maintenance: The East Asian miracle in political perspective', *New Left Review* 217, May–June: 3–37.

Watanabe, T. (1998) 'Designing Asia for the next century', in Ohno and Ohno (eds) (1998).

Williamson, J. (1990) 'What Washington means by policy reform', in Williamson (ed.) (1990).

—— (1997) 'The Washington consensus revisited', in Emmerij (ed.) (1997).

Williamson, J. (ed.) (1990) *Latin American Adjustment: How Much Has Happened?*, Washington: Institute for International Economics.

World Bank (1993) *The East Asian Miracle: Economic Growth and Public Policy, A World Bank Policy Research Report*, Oxford: Oxford University Press.

World Bank (1981) *Accelerated Development in Sub-Saharan Africa: An Agenda for Action*, Washington D.C.: World Bank.

—— (1994) *Adjustment in Africa: Reforms, Results, and the Road Ahead*, Oxford: Oxford University Press.

Yusuf, S. and J. Stiglitz (1999) 'Development issues: Settled and open', Symposium on Future of Development Economics in Perspective, Dubrovnik, 13–14 May.

2 Financial system design and the post-Washington consensus

Sedat Aybar and Costas Lapavitsas

Introduction

The role of the financial system in the development process is a central concern of the post-Washington consensus, and a major bone of contention with the Washington consensus. The rise of the post-Washington consensus has coincided with the relative decline in influence of the financial liberalisation current that was closely associated with the Washington consensus. In recent years, there has been a general shift in focus of financial research towards the institutional structure of the financial system (indicative literature includes Zysman 1983; Mayer 1987, 1988; Corbett and Mayer 1991; Mishkin 1997). The design of financial systems is increasingly thought to influence monitoring of investment, avoidance of rent-seeking and generation of entrepreneurial incentives. Facilitating the shift is an underlying transformation of microeconomic theory and the emergence of endogenous growth theory, driven by analysis of market failure due to asymmetric information and transactions costs, as discussed elsewhere in this volume. This has allowed incorporation into analysis of finance of concepts previously thought of as non-economic: trust, customs, networks, commitment and so on. This development has provided necessary underpinning for the post-Washington consensus.

In the early 1970s, theoretical treatment of the relationship of the financial system to capitalist development came to be dominated by the literature on financial liberalisation originating in the work of MacKinnon (1973) and Shaw (1973). This literature largely ignored the institutional structure of the financial system and concerned itself, above all, with determination of interest rates. As is well known, its main claim is that, if interest rates are kept artificially low by the state, savings will be low and inefficient investment will be encouraged, thus fostering underdevelopment. What matters for development is free determination of interest rates, while the design of the financial system is not an important concern. Financial liberalisation in developing countries has been exhaustively discussed during the last two decades both as theory and as policy advocated by leading international development institutions, such as the World Bank. It is now beyond question that its results in developing countries have been deeply disappointing. This has led to a gradual crystallisation of the following two currents of thought, and led to broad reconsideration of the relationship of the financial system to capitalist development.

One current, associated with the post-Washington consensus and typified by the work of Stiglitz (1985, 1994, 1996) and his associates (Stiglitz and Weiss 1981; Stiglitz and Uy 1996), claims that bank-based systems that are also relatively 'repressed' (i.e. exhibiting state controls over financial prices and flows) are more efficacious at promoting development than liberalised market-based systems. By contrast, the other current, though its emergence also reflects disappointment with the results of financial liberalisation, defends the notion that a liberalised and market-based financial system can be conducive to economic development (Levine 1992; Bencivenga *et al.* 1995; Levine and Zervos 1996; Demirguc-Kunt and Levine 1996a, 1996b, 1999). Financial liberalisation is accepted but also extended and complemented, particularly through analysis of the role of stock markets in economic development. A well-developed financial system is seen as an effective cause of economic development. For that, a freely operating stock market ought to complement a freely operating banking system.

Despite their apparent differences, the two currents share common conceptual foundations. In particular, financial systems are compared with each other according to their efficiency in receiving and transmitting information, creating transparency and generally dealing with market imperfections deriving from information asymmetry in credit markets. Reliance on the concept of asymmetric information has facilitated use of cross-country and cross-section econometric techniques – particularly by the market-based current – to endogenise externalities that were previously left out, such as social capital, ethnicity and political unrest. Both currents treat information as an absolute material fact in possession of market agents, rather than as a state of knowledge among market participants that is conditional upon social, political and historical factors. Such treatment of information leads to empirical work that is inherently problematic and hinders assessment of the merits of different financial systems.

Reliance on the concept of asymmetric information, furthermore, prevents analysis of the financial system precisely as a system, that is, as an entity the various parts of which are organically related to each other and to the 'real' economy. Instead, the financial system is treated as an agglomeration of institutions, markets and assets that might or might not exhibit certain informational properties. Thus, the aim of both currents is to identify a design for the financial system that has optimal informational and other properties for development of the 'real' economy. By this token, there is limited analysis of the two-way interaction between the financial system and the process of capitalist accumulation, and the literature shows scant appreciation of transformations wrought on the financial system by spontaneous changes in the 'real' economy. At a further remove, analysis is precluded of the social, historical and political context within which the financial system interacts with the 'real' economy.

The following section of this chapter analyses in detail the competing claims of the two currents, and demonstrates their common features regarding information asymmetry and lack of analysis of finance as a system. The next section offers an alternative analysis of the financial system that draws on radical political economy and stresses the character of finance as a system, the influence of the 'real' economy upon its design and the importance of social, historical and political factors in its analysis. We provide broad support for our claims through consideration of the development of the Japanese and the Turkish financial systems in the two subsequent sections. The final section draws conclusions.

Analysis of bank-based and market-based financial systems

It is shown below that both currents treat the financial system as a more or less arbitrary collection of markets, instruments and assets that derives its character from its properties in gathering and transmitting information. For both, the financial system can act as the engine of economic development.

Bank-based systems

Theoretical analysis of the merits of bank-based financial systems is usually undertaken within a principal-agent framework in which asymmetry of information allows participants in economic transactions to pursue divergent objectives. This might lead to adverse selection (lenders being confronted with a disproportionate amount of high-risk projects and thus forced to ration credit to newcomers) and moral hazard (borrowers who face credit rationing might attempt to borrow at high rates of interest by presenting banks with dishonest and fraudulent projects) (Stiglitz and Weiss 1981). Thus, in the presence of asymmetric information, the unregulated operation of banks can lead to inefficiently high interest rates, discouraging productive investment and reducing the return to lenders by attracting increasingly risky borrowers. This can also lead to increased demand by savers for existing assets, thereby artificially inflating their prices. In this light, the theoretical approach of financial liberalisation is unsatisfactory since it treats price and quantity controls imposed by the state as the only reason for the absence of non-rationed equilibrium in credit markets.

Further, it is also pointed out that the certainty and efficacy of contracting among financial institutions and productive enterprises might be worse for unregulated financial systems even with strongly developed capital markets in place (Mayer 1987, 1988). 'Commitment' by banks to enterprises is the key concept in this regard. Related to this point is the claim that stockholder meetings and the threat of take-over have significant weaknesses as monitoring devices over borrowing firms (Stiglitz 1985). Stockholders find it difficult to organise collectively and meetings can be orchestrated by better informed management. Those contemplating take-over have to contend with the costs imposed by an incumbent management and with the need to distinguish between poor performance and poor circumstance in evaluating a firm. However, doing so might incur investigative costs that benefit others (free-riding). Moreover, in the absence of 'commitment', the management of firms might be characterised by short-termism as far as the goals of investment and productivity growth are concerned.

A practical resolution of these problems is perceived through closer collaboration among contracting parties, encouraging long-term financial arrangements based on reputation and reducing reliance on anonymous market forces. Consequently, how banks relate institutionally to industry is of crucial importance for economic growth and performance.[1] Japanese banks, often with a 'main bank' in the lead, are presumed to have an intimate interaction with the firms to which they lend, monitoring performance intensively, providing long-term finance and, most importantly, securing long-term plans for restructuring in times of 'distress'. 'Commitment' reflects a systemic reputational effect, or implicit contract, on both sides. The bank is prepared to take a risk with a company in 'distress' since companies do not, on the whole, take advantage of the possibility of turning to other banks or sources of finance in better times (Aoki and Patrick 1994; see also Horiuchi and Yoshino 1992).

Empirical support, on the other hand, is usually provided by reference to the role of East and South East Asian (particularly Japanese) financial arrangements in accomplishing the 'Asian miracle'. Characteristic works in this connection, though considerably differentiated among themselves, are Chalmers Johnson (1982), Amsden (1989), Okimoto (1989), Wade (1990), Aoki and Patrick (1994), Teranishi (1996) and Aoki *et al.* (1997). Japanese 'main banks' are presumed to have intimate interaction with borrowing firms, monitoring their performance, lending long-term and providing funds in periods of distress (Aoki and Patrick 1994). 'Commitment' creates a reputational effect and both companies and banks are unwilling to disturb their relationship by seeking new partners. This is in contrast to Anglo-Saxon banking practices whereby banks and companies relate to each other at arm's length and on terms dictated largely by prices and conditions specified on market contracts. By implication, a bank-based financial system that exhibits 'commitment' tendencies can prove an efficient cause of rapid capitalist development.

In this light, lifting of state controls over credit prices, removal of direction of credit flows and dismantling of quantitative restrictions over finance run counter to successful capitalist accumulation and development. Once again, the experience of the financial systems of East and South East Asian countries has been used to provide support for this view (Amsden 1989; Wade 1990; Stiglitz 1996). 'Mild repression' of interest rates and credit allocation presumably allowed East and South East Asian governments to channel saving to investing firms through bank-based financial systems. Funds were directed to areas of economic activity that generated high returns, ensured technological and knowledge gains, and sustained growth and development. In this way, the exceptionally high savings of the region were not squandered on housing and consumption loans, as was likely to have happened under a liberalised market-based system, but instead supported capital accumulation.

More broadly, for supporters of bank-based systems, the experience of East Asia has shown that a third paradigm of capitalist development exists, in addition to the one based on the operation of free markets and the one based on planning, namely market-friendly intervention. Market failure, typically associated with externalities, public goods, imperfect competition and incomplete markets makes market-friendly intervention both necessary and appropriate.[2] According to Stiglitz (1996), governments in East Asia used and created markets to promote the generation of saving, more efficient resource allocation, equality, the accumulation of physical and human capital, investment and, ultimately, higher growth. Stiglitz and Uy (1996) claim that market-friendly state interventions in the sphere of finance had the following two objectives. First, the absence of efficient capital markets meant that firms had to rely on internally generated funds and private returns to investment diverged among firms. Thus, interventions had to make markets and institutions work better in this respect. Second, even in the presence of well-functioning capital markets, governments had to intervene to equalise private and social returns to investment. Thus, the desirability of moving towards a bank-based and more regulated financial system, along the lines of Japan or Germany, is proclaimed.[3] However, the exact nature of a move towards a bank-based system is not readily discernible, either in the reforms of the financial system itself or in its relations with other institutions within the economy.

The recent economic crisis in East and South East Asia inevitably poses a major analytical and empirical problem for advocates of bank-based systems: the crisis originated in the financial system, and appears to have been exacerbated by the strong 'relational' aspect of finance in those countries. Interestingly enough, the current response is to attribute the crisis partly to the unravelling of the 'relational' and bank-based character of East and South East Asian financial systems in recent years. Thus, Wade and Veneroso (1998) argue that bank-based systems have proven particularly suitable for channelling the exceptionally high savings of Asian societies into investment. However, foreign pressure (often associated with international organisations, and even involving bribes for local officials) are perceived to have encouraged these countries to adopt several features of market-based systems, especially to remove controls over international capital flows. This led to a dilution of the monitoring and control properties of their financial systems, and contributed to the crisis. The plausibility of this argument notwithstanding, it is notable that the problematic and crisis-inducing change of these financial systems (seen as models for development) is attributed exclusively to foreign pressure exerted on otherwise unproblematic bank-based systems.

Market-based systems

Exponents of the merits of market-based systems typically claim that rising stock market activity tends to accompany rising 'real' activity (Levine and Zervos 1996). Financial development and stock exchange development are seen as contributing to current and future growth, and to capital accumulation (Atje and Jovanovic 1993). The literature is, in part, an attempt to rationalise the recent explosive growth of stock markets in several developing countries, given that stock exchanges were largely absent from the main corpus of financial liberalisation theory.[4] The development of stock markets is now treated as one element in a sequence of financial reforms: successful liberalisation depends on the development of stock markets to complement existing financial markets and intermediaries (Fry 1997).

More broadly, the literature tends to argue that financial development (of which stock markets are but an important part) is an effective cause of economic growth and development. Thus, for Levine (1997), finance benefits development in five ways: risk trading, resource allocation, monitoring, savings mobilisation and facilitation of the exchange process. In this context, well-developed stock markets are supposed to provide firms with services additional and complementary to those provided by banks. Thus, financial systems without well-developed stock markets are less capable of sustaining firm expansion into risky areas, and less capable of monitoring firm management (Demirguc-Kunt and Maksimovic 1996).

Much of the work of this current is empirical and employs cross-country econometric analysis, along the lines of King and Levine (1993). Thus, Levine and Zervos (1996), using cross-section regressions for several countries, claim that stock market liquidity is positively and significantly correlated with economic growth, accumulation and productivity increases. For successful long-term growth, a financial system must contain well-developed banks and stock markets. In this view, there are no negative effects on private savings or on long-term growth arising from stock market liquidity, international integration or volatility. Nor are there negative effects on bank credits arising from a fall of stock prices, as may be the case in stock markets where listed companies rely heavily on the banking sector for loans and credit guarantees (OECF 1999). There is, finally, no room for 'repression' in this view of the financial system.

Empirical work also purports to show that stock market development complements and enhances bank intermediation by enabling a higher debt/equity ratio for firms (Demirguc-Kunt and Maksimovic 1996). If the financial system lacks a developed stock market, firms might choose their financial strategy on the basis of tax advantages rather than risk-return trade-off, hence leading to sub-optimal investment in production activities subject to long-term risk. Moreover, reliance on borrowing might discourage managers from exploiting risky but profitable projects, if the firm's creditors capture the resulting increases in value. Finally, stock markets generate information about firms that may be freely used by creditors, leading to cheaper monitoring.[5] Empirical results of this type by Demirguc-Kunt and Levine (1996a) similarly conclude that stock market development does not prejudice development of other financial intermediaries (while stock market volatility does), and that countries with internationally integrated stock markets tend to have larger banks and better developed financial systems.

On this basis, stock market development complements other aspects of financial development, and stock markets are instrumental in boosting economic growth (Demirguc-Kunt and Levine 1996b). Stock market development not only complements debt financing but also increases it Demirguc-Kunt and Levine 1996b, p. 234):

> These findings are consistent with the view that at early stages of market development, improvement in stock market functioning tends to improve information quality, monitoring, and corporate control, such that these improvements induce creditors to lend more. For these firms, debt and equity finance are complementary.

Accordingly, governments in developing countries should remove barriers to developing stock markets, but also abstain from adopting tax and other measures that might foster their growth. Finally, Levine and Zervos (1998) find that stock market development and greater ease in trading equities appear not to reduce savings, indeed not to influence savings at all. However, in line with the general position of this current, they also find that though both banks and stock markets influence long-term growth positively, they appear to do so independently of each other by providing different sets of services to enterprises. Hence, they acknowledge the need for separate but parallel analyses of banks and stock markets.[6]

This favourable view of stock markets has outspoken critics. The main argument against it, in a nutshell, is that stock markets in developing countries tend to have low capitalisation, high volatility and heavy dependence on world markets. Hence, developing-country stock markets are liable to be fragile and could seriously increase risk for the financial system as a whole. Moreover, high volatility causes short-termism that might impede the appropriate pricing of fundamentals and distort the take-over mechanism, creating a 'casino' effect that adversely affects economic growth. Singh (1997), for instance, claims that stock market prices in developing countries are often dominated by noise and do not reflect fundamental values. The take-over mechanism fails to work as suggested by theory because size is more important than performance: weakly performing large firms have more chances of survival than small efficient firms. In addition, international capital flows, such as those directed at stock markets, could increase financial instability and make the national economy more vulnerable to international macroeconomic fluctuations (Singh 1992).

In a similar vein, Akyuz (1993, p. 33) draws attention to the rise in instability generated by the close link between capital and currency markets since movements in foreign exchange rates condition the expected returns of foreign investors. Deterioration in the terms of trade, for instance, makes devaluation appear inevitable and might lead to a sharp decline in equity prices and capital outflow. Similarly, both optimistic and pessimistic expectations in equity markets can exert strong influence on exchange rates, leading to large-scale foreign currency transactions by non-residents. The resultant currency crisis might lead to sharp reversals in stock prices, as is the case in the recent South East Asian crisis (Krugman 1998, 1999).

Political economy of financial system design: a result of and stimulus to capitalist accumulation

The theoretical work on financial systems, reviewed above, typically proceeds by construing finance as a set of archetypal assets (for example, short- and long-term loans, or bonds as opposed to equity) and a set of institutions and markets (for example, money and bond markets, or commercial and investment banks). To this is usually added analysis of state regulation of the financial system (prudential and other) and of the degree of intervention in the direction and allocation of credit. Correspondingly, market-based as opposed to bank-based systems are readily associated with the predominance of different types of assets, institutions, markets and regulations.

In practice, however, the distinction between the two forms of finance is not so readily distinct. Financial systems, at least in developed countries, appear to possess essentially the same types of institutions, markets and assets. The relative weight of particular types of assets in such systems often contradicts their conventional characterisation as bank- or market-based (Corbett and Jenkinson 1996). In Japan, for instance, market-based finance for investment purposes has been surprisingly high throughout the post-war period. Analogously, both German and US corporations rely heavily on internally generated funds for investment (Corbett and Jenkinson 1997). Thus, categorisation of financial systems on the basis of formal differences in institutions, assets, and so on will often result in misleading conclusions. It follows that differences among financial systems ought to be examined in the context of the broad systemic relationship between industry and finance, in which government plays a vital role.

By the same token, theoretical analysis tends to be based upon a variety of functions undertaken by financial institutions in sequence over the lifetime of investment projects. Purely in the relations between finance and industry, this involves screening proposals, constructing particular terms and conditions for contracts, monitoring outcomes and dealing with them when they fall outside contractual stipulations. Once again, however, such functions do not necessarily correspond consistently with one another along a continuum between a market- and bank-based financial system. The specific social, historical and political context within which particular financial systems relate to industry is of critical importance in this respect, and has to be explicitly acknowledged. More specifically, the requirements imposed by the 'real' economy on the financial system differ over time and at different stages of a country's economic development. This has profound (and to a large extent spontaneously arising) implications for the design of financial systems. Thus, it is probable that the virtues of bank-based systems are less significant once large-scale corporations and conglomerates have been established that have the capacity to command sufficient long-term finance from a variety of diverse sources.[7]

Despite their formal differences, both theoretical currents regard the operations of the financial system as an effective cause of successful capitalist development – financial development drives economic growth and development. Debate and differences of analysis and opinion are about the institutional structure, and the process of determination of prices and quantities of credit, which would best enable the financial system to fulfil its putative role of spurring economic development. In analysis of the requisite institutional structure, moreover, both currents focus on the contractual arrangement between lender of money (individual or institution) and borrower of money (enterprise). Drawing on analysis of the informational content of money lending, some contractual arrangements might be seen as better than others in allowing the lender to screen and monitor the borrower (the latter being assumed to possess more information about investment projects than the lender). Analogously, some forms of state intervention might enable lenders to procure funds where none would have been forthcoming under freely determined contractual relations. This can then be construed as either beneficial or inimical to capitalist accumulation. In this light, the task of economic theory appears to be to propose a design of financial system that complies best with the underlying relation between lender and borrower of money.

This is a misleading way to approach the design of the financial system. Far from being the driving force of accumulation, the financial system is an outgrowth of the accumulation of industrial and commercial capital. It is a system of institutions, markets and instruments, which is structured in a specific way analysed below, and which arises from foundations provided by the operations of industrial and commercial capital. Equally, the relationship between lender and borrower of money, though critically important, is neither the only nor the most important economic relationship determining the characteristics of the capitalist credit system. It is shown below that trade credit among capitalist enterprises is analytically prior to money lending in theorising the design of the financial system. From this analytical standpoint, it is possible to show why historical, social and political factors specific to each country play an exceptionally important role in shaping the financial system. The following related points are important in this respect.[8]

Trade (or commercial) credit arises constantly and spontaneously among industrial and commercial capitals, irrespective of the existence of banks and other financial institutions. Analytically, trade credit relations (i.e. 'buy now, pay later') are not those of lender and borrower of money but those of seller and buyer of commodities against a promise to pay. Informational asymmetries implicit to the relationship between owner of money and owner of investment project are irrelevant to the relationship between seller of commodities (who wants to complete one circuit of industrial capital) and buyer of commodities (who wants to start or continue another). Firms that extend trade credit to each other are already connected through the process of production and circulation of a particular commodity. Trade credit advance is predicated upon relations of trust and commitment arising from regular buying and selling, as well as relations of power (market and otherwise) among enterprises. Moreover, the material and technical aspects of one capital circuit locking into another (above all, the period and the rate of turnover of both capitals) critically affect the terms on which trade credit is advanced, especially the term to maturity (Itoh and Lapavitsas 1999, ch. 4). These terms are also affected by the institutional arrangements among capitalists for the clearing and settlement of trade debt.

Trade credit relations are a spontaneously emerging foundation on which the capitalist financial system is constructed. Inter-firm credit generates instruments (bills and other), and a concomitant need to transfer money and clear balances, which provide business opportunities and an appropriate environment for banks systematically to undertake money lending. The first and continually vital role of banks is to provide order to the flows of trade credit, facilitating the clearing of balances and transferring money (Itoh and Lapavitsas 1999, ch. 4). By this token, relations of banks with their clients are not determined simply by screening and monitoring of loans for particular projects but also by systematising and extending pre-existing networks of trade credit among their customers. Consequently, for banks, trust, commitment and obligation in their relations with enterprises might well derive from the existing commercial and other relations among enterprises themselves.

At the same time, the main economic function of banks is to collect idle money across society, transform it into loanable money capital and channel it to capitalist accumulation. In this respect, bank lending is premised upon systematic generation of idle money by enterprises in the normal course of their industrial and commercial operations, which banks collect and redirect to accumulation.[9] For analytical purposes, it is vital to acknowledge the sharp contrast between trade and banking credit – the former resting on commodity capital, the latter resting on loanable money capital. Specifically, for banking credit, there are no pre-existing networks of production and circulation into which it must necessarily fit; no given interlocking circuits of capital that set limits to the terms of its advance and repayment. The terms, conditions and patterns of advance of banking credit are inherently fluid and flexible, and more so than those of trade credit. Capitalists spontaneously generating trade credit, for instance, are likely to be active in related

lines of production, often in well-defined geographical areas. In contrast, banks can, in principle, lend to capitalists in any line of business and in many geographical areas.

Efficient and flexible advance of banking credit, on the other hand, presupposes existence of credit relations among financial institutions. Inter-bank credit relations, typically in order to secure reserves, give rise to the money market. Relations between borrower and lender in the money market are quite different from those between bank and borrowing capitalist. In the money market, banking credit reaches a homogeneous form that has society-wide generality and applicability. Loanable capital is traded as a commodity that has overcome the particularities of investment project, geographical area, credit history of the borrower and lender, and so on. The informational content of bank-to-bank lending is consequently simpler and clearer than that of bank-to-enterprise lending.

Thus, the capitalist credit system has a pyramid-like structure. It comprises the following layers, from the bottom up: inter-firm trade, individual banking credit and money market credit.[10] The pyramid rests upon indus-trial and commercial accumulation both in terms of spontaneous generation of inter-firm trade credit and in terms of systematic creation of idle money available for lending. At the same time, the credit system evidently sustains capitalist accumulation in several ways. It provides clearing and payment services that reduce the costs of circulation of capital and accelerate its turnover. It mobilises money that would have lain idle, while reducing the need for individual capitalists to keep reserves of money in order to confront trade fluctuations. It channels money capital to areas of expected high prof-itability, thus equalising returns across the economy. It also facilitates the financing of investment, thus making possible the reallocation of resources in order to meet the needs of the future. Thus, the relationship between the credit system and capitalist accumulation runs in both directions: the credit system derives its fundamental design from relations of accumulation but also promotes development of these relations.

The capitalist financial system is complete when a stock market emerges to supplement the pyramid-like credit system. In the stock market, capital is mobilised on the basis of joint investment (equity) rather than debt, a difference that arises primarily because of the material characteristics of the activities that seek stock market funding (Itoh and Lapavitsas 1999, ch. 5) Typically, operations with great fixed-capital requirements and (often related) slow turnover present levels of uncertainty and risk that result in prohibitive rates of interest for loan finance. Joint-stock capital, since it is based on ownership rather than debt, allows for a more general mobilisation of idle money across society, including very small sums. Since it rests on property, equity obviously makes for quite different relations between coun-terparties compared to debt. However, the credit system and the stock market share the sources of loanable money capital. Thus, the rate of interest is able to act as benchmark for determination of prices of stock market assets, despite it being determined through the operations of the credit system. Moreover, fluidity and depth in the operations in the stock market depends on the availability of credit supplied through the credit system.

The most important theoretical conclusion from this analysis of the financial system is that relations of finance are intrinsically fluid and flexible. The volumes, prices and terms of repayment of trade credit bear no necessary relationship to the rhythms of production and circulation of commodity output, though they depend on those. On the other hand, availability of trade credit might encourage production to continue when little possibility exists of successful sale of final output (hence of repayment of credit.) Analogously, volumes and prices of banking credit depend on the rhythm of industrial accumulation but loanable capital can 'stretch' accumulation and generate conditions for its own repayment and reconstitution. Put differently, while prices, output volumes and rates of return of industrial capital are constrained by real wages, technology of production and turnover rate of capital, for the operations of finance no significant constraints of this type exist. A given financial structure can provide very variable volumes of credit under widely different terms to the same process of capital accumulation.

Fluidity and flexibility mean that few abstract statements can be made about the design of the financial system, other than those relating to the pyramid-like ordering of financial relations. Sufficient generality does exist in financial relations to provide for broad similarity across financial systems (in their formal structure, financial systems across the developed world are remarkably similar). However, the inherent fluidity of finance and the relative weakness of constraints placed upon it by real wages, technology and so on mean that key features of it do not admit of general theoretical determination. Aspects such as the typical time to maturity of trade credit and its availability in particular geographical areas, access to banking credit, rolling over of maturing bank debts and toleration of non-payment of interest cannot be determined theoretically but depend on institutional, historical and social factors.

The disproportionately important role of institutional, historical and social factors in the operations of finance also means that the design of financial systems reflects conditions specific to each capitalist country. The relationship of the financial system to capitalist accumulation cannot be fully ascertained in abstract terms, and it does not always run in one direction (i.e. finance driving capitalist accumulation). Rather, the relationship is transformed according to changes in the process of accumulation itself, and according to alterations in the social, historical and political conditions within which accumulation takes place. Below we substantiate these conclusions further by briefly considering the recent evolution of the Japanese and the Turkish financial systems.

Evolution of the Japanese financial system

'Repressed' post-Second World War Japanese finance was characterised by tight regulation of interest at low levels to promote industrial investment, rigid functional specialisation among institutions and effective isolation of the financial system from the international markets through foreign exchange controls. Three factors led to the demise of 'repression' and the profound transformation of Japanese finance since the middle of the 1970s, two of which are domestic (Lapavitsas 1997). First, sections of the company sector found themselves in possession of substantial financial surpluses that encouraged corporations to bypass banks and deal directly in open markets for loanable capital. In their early form, these were typified by the *gensaki* market (a largely open market in inter-company lending based on company-issued paper). Second, the government emerged as a substantial borrower (in its attempt to avert recession in the mid-1970s). To secure absorption of an enormously enlarged issue of bonds at acceptable prices, the authorities had to concede to banks the creation of relatively freely operating secondary markets for debt instruments. Finally, political pressure from abroad and the increasing willingness of Japanese financial institutions to compete internationally led to the abolition of foreign exchange controls in 1980. Thus, the different requirements imposed upon the financial system by the development of the economy undermined 'repression' and led to substantial financial liberalisation in the 1980s.

Throughout the 1980s and 1990s the Japanese financial system has retained many of its formal characteristics in terms of assets, institutions and markets. However, it is very different from the system that financed the rapid growth of the country, and which usually serves as paradigm for advocates of bank-based systems. Its change is best indicated by two phenomena: first, the setting of interest rates in largely free markets; and second, the blurring of the distinction between long-term and short-term financial institutions. Already from the early 1980s, 'marketisation' began to characterise Japanese finance (Tachi and Royama 1987). This is not to say that the 'relational' aspect of Japanese finance has disappeared. Indeed, one remarkable feature of the protracted crisis of the 1990s is the absence of solid evidence regarding the oft-announced demise of the 'main bank' relationship. However, it is undeniable that a system, which began life as a compact mechanism for channelling loanable funds to investment via financial intermediaries, has spontaneously created room within itself for transacting funds directly between lender and borrower. That is also one of the deeper causes of the systemic crisis of Japanese finance in the 1990s, and has important implications for the nature and scope of state intervention, discussed below.

The Japanese 'bubble' of the late 1980s was partly a product of the structural change of the financial system. Banks found themselves confronted by declining profitability (liberalised deposit rates having risen) and increasingly blurred lines of demarcation between their activities. In this environment, far from undertaking superior monitoring practices, banks wholeheartedly engaged in real estate and share speculation, including even the Industrial Bank of Japan that used to be considered a pillar of respectability and a signal-giver to others in the years of 'repression'. The changes in the financial system also strengthened the importance of the stock exchange in the Japanese economy. Paradoxically, this arose precisely because of the 'relational' aspect of Japanese finance, i.e. the prevalence of interlocking shareholding among enterprises and banks. To cement their long-term relationship, Japanese banks and enterprises hold each other's shares, which they typically do not trade. As the stock market rose tremendously in the 1980s, there were large hidden gains made by banks on their share holdings, which operated as hidden reserves. These facilitated further bank lending and so fed the bubble. Conversely, when the stock market collapsed in the 1990s, the implicit losses by banks on the shares they held seriously damaged them and impeded their necessary restructuring. One of the greatest ironies of the Japanese crisis of the 1990s is that the overall health of Japanese finance has come to depend greatly on the state of the stock exchange, despite the bank-based character of the financial system and the fact that less than half of the listed equity is actually traded.

Interventions by the Japanese state in the sphere of finance until the mid-1970s typically ensured provision of cheap credit to targeted industries, and gave guarantees of solvency and liquidity to banks. The practice of 'overloan' characterised the behaviour of Japanese banks throughout this period. Banks were encouraged by the state to expand the asset side of their balance sheet almost regardless of the liability side; the Bank of Japan (BoJ) guaranteeing their solvency through regular 'soft' loans. More broadly, the state played an important role in directly designing the post-war Japanese financial system. The Ministry of Finance (MoF) exercised tight prudential control over banks, relying on its control of awarding banking licences and permits for opening new branches. The MoF has offered to banks an implicit guarantee against bankruptcy throughout this period, and has also tightly regulated the pecking order among banks domestically. The BoJ has also exercised a strong prudential influence over the banks for much of the post-war period through 'window guidance', that is, direct encouragement to lend (or not) for particular purposes. The BoJ also played a major role in the direction of credit through the above-mentioned practice of 'overloan'. Moreover, 'repression' (coupled with direct control over substantial amounts of loanable funds via the Postal Savings System) allowed effective state intervention in the direction and pricing of credit.

Increasing 'marketisation' of the Japanese financial system since the mid-1970s has entailed a profound change in the character of state interventions in the sphere of finance. The days of tight interest rate controls, of credit subsidies, of direction of credit through legislation or administrative guidance, and of guaranteeing a small but stable profitability for banks (hence encouraging them constantly to seek a larger market share) are irretrievably gone. Even the character of prudential regulation seems to be changing: from control of bank activities and rankings through regular meetings with financial institutions, it appears to be turning into a more formal regulation of risk. The Japanese state is increasingly assuming the mantle of providing a 'safety net' for financial institutions and markets in the new conditions, relying on the relatively new Deposit Insurance Corporation at least as much as it does on the MoF and the BoJ.[11] Correspondingly, the activities of both of the latter have begun to change: from 1998, the MoF has started to devolve some of its supervisory role, and the BoJ, relying much more on open-market operations than before, has acquired much greater independence, concentrating on control of inflation.

In this respect too, the manner in which the Japanese financial crisis of the 1990s has been handled by the state indicates both the state's new role and the limits within which it operates in the realm of finance. The system of lifetime employment and welfare benefits through corporations, which prevailed in Japan for most of the post-war period, made corporate or affiliate bankruptcy difficult, since that would have implied unacceptable social and economic costs for the workforce. Consequently, industry and finance were constrained to restructure corporations in distress in ways that avoided high unemployment. This has meant an inability to countenance rapid deflation of bad debts and the consequent bankruptcies, lay-offs and so on. As a result, the Japanese state adopted a piecemeal approach in confronting the crisis of the 1990s, dealing gradually with the worst cases of bad debts while hoping that aggregate demand expansion would lessen the magnitude of the problem as a whole (Lapavitsas 1997). However, given the transformation of finance and the exceptional severity and length of the crisis, by the late 1990s the state could begin to countenance the previously unthinkable bankruptcy of large financial institutions. The failure of the very large institutions, Hokkaido Takushoku Bank and Yamaichi Securities, in 1998 indicates the new relation of the authorities with the financial system. The Japanese state now appears to treat financial institutions similarly to other capitalist firms – it concerns itself primarily with maintaining orderly conditions in the financial markets and does not assign an outstanding role to banks in the development process.

Evolution of the Turkish financial system

Turkey is also an appropriate case for demonstrating the importance of country-specific social, historical and political factors in shaping the financial system, as well as the two-way interaction between finance and capitalist accumulation. It is a developing country with a large and sophisticated financial system that embraced financial liberalisation avidly in the 1980s. Further, it possesses a varied and growing industrial sector and has a tradition of strong state intervention in the economy.

The early history of Turkish (Ottoman) finance is one of gradual establishment of a German-type bank-based financial system. The reasons for that were clearly social and political. Impressed by Germany's efficiency and technique, the Ottoman bureaucracy expanded military co-operation and undertook reform guided by Germany. German firms began to dominate Ottoman banking and railway construction at the expense of both British and French ones (Ortayli 1983), and German banks provided funds for military purchases in contrast to British and French ones (Blaisdell 1929). A turning point in the development of Turkish finance came in 1908, the year of the Young Turk revolution, and the reasons were again social and political (Ahmad 1969; Hanioglu 1995). Inspired by nationalist ideology, the Young Turks aimed at lessening the importance of foreign banks, while promoting the interests of the Turkish/Muslim element of the Empire in opposition to ethnic minorities (Greeks, Jews, Armenians and others) (Keyder 1980; Toprak 1982). Turkish/Muslim merchants, large landowners and small industrialists began to form commercial banks, mainly in Anatolia (Keyder 1978, 1987). These single-branch banks became profitable after the links with foreign credit institutions were broken during the First World War.

Thus, the early design of the Turkish financial system owed much to the presence of the state in the credit markets, as well as to the conflict between, on the one hand, merchants and financiers of minority origin and, on the other, entrepreneurs and landowners of Turkish/Muslim origin. In this sense, it is impossible to undertake analysis of the system independently of historical and social developments in Turkey. Collateral and guarantees provided by the state and direct control of credit were instrumental to the functioning of the credit markets. Private credits to trade, industry and agriculture were typically extended on full collateral and after confirmation of the repayment ability of the borrower. Absence of strong contract enforcement agencies and uncertainty surrounding economic activity led to the establishment of the closest of relationships between banks and their borrowers: entrepreneurs of Turkish/Muslim origin who were in need of credit formed their own lending institutions (Keyder 1987, Akguc 1989).

After establishment of the Republic in 1923, and in line with the new ideology of state and nation building, state-owned development and investment banks were established, benefiting from state incentives and raising funds for State Economic Enterprises (Effimianidis 1936; Yerasimos 1974; Keyder 1978). The majority of private commercial banks did not survive the world crisis of the 1930s, and the number of foreign banks was reduced to four that operated in the major industrial and commercial centres. A central bank was formed in 1930 and the equity market was clearly marginal to the financial system. Tight 'relational' networks between banks, industry and the state prevailed until the late 1970s. State-owned commercial banks provided the bulk of credit on preferential terms to selected enterprises in line with official policies of import substitution, and real interest rates remained at negative levels until the late 1970s. Privately owned banks began to be established more briskly in the 1950s (Yasa 1980; Boratav 1982). Given that entry to the banking system was restricted, private enterprises acquired ownership of existing small rural banks and expanded their operations into the major cities by opening new branches. Nevertheless,

these did not have sufficient weight to alter the design of the Turkish financial system.

The 'repressed' character of the system was disturbed by severe shortages
of foreign exchange in the late 1970s, which were exacerbated by the US
embargo on Turkey following its intervention in Cyprus in 1974. After the
first oil shock in 1973–4, the government activated the scheme of
Convertible Turkish Lira Deposits (CTLD) in order to attract worker remit-
tances from abroad. The CTLD scheme allowed commercial banks to open
foreign exchange accounts, provided that the funds were deposited with the
central bank (Artun 1975; Kafaoglu 1986). Interest rates were negotiated
between banks and depositors, and the central bank guaranteed banks and
depositors against losses arising from devaluation of the Turkish lira. Heavy
devaluation pressure in 1978 pushed the levels of guarantees to unacceptable
heights and forced withdrawal of the scheme. The resultant squeeze on
commercial bank credit encouraged emergence of private lending institutions in close collaboration with the smaller commercial banks (Artun
1983). Typical among them were old and new broking houses operating
largely outside existing controls on interest rates and credit allocation. In
that context, successive devaluations of the Turkish lira in 1979 and a
dramatic deterioration of the internal political situation made it impossible
to resist steady IMF pressure to liberalise finance (Onder *et al.* 1993).[12]

The financial reform package of 1980 was a milestone in the evolution of
Turkish finance. It aimed at contributing to the reversal of the economic
difficulties of the 1970s as well as altering the design of financial system by
loosening the tight 'relational' networks connecting the state, banks and
industry. Liberalisation was expected to shift the financial system towards a
market-based structure by removing interest rate ceilings and promoting
the role of free markets in providing investment funds to the corporate
sector. In addition, the gradual withdrawal of the state from the credit-
delivery system was expected to usher in a transparent environment that
could help raise the efficiency of financial intermediation (Uygur 1993).
Events have turned out quite differently, and relations between banks,
industry and the state have continued strongly to reflect the specific social
and historical features of the Turkish economy (Akyuz 1990).

The new relations between financial institutions, industrial corporations
and the state that began to arise after liberalisation could already be
glimpsed during the so-called 'banker' (broker) crisis of 1982 (Colasan
1984a, 1984b) . As mentioned above, the credit squeeze of the late 1970s
encouraged the emergence of private lending institutions, often spurred by
established industrial and trading conglomerates. Several of the latter
formed their own broking institutions that were funded by certificates of
deposit (CDs) received from commercial banks with established 'relational'
connections with the conglomerates. These certificates of deposit were then
traded in open markets, thus raising investment funds for the conglomerates. Liberalisation and the attendant accentuation of competition among

financial institutions led to rapid expansion of this process and eventually to the crisis of 1982. The response of the Turkish state was to re-introduce controls over deposit interest rates and credit flows.

Nevertheless, gradual relaxation of legal restrictions in the 1980s allowed commercial banks to pursue active asset and liability management. Banks generally began to engage in new activities, such as certificates of deposit, repurchase agreements, retail financing, hedge funds and securitised loans. Some state banks were restructured and privatised. Introduction of the new instruments and institutional arrangements significantly increased the risks of instability in the financial environment (Ersel and Ozturk 1990; Atiyas and Ersel 1992). In this connection, the proliferation of financial instruments and arrangements has not followed the path expected by proponents of liberalisation, and it has not been free of hindrances reflecting Turkish specificity. Commercial banks have continued to advance loans by relying on traditional factors reflecting market share, power relations, ownership structures and already existing bank–industry connections (Ozden 1996; Kaplan 1997; Aybar 1999). Nevertheless, in the highly unstable and inflationary environment of the 1980s and 1990s, banks have opted to hedge risks by lending heavily against low-risk government securities rather than expanding their lending to industry and trade (Uygur 1993; Onder *et al.* 1993).

The proliferation of new instruments has allowed the central bank to begin to control the money supply by using the indirect method of open market operations since 1987. At the same time, the fact that the banking sector has remained heavily concentrated despite the rapid growth of small banks has enabled the authorities to maintain channels of direct influence on the operations of finance. In this respect, the presence of large publicly owned commercial banks in the credit markets provides an information-rich environment for all banks, which eases the pricing of bank credits for privately owned commercial banks. Further, promotion of certain sectors and incentives provided by the state have continued to play a pivotal role in the credit decision processes of private banks (Atiyas and Ersel 1992).

Moreover, the close 'relational' links between private commercial banks and industrial corporations also determine the behaviour of banks in the credit allocation process. 'Insider lending' has been a regular feature of liberalised Turkish finance and contributed to emergence of banking crises, most recently in 1994 when three privately owned commercial banks were declared insolvent. Following that crisis, the authorities introduced prudential regulation whereby the Savings Deposit Insurance Fund fully guarantees bank deposits. Banking has become an increasingly attractive business in Turkey under the Savings Deposit Insurance Scheme. In 1998, the number of commercial banks increased to eighty-five, including foreign banks (Banks Association of Turkey 1999). As mentioned above, commercial banks at present lend heavily to the state in the money markets, thus allowing the authorities to cover the budget deficit. Returns to banks from holding government paper appear exceptionally high and have contributed to the emergence of a social layer drawing substantial incomes from financial activities, popularly called *rentiers*. Such lending is at the expense of credits advanced to the productive sector and hinders the development process.

As far as lending to industry and commerce is concerned, publicly owned commercial banks have continued to offer finance preferentially to some industrial sectors as a result of political and social influence by borrowers on the banks.[13] As a result, these credits are not commercially priced and often turn bad. Private commercial banks, on the other hand, are not in a much better condition in this respect. Linked as they are to industrial corporations through ownership, the core of their activities remains provision of finance to sister companies. It is common for such credits to turn bad. Under the Bank Act of 1985, when the bank becomes insolvent, neither sister companies nor the bank's directors and owners are held responsible for losses. Such operations are commonly known as 'emptying the bank'.

The response of the state to these pathological features of bank intermediation again indicates the significance of the broad institutional, social and political conditions within which the flows of finance occur. Interventions by the Turkish state, though critically important, have to take into account the more liberalised outlook of the system and cannot immediately assume the direct character of the past. A new law was introduced in June 1999 that scraps the Bank Act of 1985 and establishes a supervisory institution for the banking sector that will replace the central bank in this respect. New measures of responsibility were introduced for bank directors at each level of a bank's hierarchy. When a bank is in distress, its owners will be asked to increase its capital base. If the owners fail to do so, the administration of the bank will be assumed by the Savings Deposits Insurance Fund, and owners and directors (including the executive board, the general manager and the assistant general manager) will be held responsible for the bank's failure. The new law allows for such banks to be forced to declare bankruptcy and so it is hoped that it will help limit bad lending policies.

Conclusion

For the post-Washington consensus, bank-based financial systems perform better than market-based ones in promoting growth and development, and admit more easily of state intervention in the flows of finance. For the supporters of market-based systems, on the other hand, stock markets provide vital complementary services to those provided by banks; hence the stock market is an integral part of a well-developed financial system. Both currents treat financial development as an efficient cause of growth and development, and derive many of their results from analysis of the informational content of borrower–lender relations.

Lack of recognition of the social, historical and political context within which the financial system operates – particularly the system's two-way relationship with the process of capitalist accumulation – is a major weakness of this literature. That is not to deny its considerable merits in addressing empirical variation and complexity in financial systems. However, that is normally done on the narrow and technical basis of information asymmetries, incentive compatibility, and the costs and difficulties of monitoring. This results in viewing the financial system as a more or less arbitrary collection of institutions, markets and instruments. However, the financial system should be addressed precisely as an integrated system for supplying finance to the economy that arises spontaneously on foundations provided by the 'real' economy itself. On the other hand, the fluid character of both trade and banking credit means that the institutional structure of the financial system reflects social, historical and political factors specific to each country. By this token, the character of the system inevitably changes in the course of economic development. In short, analysis of the relationship of finance to industry requires a country-specific political economy approach that is much broader than the information-theoretic approach favoured by both the post-Washington consensus and supporters of market-based systems.

Notes

1 As Mayer (1988, p. 1183) concludes for the UK:

> The distinctive feature of successful financial systems is their close involvement in industry .... The fundamental challenge that faces any institution or government that can affect the practice of finance is to encourage the emergence of closer relationships and to direct the wealth of talent that has now been concentrated in British financial institutions into direct participation in corporate activities.

2 In a similar manner, Wade (1990) differentiates between market-supporting and market-supplanting state intervention.
3 Cable (1985, p. 130) argues that the UK would benefit from a move towards a German-style banking system incorporating internal capital markets but that:

> The introduction in Britain of bank lending on German terms would involve long-term structural changes rather than a mere short-run behavioural adjustment ... the German model suggests that some redistribution of existing property rights would be involved and in any event changes in company law would be required.

Singh (1992, p. 45), however, sounds a note of caution about the dangers of 'crony capitalism'; that is, of promoting domestic oligopolies through preferential access to finance and inadequate overall banking regulation.
4 For evidence on the remarkable growth in stock market capitalisation as well as growth in portfolio flows across the world in recent years, see Mullins (1993) and Demirguc-Kunt and Levine (1996a).
5 In this light, small firms might be at a disadvantage compared to large ones, thus prejudicing the financing opportunities of sectors with many small firms. State intervention might thus be necessary to maintain compatibility with broader development objectives.
6 Arestis and Demetriades (1997) have shed doubt on these empirical findings. They use time-series data for the USA and Germany and find that long-run

causality between stock market volatility and GDP may vary across countries. They also question the appropriateness of cross-country regression, which necessarily ignore the history and path of evolution of each stock market.

7 Cho and Hellman (1993) have argued that in the initial stages of development of South Korea and Japan, government-led internal organisations (GLIOs) protected industries from information imperfections by emphasising communication, co-ordination and co-operation supported by institutional arrangements. Accordingly, governments were able to select good firms and implemented credit policies facilitating their growth. However, with success in development, GLIOs gave way to privately-led internal organisations (PLIOs) (Cho and Hellman, p. 23). Thus, in the later stages of development, individual entrepreneurship and innovation became more important. Competition among PLIOs eroded the consensus regarding the direction of development as different factions of society have pursued their own socio-economic agendas and placed less emphasis on national economic growth. In those circumstances, state control of credit has less to commend it.

8 Analysis in the rest of this section draws heavily on Itoh and Lapavitsas (1999).

9 See Lapavitsas (2000) for analysis of idle-money formation in the course of turnover of industrial capital.

10 The pyramid is complete when a central bank emerges at its apex, but that is not relevant to our present concerns.

11 An account of some of these changes can be found in Itoh (1995, ch. 6).

12 For a detailed account of the significance of the devaluations of the Turkish lira in the late 1970s, see Celasun and Rodrik (1989).

13 Suffice it to mention two notorious instances of such lending. First, in 1994, criminal charges were levelled against the director of one of the publicly owned banks (Emlakbank) for receiving a large bribe in order to facilitate credit advances. Second, in 1998, the privatisation of a publicly owned bank (Turkbank) involved pressure on the government from criminal organisations connected to ultra-nationalist circles, and contributed to the downfall of the 55th government.

References

Ahmad F. (1969) *The Young Turks: The Committee of Union and Progress in Turkish Politics 1908–1914*, Oxford: Clarendon Press.

—— (1995) *Ittihatciliktan Kemalizme* ('From Unionism to Kemalism'), Kaynak Yayinlari: Istanbul.

Akguc, O. (1989) *100 Soruda Turkiye'de Bankacilik* ('Banking in Turkey in 100 Questions'), Gercek Yay: Istanbul (first edition, 1987).

Akyuz, Y. (1990) 'Financial system and policies in Turkey in the 1980s', in Aricanli, T. and Rodrik, D. (eds) *The Political Economy of Turkey: Debt, Adjustment and Sustainability*, London: Macmillan.

—— (1993) *Financial Liberalisation: The Key Issues*, UNCTAD/OSG/DP/56, Geneva.

Amsden, A. (1989) *Asia's Next Giant*, Oxford University Press: New York.

Aoki, M. and H. Patrick (eds) (1994) *The Japanese Main Bank System: Its Relevance For Developing and Transforming Economies*, Oxford University Press: New York.

Aoki, M., Kim H. K., and M. Okuno-Fujiwara (eds) (1997) *The Role of Government in East Asian Economic Development: A Comparative Institutional Analysis*, Clarendon Press: Oxford.

Arestis, P. and P. Demetriades (1997) 'Financial development and economic growth: Assessing the evidence', *Economic Journal* 107, May: 783–99.

Artun, T. (1975) 'Dovize Cevrilebilir Mevduat Hesaplari' ('Convertible Deposit Accounts'), *Maliye Dergisi*, July–Augusts Ankara.

—— (1983) *Uluslararasi Bankacilik Bunalimi ve Turkiye'de 'Serbest' Faiz Politikasi* ('International Banking Crisis and "Free" Interest Rate Policy in Turkey'), Istanbul: Tekin Yay.

Atiyas, I. and H. Ersel (1992) *The Impact of Financial Reform: The Turkish Experience*, The World Bank, Industry and Energy Department, OSP: 65.

Atje, R., and B. Jovanovic (1993) 'Stock markets and development', *European Economic Review* 37: 632–40.

Aybar, S. (1999) 'An assessment of informational operations in credit decision making processes by the Turkish banks, Paper presented at Middle East Technical University (MTU) Economics Conference III, Ankara, Turkey, 8–11 September 1999.

Banks Association of Turkey (BaoFT) (1999) *Bankalarimiz 1998*, Istanbul.

Bencivenga, V., B. D. Smith and R. M. Starr (1995) *Equity Markets, Transaction Costs, and Capital Accumulation: An Illustration*, World Bank, Policy Research Working Papers No. 1456, Washington, DC.

Blaisdell, C. D. (1929) *European Financial Control in the Ottoman Empire*, Columbia University Press: New York.

Boratav, K. (1982) *Turkiye'de Devletcilik* ('Étatisme in Turkey'), Ankara: Savas Yay.

Cable, J. (1985) 'Capital market information and industrial performance: The role of West German banks', *Economic Journal* 95, March: 118–32.

Celasun, M. and D. Rodrik (1989) 'Debt, adjustment and growth: Turkey', in Sachs, J.D. and S. M. Collins *Developing Country Debts and Economic Performance*, Chicago: University of Chicago Press.

Cho J. Y. and T. Hellman (1993) 'The government's role in Japanese and Korean credit markets: A new institutional economics perspective', The World Bank, Policy Research Working Papers, WPS 1190.

Colasan, E. (1984a) *24 Ocak Bir Donemin Perde Arkasi* ('24 January, Behind the Curtains of a Period'), Istanbul: Milliyet Yayinlari.

—— (1984b) *Banker Skandalinin Perde Arkasi* ('Behind the Curtains of Banker Scandal'), Istanbul: Milliyet Yayinlari.

Corbett, J. and T. Jenkinson (1996) 'The financing of industry, 1970–1989: An international comparison', *Journal of the Japanese and International Economies* 10(1): 71–96.

—— (1997) 'How is investment financed? A study of Germany, Japan, the United Kingdom and the United States', *Papers in Money, Macroeconomics and Finance, The Manchester School Supplement* LXV: 69–93.

Corbett, J. and C. Mayer (1991) *Financial Reform in Eastern Europe: Progress with the Wrong Model*, 603, London: Centre for Economic Policy Research.

Demirguc-Kunt, A. and R. Levine (1996a) 'Stock market development and financial intermediaries: Stylized facts', *The World Bank Economic Review* 10(2): 291–321.

—— (1996b) 'Stock markets, corporate finance and economic growth: An overview', *The World Bank Economic Review* 10(2): 223–39.

—— (1999) 'Bank based and market based financial systems: Cross country comparisons', World Bank, Policy Research Working Paper No. 2143, Washington, DC.

Demirguc-Kunt, A. and V. Maksimovic (1996) 'Stock market development and financing choices of firms', *The World Bank Economic Review* 10(2): 341–70.

Effimianidis, Y. (1936) *Cihan Iktisat Buhrani Onunde Turkiye* ('Turkey Facing World Crisis'), Istanbul: II Kitap.

Ersel, H. and E. Ozturk (1990) 'The credit delivery system In Turkey', CBRT Pub., Discussion Paper No: 9003, Ankara.

Fry, M. (1997) 'In favour of financial liberalisation', *Economic Journal* 107 (May), 442: 754–70.

Hanioglu S. (1995) *The Young Turks in Opposition*, New York: Oxford University Press.

Horiuchi, A. and N. Yoshino (eds) (1992) *Gendai Nihon no Kinyu Bunseki*, Tokyo: Tokyo Daigaku Shuppansha.

Itoh, M. and C. Lapavitsas (1999) *Political Economy of Money and Finance*, Macmillan: London.

Itoh, O. (1995) *Nihongatakinyu no Rekishiteki Kozo*, Tokyo: Tokyo Daigaku Shuppansha.

Johnson Chalmers, H. (1982) *MITI and the Japanese Miracle*, Palo Alto: Stanford University Press.

Kafaoglu, A.B. (1986) *DCM Dosyasi* ('CTLD Files'), Istanbul: Alan Yayincilik.

Kaplan, H. (1997) 'Openness to change and budgetary control in Turkish banks, Istanbul: Capital Market Board (CMB) Publ. No. 102.

Keyder, C. (1978) *The Definition of Peripheral Economy: Turkey 1923–1929*, New York: Cambridge University Press.

—— (1980) 'Ottoman economy and finance 1881–1918', in Okyar F. and I. Halil (eds) *Social and Economic History of Turkey 1071–1929*, Ankara: Hacettepe Univ. Yay, pp. 323–7.

—— (1987) *State and Class in Turkey: A Study in Capitalist Development*, London: Verso.

King, R. G. and R. Levine (1993) 'Finance and growth: Shumpeter might be right', *Quarterly Journal of Economics* 108(3): 717–38.

Krugman, P. (1998) *The Accidental Theorist*, New York: W.W. Norton.

—— (1999) *The Return of Depression Economics*, New York: W.W. Norton.

Lapavitsas, C. (1997) 'Transition and crisis in the Japanese financial system: An analytical overview', *Capital and Class* 62, summer: 21–37.

—— (2000) 'On Marx's analysis of money hoarding in the turnover of capital', *Review of Political Economy* 12(2): 219–35.

Levine, R. (1992) *Financial Structures and Economic Development*, Washington, DC: World Bank, WPS: 849.

—— (1997) 'Financial development and economic growth', *Journal of Economic Literature* XXXV(2): 688–796.

Levine, R. and S. Zervos (1996) 'Stock market development and long-run growth', *The World Bank Economic Review* 10(2): 323–39.

—— (1998) 'Stock markets, banks, and economic development', *American Economic Review* 88: 537–88.

Mckinnon, R. I. (1973) *Money and Capital in Economic Development*, Washington DC: Brookings.

Mayer, C. (1987) 'The assessment: financial systems and corporate investment', *Oxford Review of Economic Policy* 3(4): i–xvi.

—— (1988) 'New issues in corporate finance', *European Economic Review* 32(4): 1167–89.

Mishkin, F. S. (1997) *The Economics of Money, Banking and Financial Markets*, Boston: Little Brown.

Mullins, J. (1993) 'Emerging equity markets in the global economy', *Federal Bank of New York Quarterly Review*, summer: 54–83.

OECF [The Overseas Research Papers] (1999) 'The effectiveness and major issues of capital controls policy in Malaysia', OECF Research Papers No. 33, Tokyo, Japan.

Okimoto, D. (1989) *Between MITI and the Market*, Palo Alto: Stanford University Press.

Onder, I., O. Turel, N. Ekinci and C. Somel (1993) *Turkiye'de Kamu Maliyesi, Finansal Yapi ve Politikalar* ('Fiscal Policy, Financial Structure and Policies in Turkey'), Istanbul: Turk Tarih Vakfi Yay.

Ortayli, I. (1983) *Osmanli Imparotorlugunda Alman Nufusu* ('German Influence in the Ottoman Empire'), Istanbul: Hil Yay.

Ozden, U. (1996) 'Investment analysis practices in Turkey, USA and UK, Istanbul: CMB Pub. No. 52.

Shaw, E.P. (1973) *Financial Deepening in Economic Development*, New York: Oxford University Press.

Singh, A. (1992) 'The stock market and economic development: Should developing countries encourage stock markets?', UNCTAD Discussion Paper, no. 49.

—— (1997) 'Financial liberalisation, stock markets and economic development', *Economic Journal* 107, May: 771–82.

Stiglitz, J. (1985) 'Credit markets and the control of capital', *Journal of Money, Credit, and Banking* 17(2): 133–52.

—— (1994) 'The role of the state in financial markets', *Proceedings of the World Bank Annual Conference on Development Economics 1993*: 19–52.

—— (1996) 'Some lessons from the East Asian miracle', *World Bank Observer* 11(2), August: 151–76.

Stiglitz, J. and M. Uy (1996) 'Financial markets, public policy, and the East Asian miracle', *World Bank Observer* 11(2), August: 249–76.

Stiglitz, J. and A. Weiss (1981) 'Credit rating in markets with imperfect information', *American Economic Review* 71, June: 393–410.

Tachi, Y. and S. Royama (1987) *Nihon no Kinyu Atarasii Mikata*, Tokyo: Tokyo Daigaku Shuppansha.

Teranishi, J. (1996) 'Market failures and government failures: A conceptual framework and Japan's experience', background paper for the conference on 'Market and Government: Foes or Friends?', Institute of Economic Research, Hitotsubashi University, February.

Toprak, Z. (1982) *Turkiye'de Milli Iktisat 1908–1918* ('National Economy in Turkey 1908–1918'), Ankara: Yurt Yay.

Uygur, E. (1993) 'Liberalisation and economic performance in Turkey', UNCTAD, Discussion Paper, No. 65, Geneva.

Wade, R. (1990) *Governing the Market: Economic Theory and the Role of Government in East Asian Industrialisation*, Princeton: Princeton University Press.

Wade, R. and F. Veneroso (1998) 'The Asian crisis: The high debt model versus the Wall Street-Treasury–IMF complex', *New Left Review* 228, March/April.

Yasa, M. (1980) *Cumhuriyet Donemi Turkiye Ekonomisi 1923–1978* ('Republican Period Turkish Economy 1923–1978'), Istanbul: Akbank Kultur Yayini.

Yerasimos, S. (1974) *Az Gelismislik Surecinde Turkiye, Vols. I, II, III*, ('Turkey in the Process of Underdevelopment'), Istanbul: Gozlem Yay.

Zysman, J. (1983) *Governments, Markets, and Growth*, Oxford: Martin Robertson.

3 Privatisation and the post-Washington consensus

Between the lab and the real world?

Kate Bayliss and Christopher Cramer

Introduction

Privatisation is the most tangible manifestation of the withering of the state required by the Washington consensus. The policy has been gaining ground since the early 1980s (Cook 1997). About 70 per cent of all structural adjustment loans made during the 1980s contained a privatisation component (Cook and Kirkpatrick 1995). This has been especially true of structural adjustment loans to sub-Saharan Africa (Berg 1994; Bennell 1997).

The post-Washington consensus (e.g. Stiglitz 1997a, 1998a) conception of privatisation is, at first sight, different from that reflected in structural adjustment programmes of the 1980s and 1990s. The main differences include a less ideologically dogmatic attachment to privatisation as developmental panacea and a more pragmatic appreciation of the need to combine privatisation with regulation and competition policy, both of these being the preserve of the post-Washington consensus state (Kolodko 1999). Stiglitz does take account of concerns that have been central to the broader, non-World Bank literature for some time. However, some features of his and other post-Washington consensus contributions actually represent a return to themes that were significant in Bank thinking in the early 1980s. Towards the end of the 1990s the post-Washington consensus literature on privatisation expanded, in particular taking the form of a reaction to the failure of shock therapy transition in the former Soviet Union.

This chapter outlines the place of privatisation in the Washington consensus, sets out the main features of the post-Washington consensus approach and argues that there remain considerable shortcomings. Enterprises are mistakenly treated as an aggregate group, where a case by case approach is likely to be far preferable. Blanket privatisation programmes have a tendency to perpetuate precisely the kind of incoherent, unselective subsidies that World Bank interventions are supposed to eradicate. Furthermore, privatisation programmes are typically conducted without regard for the complex, specific and necessary political economies of individual late industrialising societies.

Evolution of the World Bank position[1] and the Washington consensus on privatisation

The pro-market stance has not always dominated the Bank's lending approach: 'During much of its history, the organization as a whole has had a profoundly ambivalent relationship with the private sector' (Babai 1988, p. 259). A turning point came with the Berg Report (World Bank 1981), which blamed governments for perceived development failures in sub-Saharan Africa, criticising widespread state intervention and arguing that parastatals were a drain on scarce government resources. The report recommended introducing competition and expanding the remit of the private sector. This theme was picked up in the World Bank's 1983 *World Development Report*. Privatisation was not spelt out at this stage – the focus was on state-owned enterprise (SOE) reform, market pricing and cancelling of subsidies. In fact, according to this 1983 report competition is more important than ownership. The 'key factor determining the efficiency of an enterprise is not whether it is publicly or privately owned, but how it is managed' (World Bank 1983, p. 50, cited in Cook 1997).

Until the early 1990s, the anticipated scope of privatisation was limited. However, the Bank came to see public-sector reform as unsuccessful (Shirley and Nellis 1991). Still it was emphasised that privatisation was not an end in itself but a tool to increase efficiency. A further shift came with the 1992 publication, *Privatization: The Lessons of Experience* (Kikeri *et al.* 1992), where the message now was that ownership does matter after all. It was argued that even where commercialisation had brought about improved SOE performance, improvements were short-lived. Privatisation would increase the irreversibility of reforms.

The move towards widespread privatisation was further boosted by a World Bank empirical study in 1992 that concluded that privatisation of monopolies can bring about net welfare gains (Galal *et al.* 1995). This was widely cited (Kikeri *et al.* 1992; World Bank 1995) as evidence that privatising monopolies can be beneficial.[2] This meant that the scope of what could be privatised could be widened and it became legitimate to aim to privatise more or less everything. A string of further Bank publications during the 1990s reinforced the pro-market stance and the elevation of privatisation to pride of place in reform packages. These publications included *Adjustment in Africa* (World Bank 1994), *Bureaucrats in Business* (World Bank 1995)[3] and *Privatization in Africa* (Campbell-White and Bhatia 1998). Privatisation in most of the literature in the 1990s is presented as unquestionably beneficial. The theoretical reasoning behind the policy and even its objectives are only briefly addressed. Assessment is couched more in terms of extent of implementation than in terms of how outcomes relate to objectives. The Bank has thus commonly measured the success of privatisation programmes by how rapidly programmes were implemented and by the number of privatisation transactions.

Initially a response to policy failures in other areas, privatisation began to acquire a momentum of its own and became a panacea for all sorts of economic ills. Privatisation programmes in developing countries have in fact been overloaded with objectives, and these have at times proven contradictory.[4] Long-term developmental goals and short-term fiscal fixes, even if these did work, are not obviously compatible. A frequently stated goal of privatisation programmes is to maximise domestic private-sector development and national ownership, yet the pressures of loan conditionality, of fiscal deficits and a range of other factors commonly lead to the greatest value of privatisation transactions being accounted for by foreign investors.

Critics have emphasised that the Washington consensus greatly exaggerated both the ease of implementing privatisation and the gains from privatisation (Cook 1997; Heald 1992, cited in Cook and Kirkpatrick 1995, p. 22). Also, the World Bank itself has found that efforts to encourage privatisation have been among the most disappointing of all structural-adjustment policies (Helleiner 1994). The post-Washington consensus recognises that privatisation was not well planned: 'From today's vantage point, the advocates of privatisation may have over-estimated the benefits and underestimated the costs' (Stiglitz 1997a, p. 19). In Stiglitz's view, most people at the time would have preferred to have proper regulatory systems and competition in place before privatisation, but the reason it was pushed through was that 'no-one knew how long the reform window would stay open' (Stiglitz 1997a, p. 20). In this situation privatising without the appropriate prerequisites in place 'seemed a reasonable gamble'.

What is the post-Washington consensus view of privatisation?

Given the association of the post-Washington consensus with Stiglitz, it is reasonable to look for the theoretical roots of the post-Washington consensus view of privatisation in Stiglitz's own work. Certainly, there is little elaboration in the WIDER lecture or the more recent Prebisch lecture by Stiglitz (1998d) on privatisation. What there is makes the following point: privatisation has been treated as an end in itself rather than a means, whereas the critical point is that privatisation should be accompanied by, or even subservient to, competition policy.

In his earlier work (1994), Stiglitz argues that traditional mainstream theory on privatisation is weak, that it is based on perfect competition assumptions and neglects information imperfections. There is, he argues, no strong theoretical justification a priori for privatisation. However, in practice there *are* substantial benefits to privatisation: privatisation increases the transaction costs of securing government protection and subsidy; there probably *are* better management oversight possibilities within the commercial sector; and privatisation allows for selection of efficient entrepreneurs through market-orchestrated weeding out. However, argues Stiglitz, privatisation may not be the most important policy – and here he points out that Chinese rapid economic growth has not been driven by privatisation (1998b). To the extent that privatisation is still extremely important, what really matters is that it is folded into a competition policy. In other words, privatisation is subservient to creating an effective competitive environment that still needs to be watched over by the state.

Stiglitz on competition and competition policy

The fundamental argument made by Stiglitz is that privatisation is far less important than market structure. Market structure is highly unlikely to resemble the rarefied world of perfect competition imagined by the neo-classicals. Instead it will be a world of imperfect competition, whose imperfections are heightened once we acknowledge the role of information gaps and asymmetries. None the less, in many cases this market structure need not contain *no* competition. There is a reality in-between perfect competition and pure monopoly. This murky world of real competition, taking various forms, is ill served by traditional theory. However, once examined closely it becomes clear, to Stiglitz, that contests between a handful of firms in a given market do yield efficiency gains. It is here, in maximising the degree of competition within imperfectly competitive markets, that theory and policy should be concentrated. Policies include regulatory oversight mechanisms and anti-trust competition policy.

How far does Stiglitz move from the Washington consensus?

If we return from these intellectual foundations of Stiglitz's own views on privatisation and competition to the broader brush strokes that he paints in his recent vision of a post-Washington consensus, there are three points to stress. First, despite critical remarks about the obsession with inflation reduction etc., the post-Washington consensus is really characterised by a broadening of policy tools around a slightly more relaxed version of basically the same core ideas contained in the Washington consensus. Thus, Stiglitz (1998b) argues that policy reforms should still contain liberalisation, privatisation and macroeconomic adjustment. This may be significant when we further consider the constraints on effective privatisation in developing or transitional economies (see below). It is also clear from both Stiglitz's work specifically on privatisation and competition, and his vision of a post-Washington consensus, that state subsidy and protection are, under no circumstances, worthwhile policies to adopt. The major benefit of privatisation is that it reduces the temptations for such protection.

Second, Stiglitz's notion of the relationship between state and markets is one of balance, to be determined in specific cases by weighing up the relative strengths and weaknesses of the two, supposedly discrete, sectors. Thus, implicitly, the public sector has more of a role where state capacity is strong;

but where the state is weak (however this weakness is defined) *relative* to the private sector, then markets should take on a greater role. Following this idea, the implication would seem to be that privatisation has a significant role in countries with weak governmental capacity, provided, of course, that these governments still implement and monitor what Stiglitz generalises as competition policy. This is a conception of state and market relations that we shall criticise shortly. For now, it is simply worth noting that this argument suggests a naturally occurring inverse proportion of strength and weakness between the state and the private sector.

Third, there is an analytical movement in Stiglitz's work, which belies the claims to radicalism that he appears to make. Typically, he begins with a trouncing of traditional mainstream theory and a strong argument in favour of developing theories and policies based more solidly in reality. However, just as typically he then tends to arrive at conclusions that are not so different from the mainstream position after all. Flip assumptions are made, for example, about the values of openness, without empirical justification or even acknowledgement of the work done within the World Bank, by Pritchett (1996), questioning the very basis of the concept of 'openness'. While Stiglitz accepts that competition can be wasteful and destructive, this is regarded as exceptional and its implications, especially for poor countries, are left unconsidered. To give another example, Stiglitz argues that privatisation allows inefficient enterprises to be weeded out, and suggests reasonably that it is possible for essentially good firms to be weeded out through bad luck, and for bad firms to survive through good luck. However, he comes to the summary conclusion that this is socially acceptable since on average enterprise quality will improve. Only in his most recent contribution, on privatisation and reform in Russia (1999), does Stiglitz begin to shift from this position.

A conclusion, thus far, might be that the putative post-Washington consensus promises a more subtle understanding of the costs and benefits of privatisation, and equips policy makers with better tools for designing reforms that may or may not involve privatisation. However, it is also clear that this post-Washington consensus view is driven by fundamental ideas that economies should avoid 'distorting' markets by means of subsidies and protection, that openness is to be valued above virtually all else and that policy should ensure that there is as much competition as is imperfectly possible. None the less, literature in the post-Washington consensus vein represents a significant improvement upon the orthodoxy of the 1980s and early 1990s. This is particularly so in its acknowledgement of the importance, not as a side issue but as a central priority, of institutional change if privatisation and other economic reforms are to work (Stiglitz 1998a; Nellis 1999; Kolodko 1999),[5] and in its rejection of shock therapy radicalism. Kolodko (1999) adds the insight that the time question is not simply one of shock therapy versus gradualism, each taken as an exogenous choice, but rather is a function of the fact that complex economic, institutional and cultural changes are by their very nature time-consuming. Questions remain, however, over whether this recent literature goes far enough to address the analytical and policy challenges associated with privatisation, transition, enterprise restructuring and industrialisation.

What is wrong with privatisation?

We aim in this section to discuss some of the key areas of weakness in the Washington consensus regarding privatisation and to consider the extent to which these are addressed by the post-Washington consensus.

Theory

The essence of privatisation theory is that the process streamlines the relationship between enterprise owners and managers, and thereby improves performance. There are two main theoretical strands from which more detailed arguments follow. First, according to property rights theory a private owner, with the right to residual income (i.e. profit), will exercise greater monitoring effort than a public-sector counterpart with no such direct rights. Second, public-choice theory in the New Political Economy tells us that privatisation reduces the scope for manipulation of an enterprise for political (and inefficient) ends.[6] Privatisation simplifies the relationship between agent (i.e. an enterprise manager) and principal (i.e. a shareholder in a private company or the government in a state company). This theoretical basis of privatisation has been criticised extensively[7] and will not be discussed here. Most criticisms apply equally to the post-Washington consensus. However, it is worth stressing that Stiglitz acknowledges that conditions rarely even approximate those of neo-classical assumptions and argues that, because market imperfections are rife, theory gives little guidance (Stiglitz 1997a).

Competition, regulation and state/private-sector relations

Despite this greater realism (informed by East Asian industrialisation experiences and, more recently, by international financial volatility and the obvious failure of shock therapy transition in Russia), the post-Washington consensus remains analytically narrow, naïve and weakened by internal contradictions.[8] There is little analysis of how states assist in constructing markets or in encouraging capital accumulation in the private sector.[9] Nor does the post-Washington consensus consider in detail how privatisation relates to the transformation of a state-owned enterprise into a capitalist firm, if the latter is defined as an enterprise driven by independent initiative taking behaviour (Yamin 1998). There is little sense that the state and private sectors are not just nicely calibrated by relative strength and weakness, with a generally inverse relationship between the properties of the two, but are jointly determined by the political economy from which they arise. Also, despite acknowledgement of some of the realities of state intervention in East Asian industrialisation, the common strand of advice in post-Washington consensus literature to other developing countries is 'don't try this at home'.

A central argument of the post-Washington consensus is that the state should match its intervention to its capability (Stiglitz 1998a; World Bank 1997). The argument is that government should not overstretch itself but should concentrate on what it does best. For low-income countries, this line of reasoning takes us back to the Washington consensus days of the minimalist (rather than effective) state. Some states are so weak in capabilities that such a policy would mean that they did not carry out even core functions (Martinussen 1998).[10] The implication is that poor performance of states is due to their being involved in too many areas and if they cut back on some they will improve in those remaining. However, the notion that reducing the range of public-sector activities is sufficient to improve performance contradicts the idea put forward by Stiglitz that the size of the government does not matter as much as the way in which it operates.

This argument that government intervention should be less where capabilities are more scarce ignores the extent to which structural adjustment policies have themselves created scarcity of state capabilities by insisting on trimming the state directly, and through donor support to NGOs that have frequently lured away state employees with promises of computers, vehicles, foreign trips, etc.[11] In sub-Saharan Africa, for example, stabilisation and adjustment policies have brought about a significant decline of the number of people employed by government in absolute terms and as a percentage of the population. Real wages in the public sector have also fallen sharply. The 1 per cent of the sub-Saharan African population employed by government is extremely low by comparison with other LDCs, not to mention OECD countries. None the less, the IMF, in late 1997, was arguing that there was 'still scope for further downsizing' (Lienart and Modi 1997, p. 32).

The post-Washington consensus concept of state capacity or capabilities is both too vague and too narrowly technocratic: it abstracts from the political capabilities of the state, replacing these with a simple notion that too easily can be interpreted as having the skills required to implement structural adjustment policies. The concept of state capacity in the post-Washington consensus abstracts from the dynamic experiences that generate varied forms of capacity. Thus, for example, a belated and partial acceptance that the state was significant in, say, South Korea, completely ignores the actual historical dynamic of conflict and co-operation, of trial and error, and of institutional learning-by-doing through which the so-called developmental state emerged in South Korea (see, for example, Chang 1994). Stiglitz (1998a) briefly discusses the relative performance of Russia and China to demonstrate the significance of competition relative to privatisation. However, he conducts this discussion in abstraction from the historical influences on each country, the differing political economies of the two countries and the characteristics of the emergence of a 'developmental state' in China. The real questions – to do with why some states and markets come to interact in a value-enhancing, dynamic fashion where others do so less well – are far more complex and cannot even be raised within this technical notion of state capacity.

Furthermore, the notion of matching the state's role to its (measurable) capability implicitly assumes that there is a market to fill the gaps left by the state. This is problematic because weak states tend to correspond with weak markets (Cornia 1998). Further, weak states are commonly in lower-income economies that tend to be more monopolistic. This is acknowledged by Stiglitz (1996, p. 158) himself, recognising that market failure is more common in developing countries. This means that low-income markets require greater reliance on regulation, competition and anti-trust legislation for privatisation benefits to be achieved. Therefore, taken to its logical conclusion, markets in low-income countries need to rely *more* on intervention. However, it is for these countries that Stiglitz is prescribing that the state's role should be matched to capability and, therefore, reduced. Thus, this approach is inconsistent and meaningless when applied to low-income countries.

For Stiglitz, the key to development lies not just in the private sector taking up activities beyond the state's capacity but in the private sector being competitive. Beyond the Washington consensus emphasis on trade liberalisation and ownership change, Stiglitz's view is that the full benefits of liberalisation will not be realised without 'creating a competitive economy' (1998a, p. 18). Further, contradicting his glib preference elsewhere for openness, he argues that protectionism *per se* has not been the cause of stagnation, but that the failure by the state to create a competitive economy has been more important. In shifting the emphasis towards domestic competition, Stiglitz appears to subscribe to the 'quantity theory of competition', i.e. that even if perfect competition is only a Platonic dream, in the real world the more competition the better (Weeks 1994).

If Stiglitz is correct in criticising the Washington consensus for identifying privatisation too closely with its supposed ends, he may repeat the error by over-identifying a basic notion of competition with developmental objectives. In this process, what is lost is the possibility that competition is only one means, though a significant one, and also the possibility that there are complex nuances to competition and its 'fairness'. *Whither Socialism?* draws on the reality of transition economies simply to state that there is likely to be resistance to the orderly expansion of competition. What the analytical underpinning of the Washington approach misses is that restricted competition, industrial regulation aimed not at stimulating maximum competition but at reducing some dimensions of competition while perhaps stimulating rivalry, and indeed policies to provoke co-operation, might be highly effective within the context of meeting the challenge of technological upgrading. There is, of course, well-known evidence that governments in East Asian NICs such as South Korea tried to restrict competition in some sectors, for example where large sunk costs might give rise to short-term price wars or extreme investment cycles (Chang 1994). Another issue here is that there may be a distinction between domestic, internal competition and external, international competition. This is not a distinction made by Stiglitz. However, there may be a rationale for closer competition of domestic producers with a view to enhancing international competitiveness. This has been a feature, for example, of some horticultural export drives and it has always required state intervention to manage co-operation up to the point of export.[12] For instance, Madagascar's government intervened in the vanilla sector in the 1960s to ensure quality and regularity of supply, helping the country to take a share of the world market, rising to more than 90 per cent by the 1980s. Chilean high-value primary-commodity export growth is also well known to have thrived on government support that technically tainted the purity of competition. Other examples include policies setting competitions for licences. Some recent research in European industry stresses the beneficial role of co-operation in generating production efficiencies (Milne 1997). At a broader level, Stiglitz fails to take account of the range of capitalist growth experiences, which may have involved greater co-operation and different forms of competition.[13]

According to Stiglitz, privatisation can assist in creating an efficient, competitive, private-sector-led economy, principally by reducing the scale and scope of rent-seeking. Now, Stiglitz puts forward a richer understanding of how private sectors operate than the simplistic notions of the Washington consensus. The latter suggested that privatisation would inevitably unleash a pent-up entrepreneurial *élan*, a competitive spirit and a thirst for *x*-efficiency independent of any state intervention. Stiglitz in theory recognises that there are more similarities between public and private sectors than this view accepts, and he does acknowledge private-sector impulses towards rent-seeking. None the less, he maintains the argument that the major benefit of privatisation is that it raises the transaction cost of seeking protection and subsidy from the state. However:

- Protection and subsidy may be a critical part of successful productive growth; they certainly have been in virtually every successful industrialisation experience.
- There is no room in the post-Washington consensus for consideration of the complex policies that are required for effective sectoral growth. These go beyond relative prices to marketing, branding, quality, R & D, raw-material supply renovation, supportive infrastructure, diverse relationships between participants in an industry or a commodity chain and organisational capabilities. Responses to these issues tend to involve the *creation* of imperfect competition structures rather than regulation to respond to the sorry inevitability of imperfect competition by ensuring fairness.

- There is a double illusion in Stiglitz's application of information and transactions cost ideas. For SOEs' pursuit of state support is not necessarily costless: managers of state enterprises are, even where there are soft-budget constraints, engaged in a competition for resources; and the private sector frequently appears undaunted by the costs of seeking protection. Indeed, it is peculiar that Stiglitz suggests this because elsewhere he is clearly aware of the realities of imperfect competition, and of firms' willingness to waste on advertising, raising rivals' costs, etc.

Both domestic capitalist enterprises and international firms in developing and transitional economies are extremely adept at pressing for state support of one variety or another. Research into the emerging capitalist sector in Africa reveals that the entrepreneurial class relies strongly on clientelist links, for example in Tunisia (Bellin 1994) and Nigeria (Lewis 1994b). In Nigeria, privatisation has been highly politicised, with an emerging entrepreneurial class seeking and securing close protective ties with government (Lewis 1994b). Tangri (1995) cites evidence that privatisations in Côte d'Ivoire, Guinea and Zaire were used to reward political supporters. In Senegal, the government had to reinstate protection measures that had been removed in the name of structural adjustment simply in order to entice investors and get privatisation off the ground. With respect to multinationals, Bennell (1995) found that UK manufacturing firms divesting from Sub-Saharan Africa during the 1980s was cited as a major reason for the dismantling of protection of industries in which they had been involved. In Eastern European transitional economies, multinational firms, alone or in joint ventures with domestic partners, have proved especially dogged in pressing for protection of enterprises they have taken over (Amsden *et al.* 1994). Privatisation clearly does not reduce the scope for interventionism. In many countries the government is closely involved in private enterprise, if unofficially, and in most countries the government can bail out the private sector in key areas (Chang and Singh 1997).[14]

One implication of this weak analysis of state–private-sector relations is that naïve privatisation analysis and programme design may well encourage *incoherent* protection. Without a policy framework or rationale for selecting the beneficiaries of protection and negotiating the conditions under which this protection might be offered, it is more likely that weak developing-country states will cave in haphazardly to pressure from the former *nomenklatura*, from other powerful domestic elites or from TNCs. There are other ways too in which privatisation can easily entail an undiscriminating form of subsidy. It is common for privatisation in LDCs to take the form of payment by instalments. This method is chiefly adopted to make possible the sale of publicly owned enterprises to national capitalists (which is known as broadening ownership). Now, where there is inflation, where there are significantly delayed payments, and where there is default on instalments – all of which are common in privatising LDCs – then effectively the state has subsidised the privatisation process (Cramer, forthcoming). Aside from the public finance aspects of this, the point is that there is no economic, strategic *coherence* in this form of subsidy. Rather, outcomes are determined incoherently and are defined by how accurate the sale price of the enterprise is, by the access to capital and other resources of the purchaser, by interest rate levels and undoubtedly also by political connections. Therefore, there is an argument that the World Bank is basically supporting privatisation programmes that subtly reproduce precisely what they claim to be trying to replace.

Privatisation, in the post-Washington consensus, will be effective if it is part of the creation of a competitive economy. Competition and regulation policies are central to the post-Washington consensus, having been peripheral at best to the Washington consensus. The principal policy objectives must be either to increase the amount of competition or to replicate the presumed effects of competition by regulation, where it is not possible to inculcate a competitive market structure (Stiglitz 1998c). Regulation, we argue, is indeed critical to effective privatisation. However, as with the notions of competition and private-sector behaviour *vis-à-vis* rent-seeking, the concept of regulation in the post-Washington consensus is rather limited. It tends not to take account of the implications of creating effective regulatory authorities, it tends to play down the politics of regulation issues and it tends to restrict regulation to a narrow issue of replicating competitive market structure.

Low-income economies – where state capacity is often weakest and where there is typically little by way of competitive market structures – have perhaps especially great need of regulatory intervention (Kumssa 1996). However, in such economies regulatory capacity is in its infancy, capital markets are weak, anti-trust legislation is fragile at best and frail regulation bodies have to confront the additional leverage pressures brought to bear by foreign participation in the private sector. By 1992 only sixteen developing countries had restrictive business practice legislation and only one of these – Kenya – was in Africa (Bennett 1993, cited in Cook and Kirkpatrick 1995). Regulation has not formed part, typically, of policy conditionality in structural adjustment loans. Presumably this is because liberalisation is expected to induce competition (Cook and Kirkpatrick 1995).[15] Indeed, regulatory reform in transitional economies seems to be regarded more as a means of attracting private investment by ensuring good returns than of promoting competition and efficiency (Cook and Kirkpatrick 1995).

Regulation is problematic in industrialised countries and is much more difficult in developing countries where asymmetries both in information, technical skill and political power between regulator and enterprise may be greater. Enforcement difficulties may arise when foreign technical expertise is no longer available and when the negotiating strength of the regulator may have considerably weakened. Commenting on privatisation in Latin America, Ramamurti (1996a and 1996b) expects that regulatory agreements negotiated at the time of sale will become increasingly obsolete. The regulator needs to be able to adapt the rules in circumstances of uncertainty and change, but must have the authority to impose regulation policy. Few developing countries will be able to satisfy these conditions. In Argentina, the break-up and privatisation of the national railway network has been beneficial in the short run, with major increases in productivity. However, there are concerns about the long-term regulatory capacity of the government. Concessionaires were seeking deviations from negotiated agreements within months when they were supposed to be firm for five years. Also, the bargaining power of the government has considerably diminished: neither bankruptcy nor re-nationalisation is a credible threat against non-compliance of the concessionaires (Ramamurti 1997).

Much of the post-Washington consensus (e.g. the World Development Report 1997) discusses regulation only in terms of utilities, the environment and the financial sector. There is no mention of anti-trust legislation. The advice is that regulatory options are limited to capability and this is put against the alternative of inefficient public ownership. The focus is on matching the government's role to its capabilities first and then increasing capability through technical measures. However, this is an invalid approach since regulation is difficult to change after privatisation without increasing policy uncertainty. This is acknowledged by Stiglitz, whose work on this issue represents genuine progress.[16] He mentions anti-trust legislation for the first time, arguing that its application to developing countries has not been examined adequately and that US systems may be too complex to apply directly.

These challenges to the problem of regulation are compounded by the fact that there is evidence that privatisation programmes have lowered public-sector morale. Regulatory problems are also increased by the fact that privatisation tends to absorb scarce state resources itself. In other words, if privatisation is meant to yield a 'transition dividend', this is partly undermined by the 'conversion costs'.

To sum up, there is more to competition and competition policy than meets the eye of the post-Washington consensus; the private sector has a greater proclivity to rent-seeking activities than this still partly inchoate consensus acknowledges. Partly as a result of these two facts and partly given the economic structure of developing and transitional economies, the requirements of regulation policy are complex and demanding. There is therefore likely to be a need for determined and substantial state intervention to tackle these issues, if privatisation is to be effective. However, the post-Washington consensus rests on the assumption that the state should not intervene beyond its 'capacity', an apparently technical property in very short supply in low-income economies. Regulation is costly and complex. It is also highly political, as of course is the whole question of the origin and nature of 'state capacity'. Furthermore, however, regulation is surely a matter of how the state intervenes to encourage private-sector activity to support technological change, organisational restructuring and industrialisation. It is, in other words, a broader and more challenging issue than the legalistic version presented in the post-Washington consensus literature.

This is because the post-Washington consensus literature on privatisation, competition and regulation is extremely weak when it comes to discussion of industrial policy. There is little or no evidence that the post-Washington consensus conceives of the relationship between privatisation and industrial policy any differently from the Washington consensus. In the latter, privatisation was not one among a set of potentially appropriate tools of industrial policy; it simply was industrial policy, particularly if backed by removal of all subsidies and opening to trade liberalisation. For example, there may be a clear justification for the Bank insisting as a loan condition that subsidies to chronically unprofitable state-owned enterprises be reduced. However, as Amsden *et al.* (1994, p. 117) argue for Eastern Europe:

> [I]t is quite another matter for the Bank to insist that sovereign governments take no part in restructuring promising state-owned enterprises through industrial policy and the provision of supports to these enterprises with strict conditions determined by the governments themselves rather than the Bretton Woods institutions. The Bank, however, insisted on both.

In another example, in Mozambique the World Bank first insisted on privatisation of the cashew-processing sector and then, subsequently, put intense pressure on the government to rapidly liberalise the external trading regime protecting domestic processors. This amounted not to an industrial policy but to an explicit abrogation of industrial policy (Cramer 1999).

The post-Washington consensus likewise conceives of barriers to entry and other imperfections in the structure of competition exclusively as constraints. Stiglitz also favours export promotion on the standard grounds that it will encourage specialisation in line with comparative advantage. On this latter point, he neglects the argument that industrialisation is driven by active efforts to change comparative advantage (OECF 1998), a strategy typically requiring departures from *laissez-faire* policies. On the former point, while it is of course important to acknowledge the potential role of competition, others have stressed that market imperfections can be advantageous in industrialisation. Amsden (1997), for example, stresses the role in successful industrialisation of creating effective market imperfections, not just correcting for their unfortunate presence. Again, this development of 'competitive assets' has commonly involved states and markets, and has also commonly been a politicised process. Furthermore, learning-by-doing and related arguments are simply brushed aside by Stiglitz.

Rather than attempting to theorise some institutional set-up by which there is no rent-seeking, no subsidy or protection, analysis of state and private-sector economic activity would be better off asking under what circumstances close ties between states and private-sector entrepreneurs are creative, value-generating relationships and under what conditions they tend to be less constructive. The argument here is that it is not necessarily a terrible outcome – contra both the Washington consensus and the post-Washington consensus – to have directed credit, protection, subsidies and other frightful distortions.

Analytical weaknesses

The World Bank has been adept in using methodologies of analysis that ensure privatisation emerges in a strong positive light. Criteria of judgement, selective use of data, analytical sleight of hand and over-aggregation of the issues are among the typical analytical tools that need to be critically highlighted. At the end of the 1990s, there has been little shift in these dimensions of World Bank analysis of privatisation.

First, the Bank applies rules and criteria ensuring that almost every outcome is a positive manifestation of the benefits of privatisation. For example, privatisation is deemed beneficial if enterprise performance improves after ownership change. If enterprise performance deteriorates and bankruptcy follows, this is also a beneficial result as it demonstrates the fact that the enterprise was not viable and was being propped up by the state (Campbell-White and Bhatia 1998; Kikeri *et al*. 1992).

Second, the Bank manipulates the labour implications of privatisation in particular. Some enterprises reduce employment after privatisation, often because of high staffing levels in public enterprises. The Bank commonly differentiates between reform of the public sector and privatisation, arguing that the former is responsible for lay-offs and not privatisation (Campbell-White and Bhatia 1998). This is an artificial distinction to give privatisation a better press. In reality the two are part of the same process of public-sector reform. For whatever reason, in many cases employment is reduced after privatisation and account needs to be taken of this. This is a real negative outcome of the policy representing a significant social cost. It cannot glibly be assumed that vigorous informal sectors will soak up labour shed by the enumerated, privatised sector. The closest the post-Washington consensus literature comes to taking this seriously is Stiglitz's (1999) critique of shock therapy in Russia.

Third, Bank literature (e.g. Bureaucrats in Business) tends to impose an unrealistic public/private dichotomy on the analysis of enterprise and economic performance (Bayliss and Fine, 1998). Stiglitz does delve deeper into country-specific circumstances with less rigid emphasis on the public/private dichotomy, for example in his comparison of China and Russia. He states that there is a need to examine the development of institutions and social networks (Stiglitz 1998b). None the less, the terms of the discussion remain extraordinarily vague.

Fourth, the Washington consensus adopts an aggregate approach, treating all transactions and enterprises as homogenous. In reality, the term privatisation covers a spectrum of transactions from sale of 100 per cent equity to leasing assets. Likewise, privatisation covers a huge range of enterprises from utilities to monopolies to small-scale enterprises. The factors affecting the performance of this range of enterprises vary widely. The attractiveness to investors, the scope for competition and the implications for national development are all heavily dependent on country-, sector- and enterprise-specific factors. Moreover, the levels of efficiency to be found in SOEs vary greatly. The Washington consensus treats all SOEs on an aggregate basis. However, some SOEs do well and others do badly. Evidence from Kenya shows that about half a dozen enterprises accounted for most of the parastatal losses in Kenya (Grosh 1991). Some SOEs are profitable, and privatising these will have a negative impact on government finances.

Fifth, the use of empirical evidence in much of the World Bank literature on privatisation is highly selective and one-sided. The broader literature is less sanguine about the benefits of privatisation (e.g. Millward 1988; Adam *et al.* 1992; Chang and Singh 1992; Martin and Parker 1997). There is little unequivocal empirical support for privatisation. Evaluation of privatisation is fraught with methodological difficulties – not least the question of the counterfactual. One conclusion of the empirical literature is that the public and private sectors contain both the best and the worst performing of enterprises. The only real policy advice that can emerge is to adopt a case-specific approach.

Context and policy interactions

Much of the World Bank literature (e.g. Shirley and Nellis 1991) rightly states that privatisation should not be viewed in isolation. However, the scope of the context that receives attention under the Washington consensus is limited to the economic policy package of which privatisation forms a part. There is little consideration of the historical, economic and institutional context in which privatisation is implemented in developing countries. This is important because the objectives of privatisation are far-reaching and rely on a number of linkages if they are to be achieved.

History, the private sector and competition

Neither the Washington consensus nor its hesitantly emerging successor have shown much interest in analysing and designing privatisation programmes within a historical context. However, this can be illuminating. For example, in much of Africa, nationalisation arose as much from an absence of a capitalist class in some countries as from a commitment to socialism (Mkandawire 1994). The extent to which a domestic bourgeoisie has emerged in the meantime will affect, for example, the likelihood that a competitive environment will emerge quickly after privatisation. There may be only one or two entrepreneurs or groups that have the know-how, capital access and market connections to take up opportunities. In Mozambique, for example, the development of a large state-owned enterprise sector after independence was driven both by defensive motivations and by a more assertive nationalising ideology. During the years of war and state socialism, there was no large-scale evolution of a bourgeoisie. None the less, there was a handful of individuals or families that accumulated savings amassed by, for example, exploiting wartime trading rents. These formed the core of national buyers during the privatisation programme of the 1990s, though this is not the same thing as saying that they emerged as a ready formed, competitive private sector eager to take independent initiatives that would have value-enhancing productive outcomes (Castel-Branco and Cramer 1999).

Structural adjustment and privatisation

There has been too little awareness, in the Washington consensus literature, of the scope for complex and contradictory interactions between components of reform packages. Stabilisation and structural-adjustment programmes incorporate a range of policies that can be expected to affect privatisation. For example, fiscal policy pressures may mean that priority will be given to revenue-raising aspects of privatisation while other supposedly efficiency-enhancing measures such as competition will be compromised. Stiglitz shows some sensitivity to the constraints on investment that have been imposed by obsessional stabilisation packages. None the less, there is little in World Bank privatisation programmes, in Stiglitz's writings on privatisation and competition, or in recent World Bank publications on the subject to suggest that privatisation might be affected by macroeconomic contraction, or other possible dimensions to structural adjustment.[17]

- Privatisation, as well as re-structuring, of state enterprises in Eastern Europe suffered from the macroeconomic constraints that tightened around enterprises during the early years of shock therapy. Among the difficulties that firms faced during this period of vanishing subsidy, trade liberalisation and so on were a domestic-demand squeeze, a high cost of borrowing and a lack of quality and frontier technology capable of launching firms into open international competition (Amsden *et al.* 1994).
- Privatisation of cashew-processing enterprises in Mozambique was followed by World Bank insistence on rapid trade liberalisation, which was to take the form of swiftly reducing the tax on exports of raw cashews to India. This combination of policies, in rapid succession, amounted to a 'hospital pass' (Cramer, forthcoming). Enterprises facing very high borrowing costs, and with poor technology, a poor quality of raw material input and little experience in marketing or branding were expected to switch instantly from a highly and inefficiently protected policy environment to fully open competition against rival industries in India, Brazil and, increasingly, Vietnam. However, in none of these other industries could the policy environment be described as *laissez-faire*.

- In Ghana, privatisation of the banking sector was supposed to increase competition and thereby improve credit allocation to the private sector. Results have been disappointing because the government's fiscal deficit has meant that public borrowing has increased and Treasury bills offer high interest rates at low risk so banks are holding nearly 70 per cent of deposits in treasury bills.
- Privatisation is commonly expected to generate increased domestic and foreign investment. However, the investment response to stabilisation and adjustment policies, for example in much of sub-Saharan Africa, has been unimpressive. This should be seen within a context in which foreign direct investment to the region has shrunk significantly as a proportion of global FDI flows (African Development Bank 1997, p. 12), and in which private investment has followed the downward path of public-sector investment to less than half the level of the 1970s (Glen and Sumlinski 1998). Adjustment is likely to have a negative impact on investment through reductions in public investment and contracting real incomes reducing effective demand (Severn and Solimano 1992).[18] Privatisation is unlikely to trigger a resurgence of investment in sub-Saharan Africa, but is more likely to follow trends in investor confidence.

Risk and uncertainty

More important may be the uncertainty resulting from adjustment programmes (Severn and Solimano 1992). This is partly a question of political uncertainty (African Development Bank 1997, Box 4.1). Proceeding with privatisation in this environment means finding ways of dealing with investor uncertainty. One way is to make significant concessions on sales terms (African Development Bank 1997; Hildyard 1997, p. 21). Alternatively, one can try to limit the irreversibility of private-sector investment in a privatisation transaction through partial sale, leasing or management contract mechanisms (African Development Bank 1997). Thus, while privatisation is attractive to policy makers because of its signal of *policy* irreversibility, for investors too great an irreversibility or investment commitment, in conditions of uncertainty, may make privatisation less attractive.

There are further economic factors in the context of privatisation programmes in many developing countries that complicate the perception of risk in the private sector. On the one hand, the conditions of production, especially in smartly liberalised transition economies with fragile financial institutions, are highly risky. Furthermore, the uncertainty of production was presumably one of the reasons in many developing countries why the state nationalised firms in the first place. On the other hand, risk may in some circumstances be of too *little* concern to allow for maximum benefits from privatisation. In Eastern Europe, privatisation has been an indirect form of restructuring because it has not taken the form of the purchase by private buyers of SOEs in exchange for money, but in exchange for debt or vouchers. This has been described as pseudo-privatisation. It carries a greater risk of bankruptcy: nothing is paid for as an asset, so there is less to be lost in disposing of it (Amsden *et al.* 1994).

In poorer countries – for example in sub-Saharan Africa – privatisation has not really gone down the voucher, mass-privatisation route. However, privatisation does often involve the transfer of assets into private hands without the same conception of financial risk that might be significant in, say, UK privatisation. This is because domestic entrepreneurs may finance their purchase of state-owned enterprises by loans from commercial banks that themselves operate under a form of soft-budget constraint. The commercial banking sector in Mozambique, for example, during the period of privatisation was taken over largely by Portuguese financial organisations. Portuguese banks lending overseas are guaranteed state support in the event of bad loans, and therefore have little constraint on their lending behaviour. Alternatively, where state-owned enterprises are sold off cheaply, and where there are no institutional mechanisms supporting long-term investment lending and industrial policy, then there are temptations to convert factory premises into warehouses, to asset strip and to switch into retail or export/import depot activities.

Arguably there are underlying tensions between the process of transition or market liberalisation and the goal of transforming lumbering SOEs into vigorous private-sector firms. Yamin (1998) argues that if a firm is defined as an enterprise driven by independent initiative-taking behaviour, then a high degree of buyer and seller risk in newly liberalised economies under-mines the propensity for such initiative taking. This propensity is further weakened where privatisation transactions are not backed by significant sunk costs that would impel the enterprise to engage in 'market-making' activities. Again, this highlights the problems associated with cheap-sale or low-commitment privatisation.

Loan conditionality

An outstanding feature of the context of privatisation programmes in devel-oping countries is the presence of donors and in particular the World Bank and IMF. Privatisation has formed a part of loan conditionality in numerous structural adjustment packages. The greater a country's reliance on the Bank, the greater the odds that it will be privatising (Ramamurti 1991; Babai 1988, p. 269). There are various consequences of the Bank's privatisa-tion fetish for the impact of privatisation. Loan conditionality tends to tie privatisation in to speed and number of transactions rather than a careful consideration of the sequencing of related reforms. Hence, the World Bank's 1998 review of privatisation in Africa (Campbell-White and Bhatia 1998) affects 'surprise' that there is not more competition policy and regulation. However, programmes that have prioritised selling off enterprises before establishing supportive institutions and policies are the direct result of Bank-led initiatives.

Political economy

Both the Washington consensus and the post-Washington consensus are couched in terms of things that work and things that don't. Stiglitz offers the idea that the post-Washington consensus needs to be more sensitive to specific conditions in each country. This is to be welcomed, but there are reasons why one might be less than enthusiastic about this. One is that the Stiglitz vision of what specific conditions means is itself limited to weighing up the relative strengths and weaknesses of states and markets, public and private sectors, and adjusting policy expectations accordingly. This would-be consensus, among other faults, is ill equipped to cope with conflict among political groups; it is naïvely apolitical in its analysis, though not necessarily in its underlying intent.

The success of privatisation, or of other technically possible policies, depends on the political economy in which they are attempted as well as just on the economic and financial conditions. To put it another way, the success of privatisation may depend on how and whether capitalism is ideologically and socially embedded. Here one needs to consider the role of the state, historically, in constructing institutions of private-sector transaction and production; and, indeed, the role of particular political economies, or political settlements (Khan 1995), in the development of the state. The former is a far more complex matter than 'enabling' the private sector by cutting red tape and instituting competition policy. States have, in developing countries, made double movements both to stimulate and to regulate markets, as Polanyi (1944) observed. However, the issue goes beyond this too, to the political economy within which both states and private-sector agents operate. For example, Gerschenkron (1961) did not just note the possibility of reaping advantages from backwardness; nor did he just note that the institutional response to the challenges and tensions of late industrialisation differed between countries. He also stressed the dramatic ideological shift that was necessary, but not inevitable or predictable, before effective social and institutional responses to these challenges could be found. It is very clear that the post-Washington consensus – with its contraptions of asymmetric information and their implications for efficient institutional development – really does not improve much on its predecessor by way of what is required for political economy analysis.

Distributional impact

Privatisation can be expected to exacerbate domestic and international inequality. Much of the literature states that indigenous populations have been taking part in privatisation programmes (e.g. Campbell-White and

Bhatia 1998). However, in low-income countries this is usually at the lower end of the scale. Research in Ghana and Mozambique shows that the larger and higher-value enterprises have been sold (at least in part) to foreign investors (Bayliss 1998; Cramer, forthcoming). In recognition of the potentially adverse distributional impact, some countries have established or are planning to establish privatisation trust funds to warehouse shares until such time as indigenous citizens are able to participate. This also allows the smaller investor to own a small piece of an enterprise. However, this is a limited form of participation, particularly if the owner is not a national. In Russia, policies aimed at improving the distribution of state assets (i.e. policies targeting managers and employees) have in fact become mechanisms for the transfer of wealth from poor to rich, and from pensioners and state workers to enterprise managers and employee groups (Nishimura 1998). In short, the rhetoric of broadening ownership through privatisation can easily be a euphemism for, in fact, narrowing ownership.

Absence of data makes it impossible to calculate the distribution of welfare gains and losses of privatisation in Africa (as done for high- and middle-income countries by Galal *et al.* (1995)). However, international shareholders are expected to benefit substantially from privatisation. Where there is domestic participation, this is likely to involve higher-income levels.[19] In most cases employment falls after privatisation although there is some evidence that working conditions improve for those workers retained (Bayliss 1998). The hope is that employment will increase in the long run but the response typically has been slow. In the long run, privatisation in circumstances of high formal sector unemployment can be expected to weaken workers' bargaining positions and may increase the casualisation of labour and adversely affect working conditions. Thus, retrenched workers lose out and the impact on retained workers is mixed.

The impact on consumers depends on the effect of privatisation on price, product quality and level of output. In some cases price increases have been introduced prior to privatisation to attract investors (e.g. telecommunications in Mexico; Ramamurti 1996b). The distributional impact depends on the identity of the consumers. The distributional impact of the fiscal effect depends on what happens to privatisation proceeds. Evidence from Ghana shows that revenue proceeds are another source of revenue in the government budget. Government expenditure is mainly on recurrent items.

While distribution features in some recent World Bank literature (e.g. Campbell-White and Bhatia 1998), it is not a central issue. The discussion on employment focuses on numbers employed or laid off. It does not consider wider labour issues such as the extent of casual staff, unionisation, working conditions or salaries. World Bank advice to African countries on what to do about displaced labour is to offer more generous severance packages (Wallace 1997) to buy support for privatisation.

Conclusion

This chapter has shown that many of the key problems of the Washington consensus are considered by the post-Washington consensus, but only within a restricted, over-simplifying analytical framework. Other issues such as distribution are barely touched upon, even within the avowedly participatory, pro-egalitarian sections of the post-Washington consensus literature. In practice, privatisation has created its own logic beyond the original objectives. It is used more to highlight commitment to market-oriented reforms or to comply with donor conditionalities than to increase efficiency (Pinheiro and Giambiagi 1994, on Brazil).

Privatisation programmes need to be radically adapted in the light of issues discussed in this paper. First, what is needed is clarity of objectives. The view of the Washington consensus is that efficiency should be the over-riding objective (Kikeri *et al.* 1992). This obsession with efficiency contrasts with the Japanese critique of the Washington consensus, which recommends rather that the emphasis should be on developmental priorities (OECF 1998). The post-Washington consensus offers a more realistic and careful foundation for the design of enterprise restructuring and privatisation policies, but remains limited.

Once priorities are established, a more imaginative approach is required. Much of the Washington consensus literature makes a leap from discussion of wider objectives to detailed implementation procedures that focus on detailed legal and financial issues (e.g. Campbell-White and Bhatia 1998). Privatisation agency staff are usually experienced in industrialised country privatisation, which means that wider economic, social and political issues are not addressed in LDC privatisation programmes.

The Japanese critique of structural adjustment argues that rather than seeking uniformity in policy solutions, the development community should seek consensus in methodological approaches to analysing problems of developing countries. The solutions should then be case specific. This approach would be well suited to privatisation. In this context, the specific problems of an enterprise need to be established and the means by which these can be overcome (Ohno 1998).

In the same way that Lall (1995) argues for active preparation for liberalisation reforms, preparation is needed for privatisation. Widespread liberalisation exposed all enterprises to competition from imports. This approach has wiped out potentially profitable as well as inefficient industry in sub-Saharan Africa and in Eastern Europe (Lall 1995; Amsden *et al.* 1994). In current privatisation programmes, domestic investors and enterprise managers will not be able to participate, and extensive preparation is needed. The risks and benefits of privatisation need to be clearly established in the case of each enterprise (or group of enterprises), taking account of the distributional impact. It may be that some form of partnership with the private sector will be beneficial for an enterprise, or it may be more suitable for it to remain in the public sector as an autonomous entity, possibly hiring in specialist expertise.

Privatisation should fit within a carefully considered, selective-policy package for enterprise development. Once such a package is designed, then a complex competition policy may be designed, rather than the blanket application of a single, simple competition policy.

The post-Washington consensus stressed the importance of legislative regulation, but this is an issue that is complicated by technical capabilities and by the political settlement. However, beyond this, and not mentioned by Stiglitz at all, privatisation should be accompanied by promotion of voice regulation, not just to achieve consensus and not just to encourage the collective voice of industrialists, but to encourage the voice of employees and others affected by privatisation.

Notes

1   The main vehicle for promoting and informing the Washington consensus is the vast body of literature published by the World Bank. However, as a large institution with different departments and research bodies, there are inconsistencies, for example, between Bank-funded and supported research (e.g. the EDI and World Bank Research Observer) and headline policy documents. These not only undermine the notion of the Bank as monolith but also at times weaken the whole idea of consensus. A further gap appears between these and policy implementation. This summary of the evolution of the Bank's position focuses on the widely circulated research publications and those that appear to be most influential in policy advice.

2   What most references neglect to mention is that the authors of this study explicitly warn against extrapolating their findings to very poor countries where market conditions and institutional infrastructure are different from those of the sample countries.

3   These reports have been widely criticised. See, for example, Chang and Singh (1997), Cook (1997) and Bayliss and Fine (1998).

4   For example, the Government of Malaysia's guidelines on privatisation (1985, cited in Adam *et al.* 1992, p. 23) state: 'privatisation is expected to promote competition, improve efficiency and increase the productivity of the services …. [In addition] privatisation, by stimulating private entrepreneurship and investment, is expected to accelerate the rate of growth of the economy.'

5   Gillibrand (1998) identifies the need, even in competitive market structures, for a fair-trade agency, a coherent competition policy, an anti-trust or monopolies and mergers agency, and commercial courts, plus quality standards agencies and self-regulating sectoral associations, and professional institutes for accountants, lawyers, bankers, engineers, surveyors and managers. He points out that in the UK post-privatisation regulation bodies have been estimated to employ more than 20,000 people and to cost more than £1bn a year to administer.

6   For a detailed exposition of the conventional approach, see Vickers and Yarrow (1988).

7   For critiques, see Fine (1990), Chang and Rowthorn (1995), Martin and Parker (1997) and Bayliss and Fine (1998). Chang and Singh (1992) provide a review of the theoretical and empirical position regarding privatisation in developing countries.

8   Nellis (1999) states that evidence from the former Soviet Union shows that the association between private ownership and restructuring is weak or non-existent, that firms partially owned by the state perform better than fully privatised companies, that there are few differences between performance of state-owned and private firms, and that clear performance improvements are only visible in the few firms that have been sold to foreign investors.

9   On effective Chinese support to indigenous big business, see Nolan and Xiaoqiang (1999).

10   A good example of this in practice is the contracting-out of customs services in Mozambique to the UK firm Crown Agents.

11   In Poland, for example, the Bank made sure that it undermined the capabilities and scope of the Industrial Development Agency (IDA), charged by the Ministry of Industry with enterprise restructuring initiatives. The role of the IDA was limited to loans to hire consultants to undertake 150 or so industry and enterprise studies to further the goal of privatisation (Amsden *et al.* 1994).

12   On the expansion of Taiwanese small-business bicycle exports, for example, see Chu (1997).

13   On the contrasting development of modern industrial enterprises in the USA, the UK and Germany, for example, see Chandler (1990); for a critique of the orthodox failure to learn from the varied history of industrialisation and economic growth, see also Nolan and Xiaoqiang (1999).

14   This ought to be even more obvious in the light of the asymmetric adjustment to international financial crisis during 1997–8, in which advanced-country creditors have been bailed out by concerted government intervention (see Palma 1998).

15   On legislative regulation, market regulation and voice regulation as different types, see Standing, Sender and Weeks (1996).

16   Stiglitz (1999) argues that the 'privatise, then regulate' approach creates a vested interest in blocking later regulation and competition.

17   A significant exception is in Stiglitz's (1999) critique of shock therapy in Russia, pointing out that privatisation combined with liberalisation of the capital account increases incentives to strip assets in newly privatised enterprises rather than to restructure firms.

18   For further discussion of investment trends and the crowding-in versus crowding-out debate, see Fischer *et al.* (1998, table 2) and Fontaine and Geronimi (1995).

19   In Mexico all but one of the large-scale privatisations were sold to a group of thirty-seven businessmen who, between them, controlled 22 per cent of the country's GNP (Hildyard 1997).

References

Adam, Christopher, William Cavendish and Percy Mistry (1992) *Adjusting Privatisation: Case Studies from Developing Countries*, London: James Currey and New York: Heinemann.

African Development Bank (1997) *African Development Report 1997: Fostering Private Sector Development in Africa*, Oxford: Oxford University Press.

Amsden, Alice H. (1997) 'Editorial: Bringing production back in – understanding government's economic role in late industrialization', *World Development* 25(4): 469–80.

Amsden, Alice H., Jacek Kochanowicz and Lance Taylor (1994) *The Market Meets Its Match: Restructuring the Economies of Eastern Europe*, Cambridge, MA: Harvard University Press.

Aryeetey, Ernest (1994) 'Private investment under uncertainty in Ghana', *World Development* 22(8): 1211–21.

Babai, Don (1988) 'The World Bank and the IMF: Rolling back the state or backing its role', in R. Vernon (ed.) *The Promise of Privatisation: A Challenge for American Foreign Policy*, New York: Council on Foreign Relations Books.

Barad, Robert (1994) 'Privatisation of state-owned enterprises: The Togolese experience', in Grosh, B. and R.S. Mukandala (eds) *State-Owned Enterprises in Africa*, Lynne Rienner Publishers.

Bayliss, Kate (1998) 'Privatisation in Ghana: Post-privatisation response of enterprises', fieldwork report, London: School of Oriental and African Studies.

Bayliss, Kate and Ben Fine (1998) 'Beyond *Bureaucrats in Business*: A critical review of the World Bank approach to privatisation and public sector reform', *Journal of International Development* 10: 841–55.

Bellin, E. (1994) 'The politics of profit in Tunisia: Utility of the rentier paradigm?', *World Development* 22(3): 427–36.

Bennell, Paul (1995) 'British manufacturing investment in sub-Saharan Africa: Corporate responses during structural adjustment', *Journal of Development Studies* 32(2): 195–217.

—— (1997) 'Privatisation in sub-Saharan Africa: Progress and prospects during the 1990s', *World Development* 25(11): 1785–803.

—— (1998) 'Fighting for survival: Manufacturing industry and adjustment in sub-Saharan Africa', *Journal of International Development* 10: 621–37.

Berg, Elliot (1994) *Privatisation in Sub-Saharan Africa: Results, Prospects and New Approaches*, Maryland: DAI.

Campbell-White, Oliver and Anita Bhatia (1998) *Privatisation in Africa*, Washington, DC: World Bank.

Castel-Branco, C. and C. Cramer (1999) 'Privatisation in Mozambique in the context of underdevelopment, transition and reconstruction', paper for UNU/-WIDER project on Underdevelopment, Transition and Reconstruction, Helsinki: UNU/WIDER.

Chandler, Alfred (1990) *Scale and Scope: The Dynamics of Industrial Capitalism*, Cambridge, MA: Harvard University Press.

Chang, H.-J. (1994) *The Political Economy of Industrial Policy in South Korea*, London and Basingstoke: Macmillan.

Chang, H.-J. and Robert Rowthorn (1995), 'The role of the state in economic change: Entrepreneurship and conflict management', in Chang, H.-J. and R. Rowthorn (eds) *The Role of the State in Economic Change*, UNU/WIDER Studies in Development Economics, Oxford: Clarendon Press.

Chang, H.-J. and A. Singh (1992) 'Public enterprises in developing countries and economic efficiency: A critical examination of analytical, empirical and policy issues', *UNCTAD* 48, August.

—— (1997) 'Can large firms be efficiently run without being bureaucratic? Policy Arena', *Journal of International Development* 9(6): 865–75.

Chu, Wan-wen (1997) 'Causes of growth: A study of Taiwan's bicycle industry', *Cambridge Journal of Economics* 21: 55–72.

Commander, S. and T. Killick (1988) 'Privatisation in developing countries: A survey of the issues' in Cook, P. and C. Kirkpatrick (eds) *Privatisation in Less Developed Countries*, Hemel Hempstead: Harvester Wheatsheaf, pp. 91–124.

Cook, P. (1997) 'Privatisation, public enterprise reform and the World Bank: Has *Bureaucrats in Business* got it right?', *Journal of International Development* 9(6): 888–97.

Cook, P. and C. Kirkpatrick (1995) 'The distributional impact of privatisation in developing countries: Who gets what and why', in Ramanadham, V.V. (ed.) *Privatisation and Equity*, London and New York: Routledge.

Cornia, Giovanni Andrea (1998) 'Convergence on governance issues, dissent on economic policies', *IDS Bulletin* 29(2): 32–8.

Cornia, G.A. and G.K. Helleiner (1994) 'Introduction', in Cornia, G.A. and G.K. Helleiner (eds) *From Adjustment to Development in Africa: Conflict, Controversy, Convergence, Consensus*, London and Basingstoke: Macmillan Press.

Cramer, Christopher (1999), 'Can Africa industrialise by processing primary commodities? The case of Mozambican cashew nuts', *World Development* 27(7): 1247–66.

—— (forthcoming) 'Privatisation and liberalisation in Mozambique: A "Hospital Pass"?', *Journal of Southern African Studies*.

Evans, Alison and Mick Moore (1998) 'Editorial introduction: The Bank, the state and development; dissecting the 1997 World Development Report', *IDS Bulletin* 29(2): 3–13.

Fafchamps, Marcel (1997) 'Introduction: Markets in Sub-Saharan Africa', *World Development*, 25(5): 733–4.

Fine, Ben (1990) *The Coal Question*, London and New York: Routledge.

Fischer, Stanley, E. Hernandez-Catá and M.S. Khan (1998) 'Africa: Is this the turning point?', IMF Papers on Policy Analysis and Assessment 98/6, IMF: Washington, DC.

Fontaine, J.-M. and V. Geronimi (1995) 'Private investment and privatisation in Sub-Saharan Africa', in Cook, P. and C. Kirkpatrick (eds) *Privatisation Policy and Performance: International Perspectives*, New York: Prentice Hall.

Gaddy, Clifford and Barry Ickes (1998) 'Underneath the formal economy: Why are Russian enterprises not restructuring?', William Davidson Institute Working Paper No. 134.

Galal, Ahmed, Leroy Jones, Pankaj Tandon and Ingo Vogelsang (1995) *Welfare Consequences of Selling Public Enterprises: An Empirical Analysis*, Washington, DC: World Bank, Oxford: Oxford University Press.

Gerschenkron, A. (1961) *Economic Backwardness in Historical Perspective*, Cambridge, UK: Cambrige University Press.

Gillibrand, M. (1998) 'Privatisation and post-privatisation in Africa', in *The Commonwealth African Investment Almanac*, Hanson Cooke Ltd and the Commonwealth Secretariat for the Commonwealth Business Council.

Glen, Jack D. and Mariusz Sumlinski (1998) 'Trends in private investment in developing countries: Statistics for 1970–96', IFC Discussion Paper No. 34, IFC: Washington, DC.

Grabowski, R. (1994) 'The successful developmental state: Where does it come from?', *World Development* 22(3): 413–22.

—— (1998) 'Development, markets and trust', *Journal of International Development* 10: 357–71.

Greenidge, Carl (1997) 'A case of the curate's egg: The political economy of privatisation in Guyana', in Bennett (ed.) *How does Privatisation Work? Essays in Privatisation in Honour of Professor V.V. Ramanadham*, London and New York: Routledge, pp. 105–37.

Grosh, B (1991) *Public Enterprise in Kenya: What Works, What Doesn't and Why*, Boulder and London: Lynne Rienner Publishers.

—— (1994) 'Kenya: A positive politics of parastatal performance', in Grosh, B. and R.S. Mukandala (eds) *State-Owned Enterprises in Africa*, Boulder and London: Lynne Rienner Publishers.

Helleiner, G.K. (1994) 'From adjustment to development in sub-Saharan Africa: Consensus and continuing conflict' in Cornia, G.A. and G.K. Helleiner (eds) *From Adjustment to Development in Africa: Conflict, Controversy, Convergence, Consensus*, London and Basingstoke: Macmillan Press.

Hildyard, Nicholas (1997) *The World Bank and the State: A Recipe for Change?*, London: Bretton Woods Project.

Hoshino, Taeko (1996) 'Privatisation of Mexico's public enterprises and the restructuring of the private sector', *The Developing Economies* 34(1), March 1996.

Khan, M. (1995) 'State failure in weak states: A critique of new institutionalist explanations', in Hunter, J., J. Harriss and C. Lewis (eds) *The New Institutional Economics and Third World Development*, Routledge: London.

Kikeri, Sunita, John Nellis and Mary Shirley (1992) *Privatisation: The Lessons of Experience*, Washington, DC: World Bank.

Kolodko, Grzegorz (1999) 'Ten years of post-socialist transition lessons for policy reform', Policy Research Working Paper 2095, World Bank: Washington, DC.

Kumssa, A. (1996) 'The political economy of privatisation in sub-Saharan Africa', *International Review of Administrative Sciences* 62: 75–87.

Lall, Sanjaya (1995) 'Structural adjustment and African industry', *World Development* 23(12): 2019–31.

Leinart, I. and J. Modi (1997) 'A decade of civil service reform in sub-Saharan Africa', IMF Working Paper, Fiscal Affairs Dept, IMF: Washington, DC.

Lewis, P. (1994a) 'Introduction to special section: Rentiers, capitalists and the state in Africa', *World Development* 22(3): 423–5.

—— (1994b) 'Economic statism, private capital, and the dilemmas of accumulation in Nigeria', *World Development* 22(3): 437–51.

Lorch, Klaus (1991) 'Privatisation through private sale: The Bangladesh textile industry', in Ramamurti, R. and R. Vernon (eds) *Privatisation and Control of State-Owned Enterprises*, Washingthon DC: The World Bank, pp. 126–51.

Martin, S. and D. Parker (1997) *The Impact of Privatisation: Ownership and Corporate Performance in the UK*, London and New York: Routledge.

Martinussen, John (1998) 'The limitations of the World Bank's conception of the state and the implications for institutional development strategies', *IDS Bulletin* 29(2): 67–74.

Milne, S. (1997) *Making Markets Work: Contracts, Competition and Cooperation*, Economic and Social Research Council, Birkbeck College, London: University of London.

Millward, R. (1988) 'Measured sources of inefficiency in the performance of private and public enterprises in LDCs', in Cook, P. and C. Kirkpatrick (eds) *Privatisation in Less Developed Countries*, Hemel Hempstead: Harvester Wheatsheaf, pp. 143–61.

Mkandawire, Thandika (1994) 'The political economy of privatisation in Africa', in Cornia, G.A. and G.K. Helleiner (eds) *From Adjustment to Development in Africa: Conflict, Controversy, Convergence, Consensus*, London and Basingstoke: Macmillan Press.

Moore, Mick (1998) 'Towards a useful consensus?', *IDS Bulletin* 29(2): 39–48.

Nellis, J. (1999) 'Time to rethink privatisation in transition economies?', *Transitions*, February.

Nishimura, Yoshiaki (1998) 'Russian privatisation: Progress report No. 1', in Ohno, K. and I. Ohno (eds) *Japanese Views on Economic Development: Diverse Paths to the Market*, London and New York: Routledge, pp. 241–64.

Nolan, Peter and Wang Xiaoqiang (1999) 'Beyond privatisation: Institutional innovation and growth in China's large state-owned enterprises', *World Development* 27(1): 169–200.

OECF (1998) 'Issues related to the World Bank's approach to structural adjustment: A proposal from a major partner', in Ohno, K. and I. Ohno (eds) *Japanese Views on Economic Development: Diverse Paths to the Market*, London and New York: Routledge, pp. 61–9.

Ohno, Kenchi (1998) 'Overview: Creating the market economy', in Ohno, K. and I. Ohno (eds) *Japanese Views on Economic Development: Diverse Paths to the Market*, London and New York: Routledge, pp. 1–50.

Oshikoya, T.W. (1994) 'Macroeconomic adjustment and domestic private investment in selected African countries', in Cornia, G.A. and G.K. Helleiner (eds) *From Adjustment to Development in Africa: Conflict, Controversy, Convergence, Consensus*, London and Basingstoke: Macmillan Press, pp. 137–51.

Pack, Howard (1993) 'Productivity and industrial development in sub-Saharan Africa', *World Development* 21(1): 1–16.

Palma, Gabriel (1998) 'Three and a half cycles of "mania, panic and [asymmetric] crash": East Asia and Latin America compared', *Cambridge Journal of Economics* 22(6): 789–808.

Pinheiro, A.C. and F. Giambiagi (1994) 'Brazilian privatisation in the 1990s', *World Development* 22(5): 737–53.

Polanyi, K. (1944) *The Great Transformation: The Political and Economic Origins of Our Times*, New York: Rinehart.

Pritchett, L. (1996) 'Measuring outward orientation in LDCs: Can it be done?', *Journal of Development Economics* 49: 307–35.

Ramamurti, Ravi (1991) 'The search for remedies', in Ramamurti, R. and R. Vernon (eds) *Privatisation and Control of State-Owned Enterprises*, Washington, DC: The World Bank.

—— (1996a) 'The new frontier of privatisation', in Ramamurti, R. (ed.) *Privatising Monopolies: Lessons from the Telecommunications and Transport Sectors in Latin America*, Baltimore: Johns Hopkins University Press.

—— (1996b) 'Telephone privatisation in a large country: Mexico', in Ramamurti, R. (ed.) *Privatising Monopolies: Lessons from the Telecommunications and Transport Sectors in Latin America*, Baltimore: Johns Hopkins University Press.

—— (1997) 'Testing the limits of privatisation: Argentine railroads', *World Development* 25(12): 1973–93.

Sender, John (1998) 'Analysis of sub-Saharan Africa's economic performance: Limitations of the current consensus', mimeo, School of Oriental and African Studies.

Severn, Luis and Andres Solimano (1992) 'Private investment and macroeconomic adjustment: A survey', *The World Bank Research Observer* 7(1): 95–114.

Shair, Osama Abu (1997) *Privatisation and Development*, Basingstoke: Macmillan Press.

Shirley, Mary and John Nellis (1991) *Public Enterprise Reform: The Lessons of Experience*, EDI Development Studies, Washington, DC: World Bank.

Standing, G., J. Sender and J. Weeks (1996), *Restructuring The Labour Market: The South African Challenge*, An ILO Country Review, Geneva: ILO.

Stiglitz, Joseph (1994) Whither Socialism?, Cambridge, MA and London: MIT Press.

—— (1996) 'Some lessons from the East Asian miracle', *World Bank Research Observer* 11(2): 151–77.

—— (1997a) 'An agenda for development in the twenty-first century', speech, Washington.

—— (1997b) Workshop on Issues of Reform and Development in China, Tokyo, Japan, 12 December.

—— (1998a) 'More instruments and broader goals: Moving toward the post-Washington consensus', the 1998 WIDER Annual Lecture, 7 January, UNU/WIDER: Helsinki.

—— (1998b) 'The East Asian crisis and its implications for India', speech, Conference on Asset Distribution, Poverty and Economic Growth, Brazil, July.

—— (1998c) 'Creating competition in telecommunications', speech at the Conference on Managing the Telecommunications Sector Post-Privatisation, The George Washington University, Washington, DC, April.

—— (1998d) 'Towards a new paradigm for development: Strategies, policies, and processes', given as the 1998 Prebisch Lecture at UNCTAD, Geneva, 19 October.

—— (1999) 'Whither reform? Ten years of the transition', paper presented to the Annual Bank Conference on Development Economics, 28–30 April, Washington, DC.

Tangri, R. (1995) 'The politics of Africa's public and private enterprise', *Journal of Commonwealth and Comparative Politics* 33(2): 169–84.

UNCTAD (1998) *Trade and Development Report*, Geneva: UNCTAD.

van Cranenburgh, Oda (1998) 'Increasing state capacity', *IDS Bulletin* 29(2): 75–81.

Vickers, J. and G. Yarrow (1988) *Privatisation: An Economic Analysis*, Cambridge, MA: MIT Press.

Wallace, Laura (ed.) (1997), "Deepening Structural Reform in Africa: lessons From East Asia – proceedings of a seminar held in Paris, May 13–14th, 1996, International Monetary Fund and Ministry of Finance of Japan", Washington: IMF.

Weeks, J. (1994) 'Fallacies of competition: Myths and maladjustment in the "Third World"', Inaugural Lecture, School of Oriental and African Studies, London: University of London.

World Bank (1981) *Accelerated Development in Sub-Saharan Africa*, Washington, DC: World Bank.

—— (1994) *Adjustment in Africa: Reforms, Results and the Road Ahead*, A World Bank Policy Research Report, Oxford and Washington, DC: Oxford University Press.

—— (1995), *Bureaucrats in Business: The Economics and Politics of Government Ownership*, Oxford: Oxford University Press.

—— (1996) *World Development Report 1996: From Plan to Market*, Washington, DC: World Bank.

—— (1997) *World Development Report 1997: The State in a Changing World*, Washington DC: World Bank.

Yamin, Mo (1998) 'The dual risks of market exchange and the transition process', in Cook, Paul, Colin Kirkpatrick and Frederick Nixson (eds) *Privatisation, Enterprise Development and Economic Reform: Experiences of Developing and Transitional Economies*, Cheltenham: Edward Elgar.

4 From Washington to post-Washington

Does it matter for industrial policy?

Sonali Deraniyagala

Introduction

The role played by the World Bank in promoting industrial policy reform in developing countries and the substance of these reforms has been well documented (for instance, see Thomas *et al*. 1991; Corbo *et al*. 1992). In the early 1980s, the inward-looking, import-substituting policies pursued in developing countries came under attack and a new agenda based on liberalisation and outward orientation was recommended. This Washington consensus, propagated at the height of the neo-liberal resurgence in development economics, gave almost axiomatic status to arguments about the optimisation potential of freely functioning markets and free trade.

Since the late 1990s, these views are being questioned within the World Bank itself, most notably in the form of Joseph Stiglitz's 'post-Washington consensus', which claims to re-examine the earlier reliance on market-based reforms. This chapter examines the evolution of World Bank thinking on industrial policy. It examines the Washington consensus on industrial policy and asks whether the new post-Washington consensus provides a significant departure from the earlier approach.

The first section of the chapter deals with the Washington consensus, focusing on its theoretical underpinnings and relevant empirical evidence. The second section examines the extent to which the post-Washington consensus provides an adequate analysis of the process of industrialisation and the usefulness of its policy conclusions.

The Washington consensus on industrialisation

The main propositions

The widely propagated Washington consensus on industrial policy consisted of several propositions: free trade optimises welfare at both the national and global level; industrialisation in developing countries is constrained by inward looking trade policies; trade liberalisation directly leads to improved industrial efficiency; markets in developing countries will function well if microeconomic distortions are removed; government intervention in industry is distortionary; intervention is only justified to correct a highly circumscribed, narrow set of market failures; and countries with liberal trade regimes and minimal government intervention have industrialised faster than those whose governments have intervened in trade and industry.

These propositions are based on simple neo-classical economics, which posits that boosting the long-term performance of industry only requires the creation of efficient and flexible markets, thus allowing the price mechanism to allocate scarce resources in line with comparative advantage and factor endowments. Thus, trade protection distorts the allocation of resources between tradeables and non-tradeables, and rapid, across-the board liberalisation is required to 'get prices right'. Manufacturing firms are seen to respond quickly and easily to correct price signals by adopting suitable new production techniques, which enhance productive efficiency. Inter-sectoral resource reallocation following liberalising industrial and trade policy reform is expected to be smooth and rapid (Stern 1991).

Given this belief in the optimisation potential of the free market, interventionist industrial policy is given a very limited role. The only justification for intervention is to correct special and isolated cases of market failure, which can easily be rectified to restore the competitive optimum (the obvious examples being the provision of basic, primary education and physical infrastructure). Such interventions are permissible as they have a general and undifferentiated impact on industry and do not directly affect resource allocation, which is best left to the market. They are seen as distinct from 'selective' interventions, which focus on specific industrial sectors or activities and thus interfere with the market mechanism.[1] Selective interventions are also seen as entailing a high risk of 'government failure', with government failures having a greater resource-subtracting effect than market failures.[2]

Drawing on these propositions and simple theoretical assumptions, the World Bank's agenda for trade policy reform has involved trade liberalisation directed at licensing and other quantitative restrictions, high and differentiated tariffs, export taxes and heavy bureaucratic requirements.[3] Industrial policy reform has focused on removing 'policy-induced' distortions arising from various forms of state intervention and has targeted inefficient and loss-making public enterprises, entry and exit restrictions on private enterprises, price controls, discretionary tax and subsidy policies (Frischtak 1989; Meier and Steel 1989).

In the following discussion we critically examine the theoretical arguments and empirical evidence relating to trade and industrial policy reform advocated by the Washington Consensus in greater detail.

The Washington consensus: theory and evidence

The debate on the theory and evidence relating to trade and industrial policy in developing countries is vast and will not be reviewed in full here. With its agenda of liberalising trade and industrial policy reform, the World Bank has led the neo-liberal camp in this debate. Over time and despite widespread criticism, its views have acquired an almost axiomatic status among neo-classical development economists. Below, we examine some of the main arguments used to support the case for trade liberalisation and non-intervention in industrial policy, and highlight their theoretical fragility. We also show that the relevant empirical evidence relating to these arguments is weak and inconclusive.

Trade policy: theory

When the Washington consensus emerged in the early 1980s, policy discussions on industry were much influenced by the well-known studies of trade protection, which demonstrated the large costs of haphazard and high levels of protection (Little *et al.* 1970; Bhagwati 1978; Krueger 1978). These studies argued that inward-looking trade policies led to distorted price signals which caused inefficiencies in resource allocation, infant industries that never matured partly due to the lack of competitive pressures and the allocation of resources to unproductive activities, in particular rent-seeking. The policy prescription that followed was simple: across-the-board trade liberalisation to remove policy-induced distortions.

Proponents of trade liberalisation point to the static and dynamic gains it brings in terms of industrial performance. Various types of static resource reallocation gains are shown to occur from increased import competition and outward orientation: within firms (from inefficient to efficient activities), between firms (from bad to good performers) and between industries (from less efficient to more efficient sectors). It is generally acknowledged, however, that the magnitude of these static gains (which take the form of the well-known Harberger welfare triangles) is small. Empirical estimates of the welfare costs of these relative-price distortions generally do not exceed 2 or 3 percentage points of GDP (Bhagwati 1993; Pursell 1990).

Given that the static gains from liberalisation are rarely large, the neo-liberal case for trade liberalisation rests largely on dynamic, long-term gains that are seen to be considerable. The theoretical basis for such an argument, however, is shaky, as the theory of static optimisation only goes so far as to demonstrate that an increase in the *levels* of productivity and growth will follow the removal of price distortions (in this case distortions in the prices of tradeables and non-tradeables). In the standard neo-classical model, given diminishing marginal returns to investment, a once-and-for-all liberalisation of trade cannot lead to increased productivity or economic growth in the long run.[4] The proponents of trade liberalisation largely overlook this point and make several other arguments relating to the sources of dynamic gains, but they too are weakly grounded in economic theory.[5] Consider, in particular, the following points.

First, trade liberalisation is seen to result in increased *x*-efficiency and entrepreneurial effort that boost productivity growth. It is argued that by reducing competition and increasing relative prices in import-competing sectors, protection encourages entrepreneurial slack, with liberalisation, therefore acting to reduce such slack. Formal representations of this argument have revealed its fragility (Tybout 1992). It only holds when the entrepreneurial labour supply curve is upward sloping in the relevant range and when changes in work incentives operate in the same direction for both exporters and import-substituting producers.

Second, increasing returns to scale (IRS) are also frequently cited as a source of dynamic gains from liberalisation. Firms in more open trade can supposedly operate at lower costs due to higher levels of output, available through participation in world markets. This argument, however, is based on the assumption that liberalisation necessarily expands IRS activities (Rodrik 1995). If scale economies are mainly concentrated in protected sectors that decline following trade reform, this type of dynamic gain will not materialise. Another variant of this argument is that protection increases profitability and leads to the coexistence of too many firms producing at below minimum efficient scale. Liberalisation, therefore, leads to industry rationalisation and allows firms to benefit from scale effects and produce at lower average costs. Again, this argument is also questionable as it assumes easy and frictionless entry and exit into markets.

Third, and most importantly, liberalisation is seen to have a strong positive effect on productivity-enhancing technological change. This argument, in fact, dominates neo-liberal discussions of the dynamic benefits of trade policy reform. However, in much of the literature the positive effect of liberalisation on technology development is largely assumed and no precise account of the mechanism through which it materialises is given. In an influential World Bank-sponsored study of liberalisation experiences, Thomas and Nash refer to the fact that liberal trade policies induce 'the ability to take advantage of a wide range of innovations' (1991, p. 34) and an 'increased growth in the rate of technology' (1991, p. 42). In a similar vein, Edwards (1991, p. 3) asserts that 'more open economies are more efficient in absorbing exogenously generated innovations'. Also, Balassa notes that by 'creating competition for domestic products in home markets, imports provide incentives for firms to improve their operations' (1988, p. 45), implying that competitive pressures on their own are sufficient to generate dynamic technological change.

The arguments relating to the technology-related benefits of liberalisation all remain at the level of casual observation, with weak theoretical premises. There is little to suggest that increased levels of competition will generate increased innovative activity and productivity gains across all sectors. A well-established body of research on market structure and innovation questions the notion that high levels of competition unambiguously promote technological change (Evenson and Westphal 1995; Bell and Pavitt

1992). Further, theoretical and empirical work on technology suggests that technological change is a complex process determined by a range of factors including incentives, existing paradigms of scientific and technological knowledge, and firm-level capabilities (Nelson 1981; Dosi 1997). In the light of all this, to suggest that increased competition alone is sufficient to promote technological dynamism is indeed simplistic.

All the above arguments about the dynamic gains from trade share another common shortcoming, which is that they lack a convincing story of firm behaviour. The predictions that liberalisation will increase x-efficiency, lead to industry rationalisation and promote technological change all rely on economic agents and firms easily and instantaneously responding to changes in price signals and the incentive structure. This assumption derives from a very specific view of firm behaviour, which underlies the neo-classical theory of static optimisation.

According to this view, the efficient functioning of the firm only requires that we 'get the prices right', with firms responding quickly and automatically to changes in price signals. Given the correct price signals, firms are able to improve efficiency, move in and out of production activities and upgrade technology, as long as there are freely operating product and factor markets. Upgrading technology, which has a direct positive effect on efficiency, is a straightforward task that involves picking best-practice technologies from a readily accessible 'shelf' of blueprints at given prevailing-factor prices. These technologies are characterised by predetermined efficiency levels, which are generally achieved because all the relevant information is available. The implication, therefore, is that very little firm-level 'learning' is required to achieve optimal levels of productive efficiency.

This simplistic view of firm behaviour ignores theoretical and empirical work, which has examined the nature of firm-level learning and shown that the capacity of firms to respond to external incentive and inducements depends largely on internal attributes and capabilities (Nelson and Winter 1982). In this view, firms do not pick new technologies and production techniques from a given shelf of blueprints. Rather, firm-level technology upgrading and efficiency enhancement requires the acquisition of such capabilities, which is usually a slow and costly process involving firm-specific learning strategies. The extent to which firms can respond to trade liberalisation, therefore, depends partly on these internal learning strategies, which can vary considerably between firms. The firm-level response to liberalisation is no longer straightforward and smooth.

Trade policy: evidence

Empirical research has also failed to provide any conclusive evidence relating to the gains from trade policy reform. A substantial body of empirical literature has investigated the effects of trade policy and openness on growth, total factor productivity and efficiency at the country, industry and firm level. More relevant for our purposes are the industry and firm-level studies, which generally analyse industrial performance 'before' and 'after' industrial and trade policy reform, and also relate industrial performance to rates of import penetration.

Overall, the evidence from these studies is largely inconclusive. Some early industry studies found a negative (but weak) correlation between import substitution and productivity growth (Nishimuzu and Robinson 1984), others showed Total Factor Productivity (TFP) growth rates to be high in highly protected industrial sectors (Waverman and Murphy 1992), while continued and accelerating TFP growth rates in both periods of high and low protection have also been reported (Aswicahyono *et al.* 1996). Firm-level studies also fail to establish a direct causal link between trade liberalisation and improved manufacturing performance. Some studies find support for the conjecture that efficiency levels are highest among industries experiencing the largest declines in protection (Tybout *et al.* 1991), while others find exporting firms to be more efficient than their domestically oriented counterparts (Chen and Tang 1987; Haddad 1993; Aw and Hwang 1994; Tybout and Westbrook 1995; Aw and Batra 1998).

Most of these industry and firm-level studies fail to shed light on the various channels through which trade liberalisation might affect productivity and efficiency in changing populations of heterogeneous firms. A few exceptions focus on the effects of trade policy on industry rationalisation, entry and exit patterns, and cost–price ratios (Tybout 1992; Roberts and Tybout 1991), but no strong conclusions emerge. There is little evidence of an association between import penetration and entry and exit patterns, contrary to predictions that import liberalisation is likely to result in the exit of inefficient firms and the entry of low-cost ones. There is also little support for the argument that liberalisation allows firms to benefit from scale economies or promotes technology upgrading (see Deraniyagala and Semboja 1999; Latsch and Robinson 1999).

Much of this research is marked by well-known methodological problems of establishing causality, isolating the effects of reform, as well as by data inadequacies. However, they highlight the following general points.

First, there is little evidence relating to the dynamic gains from liberalisation that are so central to pro-liberalisation literature. At best, there is some evidence of a static once-and-for-all increase in efficiency following trade reform, but again it is difficult to disentangle the effects of reform from other factors. Second, it is evident that trade policy interacts with other policies, including industrial policy, resulting in a varied set of outcomes depending on the specificities of industrial sectors and countries. Third, therefore, there is little to suggest that trade policy alone is sufficient for productivity improvement. Aspects of industrial policy such as support for research and development and technology transfer, access to credit and markets, as well as macroeconomic factors (such as exchange rate stability and domestic demand) are all relevant.

Industrial policy

As noted above, the Washington consensus rejects interventionist trade policy and ascribes a very limited role to the government in promoting industrialisation. The main task of industrial policy is seen to be the creation of freely functioning factor and product markets. Any selective industrial policy that affects the market-based pattern of resource allocation is seen as distortionary.

Much of the development debate on industrial policy has also centred around the East Asian experience and in particular on the role of the government in promoting industrialisation in these countries. In the 1970s and early 1980s, the neo-liberal view was that the spectacular success of manufacturing in these countries was primarily the result of *laissez-faire* policies and getting prices right. This, in itself, was seen as sufficient justification for advocating that governments in other developing countries withdrew from intervening in industrial policy.

This neo-liberal approach to industrial policy has faced two major challenges. First, at the theoretical level, new trade theories based on scale economies and imperfect information suggest that free trade may often be less than optimal and justify interventionist trade and industrial policies. The implication is that these interventions should be selective and country and sector specific (Krugman 1984, 1986; Eaton and Grossman 1986; Grossman and Horn 1988; Reddy 1999). Second, at the empirical level, the positive scope of interventionist industrial policy has been emphasised by influential empirical analyses of industrial policy in East Asia (Amsden 1989; Wade 1990), which attributed industrial success in these countries to deliberate and extensive intervention and not to economic liberalism.

These theoretical and empirical heterodoxies, however, have generally been rejected by neo-liberal economists. The standard response has been to emphasise both the high costs of rent-seeking and the large informational requirements associated with intervention. Alternative interpretations of the effects of interventionist trade and industrial policies in East Asia have also been given, with the best example of this being the World Bank's East Asian Miracle study (World Bank 1993). We consider each of these issues in turn.

Rent-seeking

Starting with Krueger's (1974) classic article it has become commonplace to argue that import-substitution type interventions give rise to incentive distortions and resource misallocations that have been labelled 'rent-seeking'. Examples of rent-seeking in industry include resources devoted to obtaining import licenses, generation of excess capacity when imports are allocated in proportion to excess capacity and so on. The conventional Harberger triangles relating to the static gains from trade have been inflated by incorporating rent-seeking, with the focus being on the calculation of welfare losses from government trade interventions, especially the introduction of import quotas. It has been argued that the resource costs of trade interventions are multiplied several-fold by the existence of rent-seeking. Empirical estimates have shown the magnitudes of the costs to be large (de Melo and Robinson 1982; Gallagher 1991; Tarr 1992). However, these arguments do not address the issue that a move towards liberalisation and outward-orientation may not necessarily reduce rent-seeking. They did not prove that a move to a neutral trade regime and export-orientation will necessarily reduce the potential for individuals and groups to exercise political power to obtain benefits from the government. It has been noted that exporting could bring forth a new form of rent-seeking targeted at obtaining export licenses (see Onis 1991 for a discussion of this in the case of Turkey).

The informational requirements of selective industrial policy

It is also argued that selective and strategic industrial policies are especially irrelevant to developing countries due to large informational requirements, which are beyond the scope of developing-country governments (Aslam 1995). Such arguments, however, generally remain at the level of assertions with little serious analysis of what these informational requirements might be. Little attempt has been made to examine whether any developing-country governments have been successful in undertaking strategic interventions and the factors that may determine the success or failure of such interventions, especially in relation to information problems. Further, the view that the state has a limited capacity to act in the face of imperfect information has no firm theoretical basis. Recent theories have shown that an information-constrained social optimum can be reached using a varied combination of contracts and policies (Brainard and Martimort 1997).

The role of interventionist industrial policy in East Asia

Since the late 1980s, the aforementioned studies of industrial policy in East Asia have conclusively shown that so-called outward-looking liberal trade regimes in these countries were characterised by pervasive selective protection, with the price mechanism being deliberately distorted to achieve specific objectives relating to industrial performance. Governments in these countries were shown to have intervened systematically and strategically to promote manufacturing competitiveness, to enhance technological dynamism and to deepen industrial structure (Amsden 1989; Wade 1990).

Given the weight of evidence presented by these studies, neo-liberal writers, and in particular the World Bank, had to admit that East Asian governments intervened in industry far more than they had initially suggested. Despite this, they concluded that intervention was not a good idea for other developing countries, partly because it was impossible to draw a direct causal link between interventionist industrial policy and industrial performance in East Asia.

These views are expressed clearly in the World Bank's influential 1993 study, *The East Asian Miracle*. In this study, the World Bank attempted to develop the 'theoretical' arguments relating to state intervention in industry by undertaking a detailed analysis of market failures and the types of intervention they justify. The study admitted that governments in East Asia did intervene to boost industrial performance and argued that these interventions were essentially 'market friendly'. The basis for intervention was the correction of market failures. The report provided a detailed discussion of market failures, emphasising the distinction between 'generic' and 'specific' market failures. Generic market failures were seen to require 'functional' interventions, which strengthen the workings of the market without directly affecting resource allocation (such as the provision of infrastructure and primary education), while specific failures called for strategic interventions to shift the allocation of resources away from certain activities and into others.

The study departed from earlier World Bank thinking by arguing that both functional and strategic industrial policy was pervasive in East Asia. The policy conclusions it drew from this, however, were surprising. It concluded that what really mattered in these countries were functional industrial policies (such as promoting basic education and providing infrastructure) and that it was not possible to draw a causal link between selective interventions and industrial performance.[6]

Thus, while it was expected that *The East Asian Miracle* would mark a significant turning point in World Bank thinking on industrial policy (by drawing a positive causal link between intervention and performance), in the final analysis very little new was said. By dismissing the potential of strategic interventions, the study failed to deal with important issues such as the specific ways in which governments interacted with the private sector and the particular characteristics of governments that enabled them to implement strategic industrial policies with fairly successful results. It also failed to provide any insights into the ways in which various industrial policies influence micro-level aspects of industrial performance, in particular on technology strategies, learning effects, and entry and exit dynamics.

The post-Washington consensus on industrial policy

To what extent, then, does the post-Washington consensus advocated by Joseph Stiglitz provide a significant departure from the Washington consensus on trade and industrial policy?

Stiglitz claims that his approach to industrial policy departs from the old Washington consensus in a fundamental sense, which is in its approach to markets and the way they function. Whereas the old approach assumed that markets worked well if left to themselves, it is argued that the new approach is based on an understanding of why markets do not function well (see Stiglitz 1998a, 1998b). Thus, for instance, Stiglitz (1999, p. F588) argues that:

Less developed countries differ from developed countries because their market institutions work less effectively. Development strategies must be based on an understanding that markets do not function well. And while they should work to enhance the effectiveness of market institutions, public policy will be misguided if it does not take into account the limitations of markets.

The theoretical underpinnings of this approach are, of course, clear. They lie in Stiglitz's own work in informational economics and market imperfections, which questioned the assumptions about information and technology in standard neo-classical models and highlighted the limits of the market mechanism due to the existence of numerous and pervasive market failures relating to incomplete information and weak markets. In this approach, information is always imperfect and markets are never complete, which means that the market mechanism does not generally yield an outcome that is even constrained Pareto-efficient (Greenwald and Stiglitz 1986; Stiglitz 1997). For instance, information imperfections and missing markets are intrinsic to the acquisition of new technology, raising the possibility that, if left to itself, the market may under-invest in technology development. Government interventions in the market, therefore, can make some individuals better off without making anyone else worse off, even if the government faced the same informational constraints as the private sector.

Stiglitz uses these theoretical microfoundations to analyse the process of late industrialisation. Industrialisation in developing countries is seen as a move towards increasingly perfect markets, a move that entails overcoming various market failures (Stiglitz 1997). These are not the narrowly circumscribed set of market failures acknowledged by the old consensus, but the much broader set of market failures relating to knowledge, information and weak and missing markets. Given that industrialisation involves continuously acquiring and managing new technologies and new knowledge, market failures relating to asymmetric information, technological spillovers, marketing spillovers, weak capital markets and the public-good properties of knowledge are seen as especially relevant to developing countries.

Overall, the new consensus places much emphasis on knowledge creation, with knowledge being the central role in promoting industrialisation (Stiglitz 1998c). The resultant emphasis on policies directed at knowledge and technology creation and absorption is a welcome departure from the old Washington consensus that acknowledged the public-good properties of basic education, but assumed that given the correct price signals and incentives, economic agents in developing countries could easily obtain all other types of knowledge necessary to boost industrial performance. This new focus on knowledge has been evident for a while, with references to the World Bank as a 'knowledge bank' and the 1998 World Development Report being called *Knowledge for Development* (World Bank 1998; Stiglitz 1998b). In his 1998 Prebisch Lecture, Stiglitz outlines the elements of a knowledge management strategy, which includes creating capacities to absorb and adapt knowledge through investments in human capital and research institutions, investing in technologies to facilitate the dissemination of knowledge and creating local knowledge in developing countries.

Two points about this approach to industrialisation and industrial policy are noteworthy. First, while it gives the state a greater role in promoting industrialisation than did the old consensus with its commitment to a minimal role for the state, it essentially argues that that market failures provide the only valid rationale for interventionist industrial policy.[7]

Second, most (or all) of the interventions proposed by this approach operate at the level of creating relevant institutions and infrastructure, especially institutions relating to knowledge and information. Thus, for instance, Stiglitz (1999, p. F588) notes 'government plays a vital role in providing the underlying institutional infrastructure required to make markets work well'. Again, the market-based approach of the Washington consensus is criticised for 'failing to establish the institutional infrastructure required to make markets work' (Stiglitz 1999, p. F588). We return to both these points below.

Theoretical shortcomings of the post-Washington consensus

At the theoretical level, the analysis of industrialisation presented by the post-Washington consensus is flawed in several ways. Many of these shortcomings stem from the notion that the theoretical tools of the market failure approach are sufficient for analysing the complexities of industrialisation and the associated processes of knowledge and technology development.[8] Thus, Stiglitz's analysis remains essentially neo-classical in the sense that it is located in the sphere of exchange rather than in production relations. It fails to open up the 'black box' of production, which is essential for an adequate analysis of industrialisation. These points are considered in more detail below.

First, the market failure approach is not adequately based on a micro-level understanding of firm behaviour, in particular of the ways in which firms acquire knowledge. Despite the emphasis that knowledge is important, it pays insufficient attention to the processes of knowledge generation and acquisition, especially at the firm level. Several theoretical and empirical analyses of firm behaviour have provided useful insights into this issue (Malerba and Orsenigo 1996; Cohen 1995). In particular, the fact that much knowledge at the firm level is 'tacit' knowledge, which is acquired through experience, and firm-specific learning has been emphasised. In this sense, knowledge about production techniques and technologies cannot be perfectly codified and communicated fully through blueprints and manuals, as there always remains an 'unexplained' element that must be gained through experience (trial and error). This essentially means that firms interpret information in a manner that is very specific to their own learning processes; in other words, they always operate with an 'imperfect under-standing' of production and technological possibilities, and their potential outcomes (see Dosi 1997). Learning processes also vary from firm to firm due to a variety of factors such as variations in internal skills and capabili-ties, different organisational structures, different production histories and so on. Such heterogeneous learning processes mean that, even when firms are faced with identical information, their responses and behaviour can vary.

This account is at odds with the market failure approach in which correcting for informational imperfections will necessarily bring forth desired outcomes in terms of firm behaviour. Imperfect understanding and persistent heterogeneity in learning processes may mean that interventions to correct for information failure (for instance, by providing information about a new technology) may have a varied and unpredictable outcome as firms interpret the new information in very specific ways. Further, if firms have developed well-established, 'sticky' learning routines based on low levels of knowledge absorption, it is possible that exposure to new informa-tion alone will have little or no impact on their behaviour.

Second, and relatedly, despite the emphasis on technology and innova-tion, the market failure approach is also based on an inadequate understanding of the process of technology development, with insufficient attention being paid to what actually happens inside the technological 'black box'. While the approach provides theoretical tools for analysing some important issues relating to technology – in particular, of how market failures such as spillovers, imperfect information and risk can lead to under-investment in technology – failure to recognise the complexities of the process of technological change is a serious shortcoming.

Over the past twenty years or so a large theoretical and empirical litera-ture has addressed issues relating to the economics of technology, with evolutionary and behavioural theories as well as historical interpretations enhancing our understanding of the ways in which technology is generated and diffused (Dosi *et al.* 1988; Freeman 1994; Rosenberg 1994; Nelson 1993; David 1985). Innovation and technical change are continuous and complicated processes shaped by the interaction of demand-side factors such as incentives (relative prices and demand conditions), and supply-side factors such as technological opportunities and knowledge paradigms. Institutions and firm-level abilities and experience, production routines and learning processes have therefore been emphasised in the literature (Nelson 1981; Winter 1987; Silverberg and Verspagen 1994). Processes of technical change are therefore diverse and depend on the specificities of firms, technologies, sectors and countries.

Such complexities, variations and specificities are overlooked by the market failure approach, which, with its focus on imperfect information, spillovers and missing markets tells only part of the story of technology development. While the post-Washington consensus acknowledges the centrality of technology in the industrialisation process, the fact that it is not located within a coherent theory of technology development limits it's ability to deal with these issues.

Third, the general notion that successful industrialisation mainly involves the removal of market failures and a move towards well-functioning markets is questionable. In particular, it ignores the fact that market failures are often, in fact, intrinsic to the process of production (Amsden 1997). Industrialisation in developing countries involves improving growth rates, deepening market structure, acquiring new technologies and skills, and mastering new products. While it is true that informational asymmetries in many markets have to be dealt with in the course of this, reducing the entire process of industrialisation to one of correcting market failures is problematic. Both theory and evidence suggest that successful industrialisation often involves creating market failures and distortions in resource allocation, not correcting them (Amsden 1997). Examples of these distortions include creating 'assets' such as proprietary firm-specific knowledge (about technology, management, marketing etc.) and differentiated products, erecting barriers to entry and sustaining monopoly power. For instance, evidence from industrialised countries shows that firms in industries such as chemicals and machinery developed into knowledge-based monopolies largely through building and buttressing such distortions (Chandler 1997). Evidence from East Asian countries also indicates that while government policy corrected some types of market failures (for instance, in markets for long-term credit), it also deliberately created other distortions, for instance by encouraging enterprises with 'non-public' technological knowledge and preventing knowledge spillovers from these enterprises, and by erecting barriers to entry in selected industries (Amsden 1989; Freeman 1994).

Implications for industrial and trade policy

These theoretical shortcomings, especially the failure to analyse specific problems of production, are reflected in the policy prescriptions of the post-Washington consensus.

Industrial policy

At one level, the market failure approach justifies interventionist industrial policy; by highlighting a new and extensive range of market failures it suggests a role for the state that goes beyond the minimal role of the old Washington consensus. These new market failures provide a rationale for interventions to correct them, as governments are able to devise interventions that fill in for these imperfections, with the type of intervention depending on the specific market failure addressed. Stiglitz (1996) provides details of some such interventions: providing the financial infrastructure for industry (creating development banks to deal with weak and missing capital markets, especially for long-term credit, and financial market regulation to direct capital into selected activities); support for education, especially engineering and science education; promoting science and technology programmes to deal with technological spillovers and under-investment in new technology (such as science centres to provide research and development facilities for small firms); and promoting intermediate industries with potentially large information spillovers to both upstream and downstream producers.

Many of the above interventions go beyond those of the old Washington consensus, and their inclusion in the policy agenda is a positive step. The emphasis on science and technology education, for instance, is a departure from early World Bank thinking, which implied that the provision of basic education was alone sufficient to generate the generic skills required by the technologically simple industries typically present in developing countries.

Overall, however, these policy interventions all remain at the level of institutional corrections to improve the functioning of the market mechanism. In his policy discussions Stiglitz reiterates the need to 'make markets work better' and the need for interventions to 'complement markets, not replace them' (Stiglitz 1998a: 25). A key feature of these institutional interventions is that they do not fundamentally alter the market mechanism, in the sense of directly changing the pattern of market-based resource allocation. It is implied that institutional interventions alone can create perfect or near-perfect markets and in doing so promote industrialisation.

Such an approach to industrial policy does not address the problems of industrialisation with sufficient detail or accuracy. Its weaknesses are primarily related to the theoretical shortcomings discussed above. For one thing, the advocacy of institutional interventions assumes that economic agents will respond to them in a satisfactory and even fairly uniform manner. It ignores the fact that this response will depend upon heterogeneous learning processes and may often be far from satisfactory. The theory and evidence relating to micro-level learning indicates that effective interventions to promote production have to go beyond setting up relevant institutions and must address issues of knowledge, technology and the creation of competitiveness in specific sectoral and national contexts. Evidence from countries with successful industrialisation histories indicates the state played an active role in identifying industries for selective promotion, inducing (or even coercing) firms into these industries and boosting localised learning and the problem-solving capacities of these firms and industries through micro-level initiatives (Lall and Latsch 1998). The post Washington consensus has little to say on these issues.

Further, the emphasis on policies that make markets work better ignores the need to create certain types of market failures, as discussed above. An analysis of industrialisation that recognises this would advocate industrial policy which goes beyond that suggested by the market failure approach, emphasising the need for active and selective industrial policy targeting specific sectors (and even firms), and in doing so often deliberately distorting the pattern of market-based resource allocation.

The importance of selective industrial policies, especially those that aimed at 'creating winners' by identifying and developing new areas of competitiveness (i.e. areas in which there was no obvious comparative advantage) and by creating new endowments and competitive assets, has been emphasised in the East Asian context (Wade 1990). Although Stiglitz acknowledges that policies of 'creating winners' were important for these countries, he offers a very specific interpretation of them that fits neatly into the market failure approach (Stiglitz 1996). Thus, all industrial policies used in these countries are interpreted as being directed at market failures. In addition, he interprets these policies as not being necessarily selective because they focused on the export sector in general and not on particular activities or firms. The weight of available empirical evidence, however, does not support this interpretation. If the post-Washington consensus is to draw useful policy lessons from these country experiences, it must begin with a more comprehensive evaluation of the available evidence.

Trade policy and openness

In keeping with the old Washington consensus, the post-Washington consensus continues to advocate trade liberalisation on the grounds that it inevitably brings dynamic gains in terms of productivity and growth. Thus, for instance, Stiglitz (1988a, p. 33) criticises the standard neo-classical trade theory for only dealing with the static gains from trade, and notes that 'both rigorous empirical and country experience suggests that the growth effects of engagement in the global marketplace are far greater than predicted by the standard model'. He also goes on to argue that 'the main gains from trade seem to come from an outward shift of the production frontier' (1988a, p. 34) and that 'a major difference between developed and less developed countries is the difference in the efficiency with which inputs are transformed into outputs: trade reduces the discrepancy' (1988a, p. 35).

Thus, Stiglitz displays the same belief in the dynamic gains from trade as the old Washington consensus. The large, critical literature on the gains from trade liberalisation is essentially ignored by the post-Washington consensus, which continues to present the case for trade liberalisation as unquestioned conventional wisdom. Once again, it is asserted that liberalisation alone will promote technological change, with little analysis of relevant issues, such as the internal capacity of firms to undertake this change.

By stressing the gains from liberalisation, the post-Washington consensus also denies the role of strategic interventions in trade in promoting industrialisation. In particular, it overlooks the fact that knowledge generation and technology development can sometimes be promoted through selective protection, a point made clear by a substantial body of new trade theories and endogenous growth models. This, again, reflects the partial analysis of knowledge underlying the market failure approach. The basic assumption is that any problems in knowledge development following liberalisation can be dealt with through institutional arrangements to boost the provision of information. The fact that productivity-enhancing knowledge is developed through production-based learning, and that such learning may be curtailed if the intense competitive pressures associated with liberalisation have a negative effect on production, is completely overlooked.

Conclusion

The discussion in this chapter has shown that the post-Washington consensus approach to industrial and trade policy is limited in many ways. While the scope for industrial policy is extended in comparison to the old Washington consensus, in the final analysis the new consensus fails to provide an adequate understanding of the complex problems facing late industrialising countries and fails to advocate effective policies to deal with them. This is largely the result of weaknesses in the underlying theoretical approach, in particular the inability to move the analysis beyond the sphere of market-based transactions and deal with issues relating to production.

Notes

1 See the World Bank's *The East Asian Miracle: Economic Growth and Public Policy* (1993) for an exposition of this argument.
2 See Wade (1990) for a detailed discussion of selective and general industrial policies.
3 For a more detailed discussion, see Rodrik (1995).
4 See Lucas (1988) for an exposition of this argument.
5 The following discussion draws on Deraniyagala and Fine (forthcoming).
6 See Lall (1994) for a detailed critique of this study.
7 See Stiglitz (1996), where various possible justifications for interventionist policies are discussed and only those relating to market failures are seen as valid. Other reasons, such as those relating to scale economies, are not seen as providing a convincing case for intervention.
8 Stiglitz in fact extends the market failure approach to analyse a wide range of economic phenomena. See, for instance, Stiglitz (1999), which discusses 'global' public goods, which include international macroeconomic co-ordination and humanitarian assistance.

References

Amsden, A. (1989) *Asia's Next Giant: South Korea's Late Industrialisation*, Oxford: Oxford University Press.
—— (1997) 'Bringing production back in – understanding government's economic role in late industrialisation', *World Development* 25(4): 469–80.
Aslam, A. (1995) 'The new trade theory and its relevance to the trade policies in developing countries', *The World Economy* 18(3): 367–85.
Aswichayono, H., K. Bird and H. Hill (1996) 'What happens to industrial structure when countries liberalise?', *Journal of Development Studies* 32(3): 340–63.
Aw, B. and G. Batra (1998) 'Technological capability and firm efficiency in Taiwan', *World Bank Economic Review* 12(1): 59–79.

Aw, B. and A. Hwang (1994) 'Productivity and the export market: A firm-level analysis', Pennsylvania State University, mimeo.

Balassa, B. (1988) 'Interests of developing countries in the Uruguay round', *World Economy* 11(1): 39–54.

Bell, M. and K. Pavitt (1992) 'Accumulating technological capability in developing countries', Supplement to *World Bank Economic Review*: 257–81.

Bhagwati, J. (1978) *Foreign Trade Regimes and Economic Development: Anatomy and Consequences of Exchange Control Regimes*, Lexington, MA: Ballinger.

—— (1993) *India's Economy: The Shackled Giant*, Oxford: Clarendon Press.

Brainard, S. and D. Martimort (1997) 'Strategic trade policy with incompletely informed policymakers', *Journal of International Economics* 42(1–2): 33–66.

Chandler, A. (1997) *The Visible Hand: The Managerial Revolution in American Business*, Cambridge, MA: Harvard University Press.

Chen, T. and D. Tang (1987) 'Comparing technical efficiency among import substituting and export-oriented foreign firms in a developing country', *Journal of Development Economics* 26(2): 277–89.

Cohen, W. (1995) 'Empirical studies of innovative activities', in P. Stoneman (ed.) *Handbook of the Economics of Innovation and Technological Change*, Oxford: Basil Blackwell.

Corbo, V., S. Fischer and S. Webb (1992) *Adjustment Lending Revisited: Policies to Restore Growth*, Washington, DC: The World Bank.

David, P. (1985) 'Clio and the economics of QWERTY', *American Economic Review* 75: 332–72.

de Melo, J. and S. Robinson (1982) 'Trade adjustment policies and income distribution in three archetype developing countries', *Journal of Development Economics* 10(1): 67–92.

Deraniyagala, S. and B. Fine (forthcoming 2001) 'New trade theory versus old trade policy: a continuing enigma', *Cambridge Journal of Economics*.

Deraniyagala, S. and H. Semboja (1999) 'Technology upgrading and trade liberalisation in Tanzania', in Lall (ed.) (1999).

Dosi, G. (1997) 'Opportunities, incentives and the collective pattern of technological change', *Economic Journal* 107: 1530–47.

Dosi, G., C. Freeman, R. Nelson, G. Silverberg and L. Soete (eds) (1988) *Technical Change and Economic Theory*, London: Frances Pinter.

Eaton, J. and G. Grossman (1986) 'Optimal trade and industrial policy under oligopoly', *Quarterly Journal of Economics* 101(2): 383–406.

Edwards, S. (1991) 'Trade orientation, distortions and growth in developing countries', Santiago, Fourth Inter-American Seminar on Economics (Mimeo).

Edwards, S. (1997) 'Trade policy, growth, and income distribution', *American Economic Review* 87(2): 205–10.

Evenson, R. and L. Westphal (1995) 'Technological change and technology strategy', in J. Behrman and T. Srinivisan (eds) (1995) *Handbook of Development Economics*, vol. 3B, Oxford: Elsevier.

Freeman, C. (1994) 'The economics of technical change', *Cambridge Journal of Economics* 18: 462–514.

Frischtak, C. (1989) *Competition Policies for Industrialising Countries*, Washington, DC: The World Bank.

Gallagher, M. (1991) *Rent Seeking and Economic Growth in Africa*, Boulder: Westview Press.

Greenwald, B. and J. Stiglitz (1986) 'Externalities in markets with imperfect information and Incomplete Markets', *Quarterly Journal of Economics* 101, May: 229–64.

Grossman, G. and H. Horn (1988) 'Infant industry protection reconsidered: The case of international barriers to entry', *Quarterly Journal of Economics* CIII(4): 767–87.

Haddad, M. (1993) 'How trade liberalisation affected productivity in Morocco', World Bank, Policy Research Working Paper, no. 1096.

Helleiner, G. (ed.) (1992) *Trade Policy, Industrialisation and Development*, Oxford: Clarendon Press.

Krueger, (1974) 'The political economy of the rent seeking society', *American Economic Review* 68(2): 270–4.

Krugman, P. (1984) 'Import protection as export protection', in Kierkowski (ed.) *Monopolistic Competition in International Trade*, Oxford: Oxford University Press: 180–93.

—— (1986) *Strategic Trade Policy and the New International Economics*, Cambridge, MA: MIT Press.

Lall, S. (1994) 'The East Asian miracle study: Does the bell toll for industrial strategy?', *World Development* 22(4): 45–54.

Lall, S. (ed.) (1999) *The Technological Response to Import Liberalisation in Sub-Saharan Africa*, London: Macmillan.

Lall, S. and W. Latsch (1998) 'Import liberalisation and industrial performance: The conceptual underpinnings', *Development and Change* 29: 437–65.

Latsch, W. and P. Robinson (1999) 'Technology upgrading in post-liberalisation Zimbabwe', in Lall (ed.) (1999).

Little, I., T. Scitovsky and M. Scott (1970) *Industry and Trade in Some Developing Countries*, London: Oxford University Press.

Lucas, R. (1988) 'On the mechanics of economic development', *Journal of Monetary Economics* 22: 3–42.

Malerba, F. and L. Orsenigo (1996) 'The dynamics and evolution of industries', *Industrial and Corporate Change* 5(1): 51–87.

Meier, G. and W. Steel (eds) (1989) *Industrial Adjustment in Sub-Saharan Africa*, Washington, DC: The World Bank.

Nelson, R. (1981) 'Research on productivity, growth and productivity differences: Dead ends and new departures', *Journal of Economic Literature* 19: 1029–64.

—— (1993) *National Innovation Systems: A Comparative Study*, Oxford/New York: Oxford University Press.

—— (1995) 'Recent evolutionary theorising about economic change', *Journal of Economics Literature* 33: 48–90.

—— R. Nelson and S. Winter (1982) *An Evolutionary Theory of Economic Change*, Cambridge, MA: Belknap Press.

Nishimuzu, M. and S. Robinson (1984) 'Trade policy and productivity in semi-industrialised countries', *Journal of Development Economics* 16(1–2): 177–206.

Ocampo, J. and L. Taylor (1998) 'Trade liberalisation in developing economies: Modest benefits but problems with productivity growth, macro prices, and income distribution', *Economic Journal* 108(3): 1523–46.

Onis, Z. (1991) 'Organisation of export-led industrialisation: The Turkish foreign trade companies in comparative perspective', in Nas, T. and M. Odekan (eds) *The Politics and Economy of Turkish Liberalisation* (1992) London: Associated Universities Press.

Pursell, G. (1990) 'Industrial sickness, primary and secondary: The effects of exit constraints on industrial performance', *World Bank Economic Review* 4(1): 104–14.

Reddy, S. (1999) 'Dynamic comparative advantage and the welfare effects of trade', *Oxford Economic Papers*: 51(1): 15–39.

Roberts, M. and J. Tybout (1991) 'Size rationalisation and trade exposure in developing countries', The World Bank Working Paper Series, no. 594.

Rodrik, D. (1995) 'Trade and industrial policy reform', in Behrman, J. and T. Srinivasan (eds) (1995) *Handbook of Development Economics*, vol. 3B, Amsterdam: North Holland.

Rosenberg, D. (1994) 'Science – Technology – Economy Interactions', in O. Grandstrand (ed.) *The Economics of Technology*, Amsterdam: North Holland.

Silverberg, G. and B. Verspagen (1994) 'Learning, innovation and economic growth: A long run model of industrial dynamics', *Industrial and Corporate Change* 3: 199–203.

Stern, E. (1991) 'Evolutions and lessons of adjustment lending', in V. Thomas and J. Nash (eds) *Restructuring Economies in Distress: Policy Reform and the World Bank*, Oxford and New York: Oxford University Press.

Stiglitz, J. (1996) 'Some lessons from the East Asian miracle', *World Bank Research Observer* 11(2): 151–77.

—— (1997) 'An agenda for development in the twenty first century', *Proceedings of the World Bank Annual Conference on Development Economics, 1997*.

—— (1998a) 'More instruments and broader goals; Moving towards the post-Washington consensus', 1998 WIDER Annual Lecture, Helsinki, Finland.

—— (1998b) 'Towards a new paradigm for development strategies, policies and processes', 1988 Prebisch Lecture at UNCTAD, Geneva , 19 October.

—— (1998c) 'Knowledge for development; economic science, economic policy and economic advice', *Proceedings of the Annual Bank Conference on Development Economics, 1998*.

—— (1999) 'The World Bank at the millennium', Economic Journal 109, November: F577–97.

Tarr, D. (1992) 'Rent-seeking and the benefits of price and trade reform in Poland: The automobile and colour television cases', World Bank, mimeo.

Thomas, V. and J. Nash (1991) *Best Practices in Trade Policy Reform*, Washington, DC: The World Bank.

Tybout, J. (1992) 'Linking trade and productivity', *World Bank Economic Review* 6(2): 189–211.

Tybout, J. and M. Westbrook (1995) 'Trade liberalisation and the dimensions of efficiency change in Mexican manufacturing industries', *Journal of International Economics* 39(1–2): 53–78.

Tybout, J. *et al.* (1991) 'The effects of trade reform on scale and technical efficiency: New evidence from Chile', *Journal of International Economics* 31(3–4): 231–50.

Wade, R. (1990) *Governing the Market: Economic Theory and the Role of Government in East Asian Industrialisation*, Princeton: Princeton University Press.

Waverman, L. and S. Murphy (1992) 'Total factor productivity in automobile production in Argentina, Mexico, Korea and Canada', in Helleiner (ed.) (1992).

Winter, S. (1987) 'Knowledge and competencies as strategic assets', in Teece, D. (ed.) *The Competitive Challenge*, Cambridge, MA: Ballinger.

World Bank (1993) *The East Asian Miracle: Economic Growth and Public Policy*, Oxford: Oxford University Press.

—— (1998) *1998 World Development Report: Knowledge for Development*, Oxford, Oxford University Press.

5 Consensus in Washington, upheaval in East Asia

Dic Lo

East Asia in the development policy debate

In his UNU/WIDER lecture, Joseph Stiglitz (1998a, p. 3) stated that:

> The more dogmatic versions of the Washington consensus fail to provide the right framework for understanding either the success of the East Asian economies or their current troubles. Responses to East Asia's crisis grounded in these views of the world are likely to be, at best, badly flawed and, at worst, counterproductive.

In a separate lecture, Stiglitz (1998b, p. 1) went on to claim that: 'Curiously many of the factors identified as contributors to East Asian economies' current problems are strikingly similar to the explanations previously put forward for their success.' These statements reflect the complex relationship between the process of development in East Asia and the nascent views on development policy that have been critical of the so-called Washington consensus. Stiglitz's statements also highlight an essential feature of the emerging rival doctrine, dubbed the post-Washington consensus: its analytical reliance on market failure. For proponents of the new doctrine, what is problematic with the old doctrine is not its emphasis on the need for 'well-functioning markets' to achieve economic development but its adoption of 'incomplete or even misguided instruments' in achieving this end.

As far as the development of East Asia is concerned, theoretical dispute between the two currents has focused on one dimension of achieving the above end: the extent (and desirability) of integration of developing economies into the world market. East Asia has long been praised by advocates of the Washington consensus as a model of 'openness', initially in foreign trade and more recently in cross-border capital flows.[1] Such openness is posited as the all-powerful factor that has fuelled the rapid and sustained economic growth of the region. This view of the so-called 'East Asian miracle' is considered by proponents of the post-Washington consensus as badly flawed, both because it downplays the risks associated with openness and because it ignores the role of state economic intervention in East Asian economies (Stiglitz 1996 and 1998a are representative of this view). The financial and economic crisis, which has engulfed East Asia since the summer of 1997, has added a great deal of further complexity to the dispute. Did the crisis result from the very openness itself? Or was it caused by intrinsic weaknesses of East Asia's economic institutions and development policies, particularly those arising from the aforementioned state intervention? Resolution of this intense debate could offer a new and decisive turn in official thinking within the international establishment responsible for development policy design.

It is important to observe that both new and old doctrines have two vital features in common, irrespective of other differences in analysing the development experience of East Asia. First, both adhere to a notional model of the market economy, which they also use to represent the reality of the world market. Second, they compound the ahistorical character of this model by a tendency to conceptualise East Asia's development achievements (as well as its crisis) largely as a policy matter. These two features are in sharp contrast to the conclusions of a wide range of alternative studies, which analyse East Asian development in terms of historically specific structural changes in both the local and the global economies. The present chapter reviews the relationship between the current development policy debate and the East Asian development experience from a perspective that is significantly inspired by the alternative studies indicated above. The central proposition put forth below is that, in line with the emphasis on the appropriate match between economic institutions and the demand-side environment as the precondition for economic development, the economic policies prescribed by both the Washington and post-Washington consensus are likely to bring about outcomes that are at best uncertain and at worst dangerous in the long term.

The consensus in Washington and the notional market economy

It is no exaggeration that, from the outset, a central pillar of the Washington consensus was to encourage the integration of developing economies into the world market. The codeword 'openness' has been extensively used in numerous writings associated with orthodox development policy establishment, especially in various issues of the World Bank's *World Development Report* and the IMF's *World Economic Outlook*. Underpinning the call for openness is the belief that, by means of total integration into the world market, late developing economies would move along the 'natural path' of development. That is, in line with standard neo-classical theories of growth and trade, they would converge towards the income level of advanced countries via the principle of comparative advantage. This has been further enhanced by the belief – arising from policy proposals for transformation of Soviet-type economies – that, through such integration, late development economies would be able to construct 'natural (political) economic institutions' that would, in turn, guarantee development along the 'natural path'.

More specifically, 'openness' referred initially to liberalisation of foreign trade – that is, the notion of trade regime neutrality, which essentially asks developing economies to leave their foreign trade, and thus their position in the international division of labour, completely under the regulation of the world market. With the rapid progress of what the orthodox development establishment calls globalisation, policies associated with openness have increasingly shifted their focus towards the sphere of external finance. This culminated in the IMF's 1997 Hong Kong Declaration, which agreed to amend its articles in order that member countries would then be required to liberalise their capital accounts. In the meantime, the agreement to free markets for financial services negotiated in the World Trade Organization (WTO), and the negotiations on cross-border investment within the Organization for Economic Cooperation and Development (OECD) have added further impetus to the worldwide push for greater freedom of movement for capital.

East Asia's development experience has long been portrayed as fitting well with the above doctrine. Protagonists of the Washington consensus have often attributed the rapid and sustained economic growth of the region during the past decades – that is, the so-called East Asian miracle – to the region's high degree of integration into the world market. At times, and especially in the 1980s, they have gone so far as to claim that East Asia's integration into the world market has facilitated the overcoming of domestic constraints, undercut monopolistic and protectionist economic arrangements, and encouraged competition and the pursuit of technological improvement.[2] In other words, the miracle was achieved in spite, rather than because, of clear deviations from the principles of the market economy among the region's institutions (for instance, strictly controlled financial institutions) and development policies (for instance, widely employed state industrial policies); deviations that are far too prominent to be denied.

The gradual reassessment of the development implications of East Asia's extensive as well as intensive state economic intervention has led to subversion of the Washington consensus within the orthodox establishment. The World Bank's 1993 East Asian miracle project is considered as a decisive turn in the emergence of the post-Washington consensus. It concedes that state intervention, which has been indubitably market-supplanting (in the sense that it 'distorts' the functioning of the market) in many instances, has had a positive impact on economic development, though it also argues that this has been relatively rare. The project represents a break not only with the market fundamentalism of the 1980s but also the market-friendly approach of the 1991 *World Development Report*, which argues that any state intervention that has a positive developmental impact must be essentially market-conforming (that is, it must facilitate the functioning of the market). According to Stiglitz (1998a), the most important finding of the project is that, in East Asia, state intervention (i.e. creation of an appropriate financial system to mobilise savings and allocate capital efficiently, promotion of competition and investment in human capital and technology transfer) has played a positive, indeed crucial, role that would not have been automatically taken up by the market. This argument, however, also reflects the market failure character of the analytical approach of the post-Washington consensus: state intervention is understood as complementing, rather than replacing, the market. By extension, the new consensus can be thought of as complementing the market-centered development policies of the Washington consensus in achieving a common aim; that is, the formation of well-functioning markets.

The market failure-based explanation of the East Asian miracle is more fully expounded by Stiglitz (1996, p. 151) in the following statement:

> East Asia's success was based on a combination of factors, particularly the high saving rate interacting with high levels of human capital accumulation, in a stable, market-oriented environment – but one with active government intervention – that was conducive to the transfer of technology.

Underpinning this view is the argument that the market is characterised by flows of imperfect information and so it cannot promote the development process, which is associated with acquisition of new technology (new information). Hence, even in the extreme case of East Asia's famously market-supplanting industrial policy, it is conceded that: 'Increasing returns, especially when combined with capital market imperfections, provide the foundation for strategic trade policy' (Stiglitz 1996, p. 159). This argument begs the question of why capital is in short supply in the first place, which is probably related to the nature of the industries promoted by state industrial policy rather than to capital market imperfections *per se*. Nevertheless, by focusing on the nature of technological change rather than the 'natural path of development' (which is based on the stages approach to comparative advantage, and with it the assumption of well-defined production functions), Stiglitz claims that the East Asian miracle is due to productivity growth rather than the oft-mentioned factor of cheap labour. In the following section this issue will be discussed in fuller detail.

East Asia's financial and economic crisis since the summer of 1997 has pushed the development policy debate onto a new terrain. Initially, the prevailing explanation of the crisis was what Stiglitz calls the dogmatic versions of the Washington consensus. This is reflected in the repeated claim by the orthodox establishment, notably the IMF, which was responsible for the rescue programmes, that the crisis was 'home-grown'. The derogatory term 'crony capitalism' came into vogue almost overnight among Western media and politicians, as well as academics. It put the blame unambiguously on the continuing existence of market-supplanting elements of the institutions and development policies in East Asia, particularly various forms of state-initiated 'distortions' in the financial market.

In January 1999, the IMF's official statement, *The IMF's Response to the Asian Crisis*, still phrased its verdict in this way:

> A combination of inadequate financial sector supervision, poor assessment and management of financial risk, and the maintenance of relatively fixed exchange rates led banks and corporations to borrow large amounts of international capital, much of it short-term, denominated in foreign currency, and unhedged .... Although private sector expenditure and financing decisions led to the crisis, it was made worse by governance issues, notably government involvement in the private sector.
>
> (IMF 1999, p. 1)

In line with such diagnosis of the causes of the crisis, the IMF-sponsored rescue programmes have typically encompassed measures that include: pushing up interest rates, tightening government expenditure, breaking government–business links, closing down financial institutions and opening domestic financial markets to foreign participants.

These measures have been criticised by authors of various convictions, not all of whom assign the blame for the crisis to internal factors.[3] Especially influential is the conviction, which could be considered as intellectually linked to the post-Washington consensus, that the world financial markets are seriously flawed in the first place. The World Bank's 1998 special report, *East Asia: The Road to Recovery*, is representative of this conviction. Its views on the causes of the crisis are significantly different from those of the IMF:

> It is important to note that domestic policy failures explain only part of the emergence of these vulnerabilities and subsequent crisis. Failures in international financial markets in the boom part of the cycle, as well as during the crash, were no less pivotal; herd instincts in financial markets have not served East Asia well.
>
> (World Bank 1998, p. 16).

A subsequent study that deals with rescue policies goes so far as to enunciate the unspeakable: 'reforms must be comprehensive and include a combination of more flexible macroeconomic policies, tighter financial regulation and where necessary, restrictions on capital inflows' (World Bank 1999, p. xii). Moreover, the need for reforms is not limited to the domestic front but applies to the world financial markets too: 'Changes are needed in the architecture of the international financial system in view of the excessive volatility (euphoria and panics), strong contagion effects, and increased scope for moral hazard in international financial markets' (World Bank 1999, p. xii).

This view, called by Wade (1998) the story of 'panic triggering debt deflation in a basically sound but under-regulated system', attributes the crisis to inadequate regulation by East Asian states over short-term international capital flows. It considers these flows as largely speculative and prone to causing excessive volatility in currency and financial markets. The contagious spread of the crisis to the whole of East Asia and beyond, in this view, confirms that financial panic itself was the main cause of the crisis. IMF-initiated policies, particularly closing down financial institutions in trouble, are thus charged with greatly exacerbating the panic. Jeffrey Sachs, a stern critic of the rescue programmes, put it dramatically: 'Instead of dousing the fire, the IMF in effect screamed fire in the theatre' (quoted in Bullard *et al.* 1998, p. 509). Finally, it was considered that financial panic could combine with contraction of demand to form a vicious cycle of bankruptcy, financial market collapse and more falling demand, thus pushing already weak economies into deep recession. Contractionary fiscal and monetary policies advocated by the rescue programmes were thus considered even more problematic than the proposed structural reforms, which focused exclusively on domestic institutions.

The World Bank's mildly dissenting view of the East Asian crisis and the rescue programmes, indicated above, appears to be the limit of where the orthodox establishment is prepared to go. Although significantly different from the IMF in terms of concrete policies, it still sticks to the belief that, if properly managed, developing economies would benefit from their integration into the world market, including the sphere of finance. In other words, the post-Washington consensus really departs from the Washington consensus on the issue of the appropriate means for achieving such integration, given the existence of serious market failures. However, it remains ambiguous regarding the long-term developmental implications of IMF-type structural reforms, and, by extension, the significance of East Asia's economic institutions and policies that are known as crony capitalism. Thus, the general conclusion that flows from the arguments of the post-Washington consensus is much more moderate than appears at first sight:

> [G]lobalization is double-edged, bringing risks with opportunities. If East Asia had not been outward-looking it would not have enjoyed the considerable benefits brought by trade and foreign direct investment .... The crisis reinforces the belief that countries will benefit most from globalization when they have transparent, robust and well-regulated financial markets.
>
> (Stiglitz 1998c, p. 3)

The aim of achieving such financial markets is also an integral part of the IMF-sponsored programmes.

Still, even this mildly divergent view on the appropriate means for achieving the common aim is not acceptable to many within the orthodox development establishment. While agreeing early on to abandon contractionary fiscal and monetary policies, the IMF has maintained that its structural reforms are appropriate and indispensable, both in the short and long term. Stanley Fischer, the IMF's First Deputy Managing Director, has gone as far as to say that: 'financial and corporate inefficiencies were at the epicentre of the economic crisis, and have to be dealt with to restore durable growth. Indeed, the priority now should be to accelerate restructuring' (Fischer 1998). Note that this statement was made as late as October 1998, when the view that the East Asian crisis was purely due to crony capitalism had already been widely discredited, and the World Bank had proposed the alternative view described above.

The World Bank's (1999) cautious approach concerning capital account liberalisation, which states that opening the capital account and aiming at integration into the global financial markets should be contingent on adequate domestic institutional development, has also encountered orthodox opposition. In late 1998, Lawrence Summers, then Deputy Treasury Secretary of the USA, in addressing the question of how developing countries can build an adequate regulatory regime to allow for capital account opening, bravely asserted that: 'One of the best ways to accelerate the process of developing such a system is to open up to foreign financial service providers, and all the competition, capital and expertise which they bring with them' (quoted in Wade and Veneroso 1998b, p. 35). That is to say, adequate domestic institutional development is not the prerequisite for capital account liberalisation – it is rather a natural outcome of the latter. Clearly, this is no more than a reiteration of a basic tenet of the Washington consensus: that through integration into the world market, developing countries would be able to construct the necessary 'natural economic institutions'.

To recap, as far as the diagnosis of the East Asian crisis is concerned, the division within the orthodox establishment is real but of limited depth. Those associated with the post-Washington consensus have tended to ascribe the crisis to the interaction between domestic institutional weaknesses and failures in the world financial market. Accordingly, their proposed rescue policies have been of a gradualist and managed character, with the emphasis on the appropriate match between the level of domestic institutional development and the degree of opening up to cross-border capital flows. These are in contrast to those views characterised by Stiglitz (1998a) as 'dogmatic versions of the Washington consensus', presumably referring to views expressed in the IMF publications indicated above. Nevertheless, adherents to the post-Washington consensus have remained ambivalent towards the ongoing IMF-sponsored structural reforms aimed at transforming East Asia in the direction of the notional market economy. Despite recognising that East Asia's unorthodox institutions and policies have played a positive and significant role in the miracle era, they have appeared uncertain about the role of these factors in the 1990s. The ambivalent attitude towards IMF-type structural reforms, held by the World Bank and associated writers including Stiglitz and expressed in the special report, *East Asia: The Road to Recovery*, clearly reflects this position. Thus, there is the real possibility that, regarding long-term development, concrete policies based on the post-Washington consensus would turn out to be indistinguishable from those of the Washington consensus (its less dogmatic versions), or at least from those of a general market-friendly approach.

The upheaval in East Asia as history-specific process

The most crucial area of ambiguity in the policy debate within the orthodox establishment concerns the development implications of East Asia's peculiar economic institutions and development policies. This is because, as indicated in the preceding section, while adherents of the Washington consensus simply use the term 'inefficiency' to characterise the nature of these institutions and policies, those of the post-Washington consensus tend to regard them as effective remedies for market failure (on balance and mainly in the miracle era). Also, both appear to accept that, in the 1990s, these institutions and policies need to be reformed in the direction of the notional market economy.

Outside the orthodox establishment, however, there exist many dissenting views on East Asia's development experience.[4] Several influential studies regard the putative weaknesses of the region's institutions and policies as a necessary trade-off for the benefits of promoting catching-up development in late-comer countries entering the capitalist world economy; that is, development on the basis of created rather than given comparative advantage. On the side of weaknesses, Wade and Veneroso (1998a) offer a revealing answer to the question of why the crisis in East Asia has reached such an exceptionally large scale compared to other areas and economies. For them, the reason is that East Asia's 'high household saving, high corporate debt' economy is vulnerable to systemic shocks, such as high interest rates, currency devaluation or demand contraction. This is because high interest rates or currency devaluation increase the cost of servicing debts, while demand contraction reduces corporate profits. When interest payments are in excess of profits, firms have no other option but to increase total debts. However, coping with shocks in this way is not usually possible in the context of East Asia, where firms are already heavily indebted. Moreover, because debt requires a fixed level of repayment, unlike equity, which requires a share of profits, firms would be forced to bear the brunt of systemic shocks. This makes their vulnerability to systemic shocks even more pronounced.

However, vulnerability is not simply a matter of inefficiency. In a rebuttal to the orthodox notion of 'the natural path' of development, Amsden (1994) argues that unfettered regulation of local economies by the world market could well result in underdevelopment, instead of (more or less) development.

This argument is more explicitly pursued by Wade (1990), who coins the term 'governing the market' and argues that catching-up development has been a central pillar of the East Asian miracle. While accepting that labour-intensive, export-oriented industrialisation has played an important role in East Asia's experience, both Amsden and Wade argue that the development of a range of industries which exhibit strong increasing returns or techno-logical externalities has been at least of equal importance. East Asia's integration into the world market, in short, has been strategic rather than indiscriminate. The mechanism that regulated this integration process has been precisely what was derisively termed 'crony capitalism', namely the region's peculiar economic institutions.

These institutions, such as the Japanese subcontracting system, the main bank system, the practice of lifetime employment and strong government–business links are normally embedded in networks of enterprise groupings and nexuses of social and political relationships. Their most prominent char-acteristic is to emphasise long-term relationships and accountability of firms to all stakeholders, as opposed to shareholders alone. In other words, such institutions suppress regulation by the market in the 'factor' markets. In theory, institutional arrangements of this kind could have the advantage of facilitating the behavioural flexibility of firms in responding to market demand. According to this literature on East Asia, however, the develop-mental implications of the institutions are not confined to those that could be identified by the various market-failure approaches in the theoretical literature, such as economising on transaction costs or coping with informa-tion imperfections. Rather than serving as a mechanism for more efficient value allocation, the institutional arrangements serve as necessary conditions for value creation; that is, for technological progress or productivity growth in general.

The East Asian miracle was to a large extent underpinned by productivity growth, which originated in two main sources: continuous innovation and industrial upgrading. Continuous innovation partly resulted from collective learning effects. With the enterprise system being characterised by an emphasis on long-term relationships, major stakeholders in the system tend to have good incentives for learning by doing. These have been, in turn, translated into productivity growth through horizontal co-ordination mech-anisms such as quality circles and just-in-time practices. On industrial upgrading, debate in the literature has hitherto focused on the efficacy of industrial policy (the scholarly debate surrounding the World Bank's famous 1993 report is representative in this regard). What seems more important, however, is the main precondition for industrial policy to be implemented, namely high-intensity investment. This is because such investment not only deviates from 'given' international comparative advantage, but is also typi-cally of massive volume and brings slow returns. It is unlikely to materialise purely under regulation by the market. Moreover, at the aggregate level, there is also the serious problem of the sources of funds. It is precisely at this point that Wade's notion of the 'high household saving, high corporate debt' economy comes into play. Concrete manifestations of this notion in East Asia include, on the one hand, bank-based (rather than market-based) financial systems, and, on the other, restrictions imposed by the state on financial market liberalisation and frequent interventions in the sector. These combine to give rise to a development-oriented, reciprocity relationship whereby firms exchange good performance for policy favours from the state authorities.

This said, however, writers in this tradition typically do not consider the advantages exhibited by East Asia's economic institutions as being in any sense absolute. Unlike orthodox economists who tend to compare the reality with the notional market economy (and hence the notion of 'the natural path' of development), characterising any deviation therefrom as inefficiency, these writers make it clear that the development implications of institutions depend on their appropriate match or otherwise with the external environment (particularly the demand side). For Aoki (1990), in order that the institutions could promote collective learning and therefore productivity growth, the market demand environment must be continuously changing, but do so in a steady fashion. A stable market environment tends to favour USA-type big business, infused with especially serious rigidity, whereas a rapidly changing environment tends to favour atomistic firm of the arm's-length market relationship, which is highly flexible. East Asian institutions have their distinctive competitive advantage in between the two extreme market environments.

The emphasis on the appropriate match or otherwise between institutions and the external environment, it will be recalled, is precisely the central proposition of Wade and Veneroso (1998a) in their attempt to explain East Asia's financial and economic crisis. More broadly, this emphasis could be generalised to imply that East Asia's development experience is to a significant extent a historically specific process. That is to say, in line with the emphasis, one may proceed to judge that both the miracle and the crisis were caused by history-specific factors that have shaped the internal institutions and the external environment, as well as the interaction between them.

Consider the miracle. The behavioural flexibility peculiar to East Asia's rigidity-infused, long-term-oriented economic institutions was undoubtedly central to sustaining the region's continuous enlargement of its cheap manufactured exports to the US market – and hence to its rapid and sustained economic growth – in the 1960s and 1970s. However, this worked in conjunction with other, equally important, factors, including the relocation of industrial activities from the core regions of the capitalist world economy to its periphery on a massive scale, and US trade favouritism, which greatly eased the way for East Asia to take advantage of the opportunity for worldwide industrial restructuring.[5] Industrial relocation was symptomatic of the phase of production expansion of the long cycle in the capitalist world economy, while US favouritism was largely due to the fact that for several decades East Asia was on the forefront of the Cold War, and the East Asian states were in one way or another serving as junior partners of the USA. During the 1980s and 1990s, East Asia was still able to sustain rapid growth largely due to the same flexibility, which by now took the form of expanding its production base from the core economies (Japan, South Korea and Taiwan) to the region as a whole, as well as participating in global financial expansion.

The causes of the financial and economic crisis could be analysed in a similar light. On one level, the spread of the production base to the East Asian region as a whole met with increasing difficulties. The industries that were relocated from the core economies to South East Asia were mainly of an enclave nature. That was mostly due to the fact that the 'canonical' East Asian institutions (mentioned above) were heavily based on the specific social and historical conditions of post-war Japan, hence were not easily transferable overseas. To make things worse, the seriously uneven distribution of income in South East Asia hindered the formation of domestic mass-consumption markets. For East Asia as whole, therefore, economies had to be permanently 'export-oriented', meaning that both corporate profitability and economic growth had to rely heavily on acquisition of market share outside the region. Unfortunately, as far as the external environment is concerned, the condition of world market demand did not serve East Asia well in the 1990s. Following the end of the Cold War, US policy changed from trade favouritism to pressurising the East Asian states for market liberalisation, including the sphere of external finance. A further blow came from China, in the form of a squeeze in the world market share of the East Asian economies. Increasingly, due to Chinese competition, manufacturing exports from the East Asian economies were limited to a narrow range of electronic products. They were thus hit hard by the 1994–6 cyclical downturn in the world electronics market, which in large measure accounted for the stagnation of export growth in the run-up to the crisis (Hart-Landsberg and Burkett 1998; World Bank 1998).

It was against this background that the South East Asian governments adopted the kind of policies identified by the IMF as causing the crisis. The maintenance of relatively fixed exchange rates, effectively pegged to the dollar, was largely due to the fact that the economies concerned have served as extensions of the production base of Japan (and South Korea and Taiwan) for exports of manufactures mainly to the US market. The opening up of their capital accounts was largely aimed at making good the loss of steam in growth due to the redirection of Japanese and European direct investment from South East Asia to China since the turn of the decade (Bullard *et al.* 1998). In response to financial liberalisation, and in the context of worldwide excess liquidity, massive capital inflows took place, but mainly in the form of commercial lending by Japanese and European banks as well as portfolio investment in local stock markets by US financial capital. The stage was thus set for the subsequent unfolding of 'panic', and the currency collapses, financial turmoil, economic crisis and developmental disaster that followed. Stagnation in export growth served as a trigger for the crisis as well as its underlying cause.

Conclusions

East Asia is perhaps the only region in the capitalist world economy that has had a visible increase in its world income share in the half century after the Second World War. The financial and economic crisis that has engulfed the region since the summer of 1997, however, threatens to push it back to its previous position in the world income hierarchy. No wonder, therefore, that the development experience of the region has occupied such a prominent position in the development policy debate both inside and outside the orthodox development establishment. The fact that the region's development experience has been shaped by evidently unorthodox economic institutions and development policies has added a great deal of further complexity – and hence analytical challenges – for all participants to the debate.

This chapter has reviewed the complex relationship between the development policy debate and the East Asian experience from a perspective that is largely based on studies outside the orthodox development establishment. It claims that the division over explaining the East Asian experience within the orthodox establishment – a major element of the rivalry between the Washington consensus and the post-Washington consensus – is real but of limited depth. The division, in essence, refers to the appropriate means for achieving a common end, namely the (ultimately total) integration of developing countries into the world market. By adhering to this common end, the long-term development policies of the post-Washington consensus appear indistinguishable from those of the less dogmatic versions of the Washington consensus.

The alternative perspective, which has provided foundations for the analysis of this chapter, correctly maintains that East Asia's economic institutions are not intrinsically inefficient. By this token, the policies that are implied by the orthodox common end emerge as problematic, and even dangerous. It will be recalled that the central proposition of the alternative perspective is that the development implications of East Asia's unorthodox economic institutions (just like the envisioned 'well-functioning markets' of the orthodox establishment) depend on their appropriate match with the external, demand-side conditions. Hence, IMF-type structural reforms aiming at the transformation of East Asia's institutions in the direction of the orthodox 'well-functioning markets' appear as a great gamble. They prevent East Asia from continuing along its previous (and rather successful) path of development, which was based on mediation by unorthodox institutions. The promise they carry of success along the 'natural path of development' is, at best, profoundly uncertain.

Notes

1   See, for instance, International Monetary Fund, *World Economic Outlook*, May 1997, especially Chapters I and IV.
2   See Lo (1999) for a review of the mainstream literature on East Asia.
3   See Wade (1998) for a review of the literature.

4   Readers are referred to Lo (1999) for a detailed review of the relevant literature. Very selectively, key references include Amsden (1989), Aoki (1990), Best (1990) and Wade (1990).
5   Arrighi (1994) is, perhaps, the best reference in this regard.

References

Amsden, A.H. (1994) 'Why isn't the whole world experimenting with the East Asian model to develop?', *World Development*, 22(4): 627–33.
——— (1989) Asia's Next Giant: *South Korea and Late Industrialization*, New York: OUP.
Aoki, M. (1990) 'Toward an economic model of the Japanese firm', *Journal of Economic Literature* 28(1): 1–27.
Arrighi, G. (1994) *The Long Twentieth Century: Money, Power and the Origins of our Times*, London: Verso
Best, M. H. (1990) *The New Competition: Institutions of Industrial Restructuring*, Cambridge: Polity Press.
Bullard, N., W. Bello and K. Mallhotra (1998) 'Taming the tigers: The IMF and the Asian crisis', *Third World Quarterly* 19(3): 505–55.
Fischer, S. (1998) 'Lessons from a crisis', The Economist, 3–9 October, 1998: 27–9.
Hart-Landsberg, M. and P. Burkett (1998) 'Contradiction of capitalist industrialization in East Asia: a critique of "flying geese" theories of development', *Economic Geography* 74(2): 87–100.
International Monetary Fund (IMF) (1999) *The IMF's Response to the Asian Crisis*, http://www.imf.org/external/np/exr/facts/asia.htm/
Lo, D. (1999) 'The East Asian phenomenon: The consensus, the dissent, and the significance of the present crisis', *Capital and Class* 67: 1–23.
Stiglitz, J.E. (1996) 'Some lessons from the East Asian miracle', *The World Bank Research Observer* 11(2): 151–77.
——— (1998a) 'More instruments and broader goals: Moving toward the post-Washington consensus', UNU/WIDER Annual Lectures 2, Helsinki, UNU/WIDER.
——— (1998b) 'Sound finance and sustainable development in Asia', mimeo, The World Bank.
——— (1998c) 'Road to recovery: Restoring growth in the region could be a long and difficult process', mimeo, The World Bank.
Wade, R. (1990) *Governing the Market: Economic Theory and the Role of the Government in East Asian Industrialisation*, Princeton, NJ: Princeton University Press.
——— (1998) 'The Asian debt-and-development crisis of 1997–?: Causes and consequences', *World Development* 26(8): 1535–53.
Wade, R. and F. Veneroso (1998a) 'The Asian crisis: The high debt model versus the Wall Street-Treasury–IMF Complex', New Left Review 228: 3–23.
——— (1998b) 'The gathering world slump and the battle over capital controls', New Left Review 231: 13–42.
World Bank (1993) *The East Asian Miracle: Economic Growth and Public Policy*, Washington, DC: The World Bank.
——— (1998) *East Asia: The Road to Recovery*, Washington, DC: The World Bank.
——— (1999) *Global Economic Prospects and the Developing Countries*, Washington, DC: The World Bank.

6 The new political economy of corruption

Mushtaq H. Khan

The shift in the interest of international agencies and of the World Bank, in particular in the 1990s towards issues of governance, is on the face of it long overdue. It appears that, after a long hiatus, mainstream economists are returning to the political economy of growth in general and to the problems of policy implementation in particular. Evidently, the new consensus is to be welcomed as a huge improvement over the market theology of the 1980s. The state is now recognised as important, as are investments, and how effectively states and other non-state institutions, like financial institutions, work to create conditions conducive for investment must clearly have a lot to do with explaining growth and in directing policy attention when growth is poor. On the other hand, the new consensus is resistant to taking into account the role of political power in general, and in particular in explaining the patterns of corruption in different countries and the effects of this corruption. This is not because the importance of political corruption is not recognised. Economic theorists working on corruption, as well as the Bank and the IMF, have explicitly recognised the importance of political corruption. Rather, the problem is that political corruption is difficult to model and the policy implications of identifying this problem is that politics has to be targeted, a prospect that is not attractive to international institutions unless the political reform can be presented in terms familiar to their Western funding constituency.

This is why when the political underpinning of corruption has been discussed, the policy suggestions have been things like greater democratisation or the encouragement of civil society participation in monitoring the state. Typically, economists and international agencies have shied away from trying to identify the classes and groups involved in corruption in different contexts, the consequences of their corruption in each case and the possible ways in which the political structure can be changed to change the magnitude or effects of corruption. We will argue that although economic models have made a contribution to our understanding of corruption, by leaving out the political determinants of corruption, these models are not just deficient but in many cases may be misleading. The required direction of reform may often be quite different from that suggested by the emerging models on corruption.

This chapter is structured in the following way. In the first section we discuss definitions of corruption and some of the evidence that has under-pinned the recent interest in the phenomenon. In the next section we examine a number of contemporary approaches to corruption, focusing on the Shleifer-Vishny (1993) model of the effects of corruption under different institutional arrangements, as an example of the direction of research based on game theory models. Finally, in the last section we look at the impor-tance of class and group structure in determining incentives for different types of corruption, which we argue are important for understanding corrup-tion properly and responding to it in ways that have a chance of working. This section provides a critique of the new economics of corruption, which typically ignores the effects of class and group structure.

Definitions, types and the evidence of corruption

Corruption is most usually defined as a violation of the formal rules governing the allocation of *public* resources by officials in response to offers of financial gain or political support. This definition is the one we will follow. This makes corruption narrower than theft, which refers to illegal transfers of *both* public and private property, though in practice the distinc-tion is difficult to apply because the frontier between public and private is not always clear. Corruption can also refer to a vast range of different types of phenomena and it may sometimes be quite misleading to use similar analytical tools to examine the implications of each. At the very least we can distinguish between two different motivations for corrupt acts: motivations that are primarily *economic* and those that are primarily *political*. Economic corruption refers to cases where a public official has the opportunity to allo-cate a valuable resource or make a decision that affects the economic gains or losses of others, and can bargain for a payoff to make a decision of a partic-ular type. The bulk of the analysis of corruption undertaken by economists is about corruption of this type. However, corruption can be and often is politically motivated. Here the allocation of resources by the public officials, which includes politicians in power, is in response to the *political* payoffs that different constituencies can offer to the official and not just the economic payoff. The possibility of political corruption makes the analysis of corruption very difficult from the standpoint of pure economics since polit-ical and economic motivations are often combined in the same transaction.

Economic corruption appears to be endemic in developing countries and indeed there are systematic reasons why this should be the case. First, accu-mulation and the allocation of public resources in developing countries very frequently involve changes in established property rights and institutions, or the creation of entirely new ones. For these processes *not* to involve corrup-tion in the formal sense defined above, the changes in rights and institutions or the allocation and creation of new rights would have to follow legally established rules. These rules would in general be very difficult to set up explicitly given the post-colonial political settlement in most developing countries, since in most cases explicit legal rules that aim to set up capitalist classes would very likely not enjoy widespread legitimacy. Thus, there may very frequently be substantial difficulties in following this route even if developing country leaders had wanted to be explicit about the types of changes in property rights that they wanted to bring about.

If a legal framework allowing primitive allocation cannot be formally constructed, *any* allocation of rights by the state that amounted to primitive accumulation would, by definition, be illegal because it would be disallowed by a legal framework copied from countries with more advanced property rights. Thus, when subsidies or land or the permission to import capital goods is being granted by the state to accelerate the creation of a new capitalist class, these allocations are often, strictly speaking, illegal because they cannot follow the procedural rules that have been set up to administer them.

A second reason for widespread corruption in developing countries is that their states have typically played a much more important role in the economy. The role of the state has not only been large in the typical sluggish developing country, but, as has been recently recognised by many orthodox economists and the World Bank as well, the role of the state has also been extensive in the very successful industrialisers in East Asia. Apart from primitive accumulation proper, rapid development can be achieved if rights can be re-allocated in the form of subsidies and assistance to infant industries or for learning of new technologies, provided these subsidies are well-managed and are withdrawn when their usefulness has expired. However, whether or not the subsidies are well-managed, there are never enough subsidies to accommodate all those who may legitimately benefit from them. The excess demand for subsidies in various forms to emerging industrialists or rich peasants also opens up possibilities of corruption since scarce resources had to be allocated bureaucratically.

Finally, there are good reasons why political corruption should also be widespread. Development inevitably involves the creation and entrenchment of a new class of property owners who often did not exist a generation ago. These early beneficiaries of development are clearly the winners of a game of property right allocation that will have consequences for generations to come. In many cases, the individuals who succeed in establishing their property rights and benefiting from subsidies at this critical stage only do so as a result of a great deal of good fortune, being at the right place at the right time or possessing the characteristics on which the rationing is carried out (such as language or sect). Given the inherent unfairness involved in these processes, it has been relatively easy to organise opposition to the state in most developing countries.

Opposition of this sort has typically been organised by members of emerging middle classes who have been left behind in the development process. It is therefore more intense in societies where these groups are better organised and entrenched. Their opposition has often resulted in a set of political pressures that have paradoxically generated even higher levels of corruption, this time through the route of political corruption. The opposition of organised groups to the development strategies of the state has typically been bought off by payoffs from existing elites or from the state to purchase a minimum level of support or legitimacy. These transfers have had to be surreptitiously organised because (in most cases) payoffs to opponents in proportion to their ability to make trouble could not, by their very nature, be publicly recorded in the budget. Many of these flows are interlocked with economic corruption and are difficult to separate by superficial observation. We will see later how the patterns of interlocking can have significant implications for the *economic* effects of corruption.

There is a final and more incidental reason why corruption is more widespread in developing countries. In an important sense, the problem of corruption is really about a much more essential problem in capitalist societies, which is the conflict between the logic of capitalism and the logic of liberal democratic legal systems and norms. The former tells us that the ability of individuals to influence the political decision-making process is proportional to the economic power of the individual. The latter tells us that political voice *should* be equalised as it is formally represented in the ideal of 'one person, one vote'. The ways in which the economically powerful buy influence can be more generally described as rent-seeking, but most of the rent-seeking in advanced countries is legal. We have already discussed why much of the influence buying that goes on in developing countries cannot be legalised given the low legitimacy of the emerging capitalists.

This is the general background against which we need to examine the evolution of patterns of corruption in developing countries. The approach in this chapter will be to locate the processes of corruption in the context of the very different routes through which classes and property rights have been evolving in developing countries. We argue that, by so doing, we are better able to account for the differences in the apparent effects of corruption across countries. The processes of accumulation have been quite different across Asia. The rights that were being created for emerging capitalist classes and the terms under which these rights were being created differed greatly. Since the social utility of property rights depends quite a lot on which rights are created and the terms of their creation, it is not surprising that the processes of corruption in these countries were associated with a very wide range of economic performance. To say this is not to justify corruption even under those conditions where it is associated with rapid growth. Rather, it is to point out that corruption can have much more damaging effects in contexts where it is associated with growth-retarding patterns of accumulation.

Does corruption have any effect on economic performance? Even if there is a negative relationship between corruption and economic performance, what does that mean? Is corruption an independent variable that can be altered to improve performance? Or is it an indication of problems that need to be directly tackled? Table 6.1, which looks at a small subset of Asian countries, throws some doubt on the type of regression analysis relating corruption to poor economic performance, of the type popularised by Paulo Mauro (1995) and others. We will look at these countries at greater length later. However, the table confirms that when we look at *successful* developers, it is difficult to find examples of development without corruption. This does not of course mean that corruption *contributed* to development, but it does mean that we have to be careful in drawing conclusions about the effects of corruption from large cross-section regressions. Even if the successful countries were not as corrupt as, say, Nigeria, the *difference* in the scale of their corruption is *unlikely* to explain any significant part of their *difference* in economic performance. In this sense the theories that look at the differences in the *types* of corruption are more likely to be useful, though we will have to look at both.

The *relative magnitude* of corruption is difficult to assess, although it appears from journalistic, political and legal evidence that corruption was widespread in all these countries. The subjective evidence on corruption certainly suggests that the countries were quite similar in the key period of the 1970s and 1980s, when India and the South Asian countries had relatively low rates of growth compared to the East Asian countries. The *Business International* index for corruption in 1980–3 (on a scale from 0 for maximum corruption to 10 for no corruption) was 5.25 for India, 5.7 for South Korea and 6 for Malaysia (Mauro 1995). Given the crudity of these subjective indices, these differences are not very significant. Thailand, on the other hand, had a very high corruption index of 1.5 for this period, suggesting a combination of large and widespread bribes faced by prospective businessmen.

By the mid-1990s, the subjective perception of corruption had increased in most of these countries. The only exception was Thailand, which was

Table 6.1 Corruption and economic performance

Country	Corruption index	GDP growth rates	
		1970–80	1980–92
Malaysia	6.0	7.9	5.9
South Korea	5.7	9.6	9.4
India	5.25	3.4	5.2
Pakistan	4.0	4.9	6.1
Bangladesh	4.0	2.3	4.2
Thailand	1.5	7.1	8.2

Source: Mauro 1995; *World Development Report* 1994.

Note: A corruption index of 10 indicates 'no corruption', and an index of 0 indicates 'maximum corruption'.

perceived to be the most corrupt country in the group in the 1980s, but by the 1990s was perceived to be less corrupt than the South Asian countries. What is interesting, of course, is that the most significant increase in corruption in the 1990s was in the South Asian countries, which paradoxically suffered less severely from the financial crisis of 1997. To the extent that the corruption index is trustworthy, it corroborates other evidence suggesting that the 1997 financial crisis raises some special issues that should not be confused with our long-run assessment of the implications of corruption in these countries. Clearly we need to have an analytical framework that allows corruption to have differential effects in different countries. If corruption indeed has a uniform effect (whether good or bad) everywhere, this should be the conclusion reached at the end of a process of evaluation and analysis rather than a presumption made at the outset. If, on the other hand, corruption can have variable effects, identifying these differences could be of great policy importance.

New approaches to corruption

Corruption is typically the exchange of a bribe for something in return, which is usually some allocation of economic rights. If we are concerned with the *types* of corruption, we should look at the specific economic rights that are exchanged. The real difference between countries may be that corruption is associated with value-enhancing rights being created in some cases and value-reducing rights in others. However, this is not the approach that is followed in the conventional approach to corruption, where the main target of analysis is the *magnitude* of corruption. This is because it is wrongly assumed that intervention is always value-reducing, so we can simply concentrate on differences in the magnitude of corruption to explain differences in performance across countries.

This perspective has produced the most widely held of the conventional economic arguments about what causes corruption and how to deal with it. An example is the *World Development Report 1997*, which identifies the 'causes' of corruption in line with this reasoning. Countries that have higher corruption have:

1   a higher 'policy distortion index' (for which read divergence from a notional free market);
2   a lower opportunity cost of being caught in the act of corruption (in the form of lower civil service to manufacturing salary ratios);
3   a less meritocratic bureaucracy (more political appointments and fewer exam-based appointments);
4   a lower predictability of the judicial system (measured by a lower probability of getting caught and being brought to justice).

Much of this is unexceptionable but is misleading. These correlations are then combined with the Mauro-type regressions where corruption is the independent variable. The policy conclusion is that if these primary causes (such as market distortion and civil service salaries) are addressed, the implication is that growth will improve. However, if corruption has more systemic causes, this argument may well be fallacious and, in the case of some types of liberalisation, the effects may even be damaging.

Broad overviews of the corruption literature already exist (see Bardhan 1997). In the remainder of this section we will instead look at one important model of corruption in depth, which typifies the main problems faced by purely economic models in providing policy-relevant advice for tackling corruption. This is the Shleifer and Vishny (1993) model, which identifies the importance of the institutional structure of the state in determining the magnitude of corruption and therefore its economic effects. The basic result here is that centralised states are likely to engage in lower levels of corruption than more fragmented states, and in a second-best world may be better.

The model like most others assumes that the competitive free-market outcome provides the benchmark of efficiency. The state sells monopoly rights (say to import) that restrict net social product. The more of these rights they sell and the lower the price (bribe), the better it is because output increases closer to the competitive level. If state agencies sell *complementary* rights (for instance, the right to import petrol may depend on how many rights have been sold to import cars), a centrally co-ordinated state will charge lower bribes for each right and be able to collect a higher total bribe because the overall level of activity will be higher. The logic behind this is that a centralised state acts as a monopsonist and is able to pick the profit-maximising level of bribe for each sector. In contrast, a fragmented state, which has a number of independently acting agencies, will have each agency trying to maximise its profits. This leads to a prisoner's dilemma problem where each agency charges too high a bribe for its licences, and as a result the overall level of activity drops and the total bribe collected also falls. Interestingly, the best outcome in this model is the case where the state is so fragmented that the level of bribes falls to zero because many different agencies are offering each right or licence, and the price of each right offered by the state is bid down to zero!

The last point is highly misleading. A state approaching anything like that degree of fragmentation would not achieve efficiency, but rather it would descend into chaos as it would be unable to protect any rights at all. The more interesting comparison is between fully centralised and partly fragmented states. Superficially, this seems to explain why South Korea, say, had less damaging forms of corruption than, say, countries in the Indian subcontinent. However, on closer inspection, the model has a number of serious problems. First, the authors assume that state agencies are able to enforce their decisions. In fact, a particular problem in developing countries is that states, even when centralised, cannot implement the decisions they would like to. This has important implications because it means that states with *formally* centralised institutional structures can behave in a fragmented way if, for instance, powerful groups can prevent particular agencies from creating value-enhancing rights that hurt them. Thus, institutional centralisation is not *sufficient* for co-ordination. The Indian state, for example, is formally as centralised as the Malaysian state but behaves very differently.

On the other hand, states whose formal institutional structures appear to be fragmented can sometimes behave in a co-ordinated way, particularly in repeated games – which games played by the state always are. Shleifer and Vishny's analysis is of a one-shot game,which is particularly inappropriate for modelling the state–society interaction even in terms of game theory. Rational strategies in an indefinitely repeated prisoner's dilemma game are indeterminate. Agencies in an institutionally fragmented state could act in a co-ordinated way in a repeated game, provided the payoffs from co-ordination are large compared to the payoffs from non-co-ordination, and provided the time discount of officials is sufficiently low to make the future gains from repeated co-ordination worthwhile. Thus, institutional centralisation may not even be *necessary* for co-ordination to emerge in repeated games. Thus, even in South Korea, the formal centralisation of the state was actually not absolute. There were different agencies such as the Economic Planning Board, the Ministry of Finance and the President who were making decisions, but in the repeated game their decisions were effectively co-ordinated. What allowed this to happen? Looking only at the agency structure is the starting point; it cannot be the whole story. We also have to look at the distribution of power that allowed one agency to co-ordinate the others and then to implement decisions.

Of course, another major problem with the Shleifer and Vishny model is that it assumes that states only create value-reducing licences instead of often creating value-enhancing restriction, property rights, taxes and subsidies, each of which could also be the subject of corruption. In this case the analysis of centralisation becomes more complex (Aoki *et al.* 1997, p. 6; Qian and Weingast 1997; Khan 2000b). However, the problem we want to focus on now is that they do not model the significance of the distribution of power in determining how institutions actually behave.

Class and group structure and the implications for corruption

In contrast to the conventional approaches, which start with a bargaining problem between officials and citizens under different payoffs and institutional structures, we suggest that the bargaining story should be constructed *after* we have a picture of the bargaining power of the classes and groups participating in the bargain. There is a role for using some of the tools of modern game theory but they are only interesting once the bargaining context has been defined. One problem with identifying bargaining power at a high level of abstraction is that this is bound to raise many questions when we look at the evidence in detail for particular regions. Nevertheless, it is important to identify the most important features of a number of patterns, even if we are forced to ignore aspects of detail that may be important for more narrowly defined problems.

The most tractable way of fixing differences in class and group organisation is to look at differences in patterns of redistributive flows in our sample countries on the basis of the literature on regional economic history and politics. Redistributive flows are flows of resources, both legal and illegal, which are a useful starting point for searching for the political and organisational differences between countries that can explain these flows. These political and organisational differences in turn serve as the starting point for constructing a more complete analysis of why corruption is associated with different outcomes across countries. In this section we will identify a number of patterns in the distribution of power and indicate how they are relevant for explaining the association of similar amounts of corruption with very different outcomes in different countries. Before we proceed, we should say that political and organisational power changes over time, and the comparative story we are sketching is for the 1960s, 1970s and early 1980s, when the East Asian countries were performing much better than the South Asian ones.

South Asia

Despite important differences between India, Pakistan and Bangladesh there are substantial similarities in the predominant types of redistributive flows in these countries. The most important similarity is in the complexity of the networks of interlinked redistributive flows. In all these countries a great number of groups compete for redistributive rents and in all of them members of the 'intermediate' or 'middle' classes play a key organisational and leadership role within these groups. These intermediate classes include, in the main, the educated sections of the population, both employed and unemployed, and the richer peasants whose sons and daughters provide the new entrants into the educated classes through the universities and colleges, and who themselves control opinion and electoral politics in the villages. Professionals (or white-collar workers) are a subset of the intermediate classes, who have more privileged positions in the job market; political economists looking at India have frequently granted professionals a particularly important status. Bardhan (1984), for instance, identifies professionals as one of the three classes forming the coalition of dominant classes in India, together with capitalists and landlords. While we do not dispute the special position of professionals, we identify a wider and more loosely defined intermediate class, which includes college graduates and richer peasants, as the reservoir of organisational power from which leadership is provided for groups competing for redistributive rents.

The roots of the pivotal role played by the organisationally powerful intermediate classes goes back at least to British colonial times, if not earlier. The tiny number of British in India could only have ruled with the complicity of indigenous Indian classes and groups, which potentially had the power to contest the colonial power. These groups included in the first instance landed elites and later members of the emerging 'middle class', both of which later became key components of anti-colonial party machines. The colonial state responded by creating divisions between classes and groups to create a finely balanced social edifice. The object of this exercise was to ensure that claims and counterclaims were finely balanced so that the state had to deal with only a small number of malcontents at any one time. On the other hand, because redistributions were based on organisational power, there were big gains for groups that could organise cross-class alliances more effectively. This is the reason for the proliferation of linguistic, religious and caste organisations. The lion's share of the benefits were of course captured by key 'middle-class' professional organisers, but they could only succeed if they could mobilise large numbers of people around politically motivating symbols.

The political power of the intermediate groups is reflected in a state tradition of selective accommodation and incorporation of groups led by members of these classes. Subsequent institutional and political developments further strengthened these groups. Most political scientists agree that factional politics led by the intermediate classes intensified in India after the mid-1960s (see, for instance, Rudolph and Rudolph 1987). A similar intensification is observed in Pakistan and, later, Bangladesh (Khan 2000b). The inherited tradition of mobilising support by using a variety of emotive symbols was increasingly used by competing organisers to mobilise new groups of workers, peasants and the unemployed. These symbols included Western ideological symbols as well as symbols derived from local languages, castes and religions. This pattern of politics has not enriched the vast majority of the populations of these countries but *has* enabled successive layers of emerging middle-class groups to get access to rents on the basis of their ability to organise the much more numerous groups below them. Their access to rents is the result of the method of incorporation used by the state and by political leaders, which is to transfer redistributive rents to these groups. Some of these are perfectly legal (such as subsidies), while others are illegal transfers of resources or the transfer of illegally generated resources.

What is important is that a large part of the transfer (whether legal or illegal) through the state to intermediate classes of clients has been based on their political bargaining power. The more vociferous and well-organised a group, the greater the likelihood of accommodation, since resource constraints mean that not all groups could be accommodated all the time. Transfers in turn have had to be financed and state leaders have had to find resources, either in general taxation or through rent-sharing arrangements with emerging capitalists who had access to other types of rents. The latter involved state leaders extracting a share of rents from elsewhere in the economy to meet the excess demand for transfers. An example would be local or state party organisations extracting rents from capitalists in the form of bribes and taxes to run local party machines, which accommodated important local factions.

In addition, groups that could not be accommodated through the state were often directly incorporated by capitalists whose rents were threatened, since these factions could provide additional political muscle to defend the rents of the capitalist at a price. An example would be political factions offering to help particular capitalist or other rent-receiving interests in their conflicts with the state, or against other groups, in exchange for a share of the rents. These processes help to explain the dense structure of interlinked economic and political exchanges that Wade identified as characteristic of Indian corruption but did not adequately explain (Wade 1985, 1989, 1992). This type of interlinked rent flows can be explained in terms of a growing set of demands for political redistribution, which in turn leads to an interlocking of rent extraction and distribution.

Figure 6.1 shows in a simple way the potential complexity of the flows of resources between the state, capitalists and political organisers in the typical South Asian political context. Bureaucrats (B) and politicians (P) constitute two parallel hierarchies within the state. For simplicity Figure 4 distinguishes between only two social groups, capitalists (C) and non-capitalists (N), the latter being led in the main by the intermediate classes discussed earlier. The most successful non-capitalist organisers can often become political leaders or even capitalists over time. The most distinctive feature of the redistributive rent flows in the Indian subcontinent is the transfers going from politicians at different levels to groups of non-capitalist clients (the arrows from P to N). The quid pro quo from these clients to the state is not shown in Figure 6.1 because it is typically not an economic payoff but rather a 'payoff' in the form of political quiescence or support.

Like capitalists in many other developing countries, Indian capitalists have shared some of their rents directly with politicians and bureaucrats

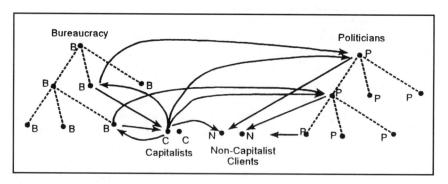

Figure 6.1 Rent flows in the Indian subcontinent: 1960s onwards

(the arrows from C to P and B) in the form of taxes or bribes. These kick-backs from industrialists have in turn been an important source of finance for the political survival strategies of subcontinental politicians. In exchange, capitalists have received allocations of new property rights, which have often amounted to primitive accumulation as well as subsidies for learning to induce industrialisation or agricultural growth (shown collectively by the arrows from B to C). Finally, there are the rent flows going from capitalists to political groups (the arrows from C to N) as capitalists buy 'protection'. We have argued that these flows in particular locked in local political power to particular rents, making structural change very slow in the Indian subcontinent compared to more rapidly developing countries.

While the networks of corruption and political payoffs in India have often been commented on, the economic implications of these complex networks is usually underestimated. An important consequence of the fact that not all demands for redistribution could be met was the construction of a dense and shifting network of localised rent-sharing between rent-recipients of all types and political organisers, both within the state and outside it. This was to have severe consequences for the efficiency and growth associated with state intervention, and in particular of the subsidies given to infant industries that the Indian state was engaged in managing. Once the interlocked networks had developed, allocations of subsidies proved very difficult to change since they were invariably protected by powerful local interests. The eventual result was the emergence of persistent subsidies for poorly performing industries and sectors, which were difficult to change in response to performance failures or changes in technologies and markets.

Thus, the *pattern* of redistributive rent flows in India can provide at least part of an explanation for the persistence of inefficient learning subsidies, which effectively became monopoly rents for many industrialists. Thus, the observed corruption in India was associated with the maintenance and protection of inefficient and growth-reducing monopoly rents locked in with redistributive rents. The experiment with liberalisation in the Indian subcontinent in the 1980s and 1990s has to be seen in this context. By reducing the amount of subsidy they were delivering, the states in these countries hoped to reduce redistributive politics and eventually the blocking effect coalitions played in processes of structural change. The likely outcome of this strategy is still in the balance. There is no evidence yet that redistributive politics have been effectively curtailed. Much of the early success of liberalisation has been due to a boom in demand for consumer durables rather than to a decline in redistributive politics. It is only if the latter is achieved that liberalisation would change the pattern of rent-seeking in India in the long run (Harriss-White 1996, Khan 1996a). The limited evidence on corruption suggests that it may actually have increased, driven by more intense distributive conflicts.

South Korea

In contrast to the large and unstable redistributive transfers in South Asia, South Korea during the 1960s and 1970s was at the other end of the spectrum in terms of the magnitude and stability of politically driven redistributive rents. The pattern of resource flows appears to have been both different and simpler. This seems to have been particularly the case in the early days of industrial policy in the 1960s when commentators emphasised the degree of autonomy that the South Korean state enjoyed from competing demands in society (see, for instance, Jones and Sakong 1980; Mason *et al.* 1980; Amsden 1989; Kim 1994, pp. 59–70; Kong 1996; Kim and Ma 1997; Khan 2000a). The broad features of the South Korean case suggest a much higher degree of concentration of political power, which allowed the political executive to extract rents from beneficiaries of new rights without having to make political side-payments to non-capitalist clients to anything like the extent observed in South Asia. Thus, although there is some redistributive rent-distribution going on throughout the 1960s and 1970s, particularly to the agricultural sector, this is not based on the political or organisational power of agrarian factions to demand redistributions as the price for political quiescence. In Figure 6.2 we therefore exclude the non-capitalist rent-recipients completely, not because they were completely absent but because they did not play a decisive role in the pattern of rent allocation in South Korea at this time.

This outline is consistent with the accounts that are by now well-known of the flows associated with industrial policy in South Korea (see in particular Amsden 1989; Kim and Ma 1997). The most important feature of the rent flows during this period was the transfer of subsidies from the state's bureaucratic apparatus (B) to emerging capitalists (C). Second, we now know that there were also in exchange substantial kickbacks from these favoured industrial groups (C) to the political leadership (P) as rents from the growing industrial sector were redistributed to the political leadership and through them to bureaucrats (B) as well (Kong 1996; Khan 1996a, 1996b). These revelations emerged during the corruption cases that surfaced in the early 1990s, from which we can piece together a story about

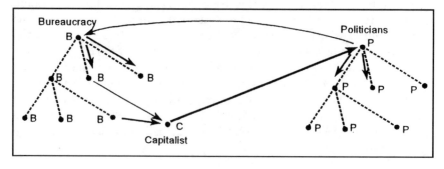

Figure 6.2 Rent flows in South Korea: 1960s and 1970s

how bribes were shared by the top politicians and bureaucrats during the 1960s, 1970s and 1980s.

The important difference of South Korean rent flows from the pattern observed in the Indian subcontinent is the absence of competing and decentralised centres of political power, which could demand rent redistribution to themselves. This had important consequences for the efficiency with which rents for learning could be administered by the central leadership of the state. Under those conditions, the inability of rent recipients to mobilise local power in protecting their rents was an important factor allowing developmental states to play a value-enhancing role. The distribution of organisational power in South Korea prevented individuals unrelated to industrial policy from bargaining for rent redistributions during a critical phase of development when the state was creating and allocating rents for learning to accelerate industrialisation (Woo-Cumings 1997).

The absence of a large number of redistributive groups led by a powerful intermediate class in South Korea can in turn be traced to Korea's social history and the nature of the Japanese colonial impact, which prevented these classes from developing or consolidating (Kohli 1994). The Japanese, unlike the British, did not rule through the creation of supporters and administrators within the local population. Instead they relied to a much greater extent on Japanese colonial administrators at all higher levels. This had much to do with Japan's geographical proximity and demographic dominance over its colonies as well as perhaps to differences in colonial ideology. The Japanese colonial state was thus responsible for far-reaching social changes, often carried out with great harshness. This kind of social engineering destroyed the power base of the landed elite. It transferred between a quarter and a third of arable land to Japanese entrepreneurs and corporations (Kohli 1994, pp. 1277–9). At the same time considerable investments took place in industry and agriculture, which created employment opportunities in the productive sector.

The Japanese colonial goal in its neighbouring colonies was not to extract a few resources and maintain a captive market at the lowest political cost, which was the objective of the British in their far-flung colonies. Instead they aimed to convert Korea into a productive base for Japan and eventually to absorb it into Japan (Kohli 1994, pp. 1272–4). The social development of Korea under Japan meant that landlords and the urban professional and middle classes, who caused the greatest political headaches for post-colonial industrialising states, remained very weak because they were never part of the political and administrative coalition that was running the colony. In contrast, the British could only run their vast and far-flung colonies by selectively accommodating groups that had organisational power. To say that South Korea benefited from this social history is not to deny the importance of the leadership role of the state under Park Chung-Hee, nor the importance of the specific institutional arrangements under which rents for learning were administered during the industrial policy phase. At the same time, we know that similar institutional attempts to discipline recipients of subsidies failed in other countries (such as Pakistan in the 1960s), which had inherited a different social organisation (see, for instance, Khan 1995, 2000b).

The pattern of South Korean rent flows shown in Figure 6.2 did not remain unchanged over time. Rapid economic development created a large middle class and a civil society, which by the 1980s became increasingly unwilling to accept the high-handed manner in which resources were being allocated by the state. Not surprisingly, by the early 1990s, revelations of corruption increased dramatically even though much of this referred to the efficient rent-creation and rent-sharing of the past. When evidence of contemporary corruption began to emerge, there were some indications that the pattern of corruption was also changing by the early 1990s. Evidence of value-reducing interlocking between political factions and capitalists begins to emerge. In 1997 the steel company Hanbo went bankrupt amidst allegations that it had continued to receive state support long after its poor economic performance had become well-known. Factions within President Kim Young Sam's party and one of his sons were implicated. In the same year, Kim Young Sam's finance minister seemed to be supporting a takeover of the automobile operations of Kia by Samsung, a strategy that many observers felt was motivated by political rather than economic considerations. The finance minister was closely associated with Samsung, which had also invested in President Kim's home town of Pusan. The episode led to a decline in international confidence and contributed to the financial crisis of 1997.

In commenting on the crisis, Chang *et al.* (1998) argue that the examples of particular corruption protecting inefficient rents, which were surfacing in South Korea in 1997, were untypical of the broad pattern of corruption in that country. In other words, they subscribe to the view that the gradual abandonment of industrial policy in the 1990s and the shift towards liberalisation was an autonomous policy decision taken by the politicians in power. They may be right, but it may also be that by the 1990s real changes were taking place in the distribution of political power in South Korea, which allowed rent recipients to form political alliances to protect their rents in ways that had not been possible earlier. If this is true, then the shift towards liberalisation in South Korea may well have been driven at least partly by the recognition by state leaders that efficient rents could no longer be exclusively protected. The growing technical sophistication of South Korean industry was undoubtedly making the regulatory problem for the state more difficult since bureaucrats had less and less competence to judge the performance achieved by recipients of learning rents. If, in addition, recipients of inefficient rents were able to protect their rents by forming alliances with politically important factions, industrial policy would have increasingly produced inefficient rent-seeking outcomes reminiscent of the South Asian countries in the 1950s and 1960s. The social changes in South Korea, which may or may not have allowed old-style industrial policy to continue, will be key issues in future South Korean policy debates.

Malaysia

The South East Asian countries provide interesting intermediate cases of redistributive rent flows. Unlike South Korea and Taiwan, which inherited fairly exceptional social structures as a result of Japanese colonialism (Kohli 1994), the South East Asian countries were closer to the South Asian pattern. Although less powerful and entrenched than in the Indian subcontinent, emergent middle classes in these countries possessed a greater ability to organise political opposition and thereby demand political payoffs compared to their North Asian counterparts. The political and institutional responses in these South East Asian countries show a wide range of variation in terms of the patterns of political side-payments organised to maintain political viability. Malaysia and Thailand provide two interesting contrasts to the South Asian case. In both of these countries redistributive rents were much more important than in North Asia but they had far less damaging effects than in the South Asian countries.

While Malaysia inherited a very similar redistributive problem as India, it solved it through a centralised and stable set of redistributions that the losers did not strongly contest. The feature of Malaysia's political economy that allowed a solution to be constructed was paradoxically the ethnic division between capitalists in Malaysia and the rest of the population, which could have spelt disaster. In the 1960s, Malaysia had a capitalist sector based on small-scale trade and production that was dominated by ethnic Chinese capitalists. An emerging Malay middle class was increasingly willing to use its political muscle to organise the Malay majority to get a larger share of the pie for itself. Luckily for Malaysia, the coincidence of ethnic identities with class ones to some extent helped the organisation of political payoffs in a centralised way.

The orderly solution to the redistributive problem emerged as an unintended consequence of the 1969 riots and the adoption of the New Economic Policy. The political consolidation that took place after the riots of 1969 established the United Malays' National Organization (UMNO), which was the Malay party in the ruling coalition as the dominant political power in the country. Unintentionally, the effect of this was to consolidate potentially competing Malay clientelist groups into a unified structure, and at the same time established their political dominance over the capitalists who would have to pay for the redistributive rents. We could therefore characterise Malay clientelism as 'centralised clientelism' compared to the fragmented clientelism afflicting the Indian subcontinent (Khan 1989) or the decentralised but capitalist-led clientelism in Thailand discussed below (see also Doner and Ramsay 2000; Rock 2000; Khan 2000a; Sidel 1996).

The main features of the rent flows in post-1969 Malaysia are shown in

Figure 6.3. The most important transfers are shown in the arrow from the mainly Chinese capitalists (C) to the political leadership of the Malay party, UMNO (P), which dominated the political system. These transfers included both taxes and illegal extractions. The rents extracted were then centrally distributed through the political apparatus to the non-capitalist clients (N) of UMNO, shown by the arrows cascading down the political apparatus to non-capitalist clients. In return, domestic capitalists received protection and, increasingly, assistance for moving into high-technology industries through the provision of some subsidies but primarily through state-assisted negotiation of backward linkages with multinationals operating in Malaysia. These rent flows are shown by the arrows from B to C. These subsidies to Malaysia's capitalists were typically not large rents for learning (as in South Korea) but they were nevertheless of economic significance.

The distinctiveness of this system compared to the South Asian system was that rent extraction from the Chinese capitalists was centralised and, initially at least, direct links between particular capitalists and political factions in the Indian manner did not exist. This has changed to some extent over time as the Malaysian economy has grown and with it the political power of competing Malay factions within UMNO. However, the picture sketched above is reasonably accurate for the late 1960s and early 1970s when Malaysia began its economic take off. As decentralised networks developed through the late 1980s and 1990s, we would expect the rent-seeking system to produce fewer value-enhancing rents, as the distribution of political power in Malaysia did not have any obvious proportionality with economic productivity.

The key difference with the South Asian patterns was the centralisation and relative stability of the flows in the 1970s and much of the 1980s,

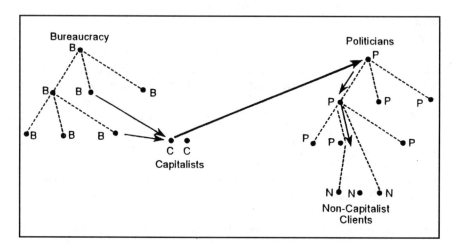

Figure 6.3 Rent flows in Malaysia: 1970s and 1980s

which prevented the build-up of dense localised networks of exchanges between capitalists and particular political factions. This can help to explain significant features of the overall pattern of rents and rights created through the corruption and rent-seeking process in Malaysia in its high-growth phase. First, the factional alliances that led to inefficient subsidies and sick industries in India were much less in evidence in Malaysia. The structure of rights and subsidies allocated by the state could be changed without a huge resistance being offered by large collections of localised intermediate groups. Malay middle-class political elites did not have to extract their redistributive rents by means of decentralised factional alliances with particular capitalists, which we have argued blocked value-enhancing changes in rights in the Indian subcontinent.

Second, the stability of rights and rents that Malaysia achieved as a result allowed it to rely much more heavily on high-technology investments by multinationals than either India or South Korea. The centralised political settlement, together with the fact that vast natural-resource rents were available for redistribution, allowed domestic redistributive demands to be met by tolerable transfers from the mainly Chinese capitalists. Multinationals could feel secure that internal redistributive conflicts would not spill over to adversely affect them. This confidence proved to have been justified. Multinationals in Malaysia believed that their profits and property rights were secure and this induced them to bring in new technology and progressively use local subcontractors. One could compare this with the successive changes in policy facing multinational power generators like Enron in India in the mid-1990s, even after the onset of liberalisation. Not surprisingly, prior to the financial crisis, multinationals in Malaysia were driving export growth and technology acquisition to a greater degree than in most other developing countries (Jomo 1986, pp. 254–6, Jomo and Edwards 1993).

However, there is some evidence that alliances between particular capitalists and competing factions within the Malay political leadership did become more common over the 1980s and 1990s (Jomo and Gomez 2000). One consequence of this may have been that the pattern of redistributive rents became more unstable and contested, and as a result the state's ability to efficiently reallocate rents and rights decreased. The push for financial liberalisation and the development of stock markets, which began to take off in the late 1980s and early 1990s, could not have happened without the political support of powerful factions within the political structure. These differences in factional interests are increasingly evident in the conflict between Prime Minister Mahathir and his deposed deputy, Anwar Ibrahim, who lost power in the aftermath of the financial crisis. Whether these conflicts are purely ideological or whether they reflect a growing factionalisation of the Malay polity as the result of the growth of a more powerful middle class, which cannot be easily accommodated through centralised rent redistribution, remains to be seen.

Paradoxically, the bipolar ethnic dimension of the redistributive conflict in Malaysia may have helped rather than hindered the construction of a relatively efficient solution, which at least worked effectively for a time. The ethnic isolation of the Chinese capitalist allowed the construction of a fairly explicit and centralised 'tax' system, which taxed capitalists for the benefit of emerging intermediate groups. The language of ethnic deprivation allowed a high proportion of these exactions to be legitimised and therefore organised through centralised and legal party and state structures without secret deals and personalised bargains. This is consistent with the observation that Malaysia was the least corrupt of the group of countries shown in Table 6.1 according to subjective corruption indices. A non-ethnic and purely welfarist argument for transfers would not have been equivalent because it would have required that the bulk of the transfers went to the poorest groups in Malaysia and not necessarily to the leading factions of the intermediate classes, who had the greatest political power. Moreover, an argument based on welfarism would probably have been more strongly contested by capitalists since they would not have accepted the redistributive threat to be credible. For these reasons it is difficult to imagine an equivalent ideology in India that could have served to justify a similar centralised transfer from capitalists to the leaders of India's contesting and diverse groups demanding redistribution.

Thailand

Thailand offers a useful contrast to the other countries in our sample. In contrast to Malaysia, the Chinese capitalists of Thailand were much more ethnically integrated with the Thai middle class. The Malaysian pattern of redistributive rents along ethnic lines did not therefore emerge in Thailand. Thailand was also different from all the countries discussed so far in not having experienced direct colonial occupation and rule. The absence of anti-colonial mobilisations explains why the political leadership of its emerging intermediate classes appears to have been weaker compared to the Indian subcontinent or even Malaysia. On the other hand, its intermediate classes were not as atomised as they were in South Korea, which was subjected to Japanese colonialism. Unlike South Korea, where Japanese land reform displaced rural power blocs, Thailand inherited powerful networks of rural politicians who had to be accommodated at a much earlier stage of development. Thus, despite its differences with India, it is quite possible that decentralised networks of patronage would have developed in Thailand to meet the political demands of powerful and largely rural clients. Instead, over the last twenty years Thailand seems to have witnessed a gradual taking over of localised political networks by local capitalists (see, for instance, Phongpaichit and Baker 1997, pp. 332–54).

The key arrows in Figure 6.4 are the ones showing transfers from capitalists (C) to political factions (P), which allowed many Thai capitalists to take over and run their own political factions to a much greater extent than in other developing countries in Asia. Some of these resources were subse-quently used in redistributions to non-capitalist groups who provided political support or votes in elections. Thailand has one of the highest numbers of businessmen in parliament and in cabinet in the region (Sidel 1996; Phongpaichit and Baker 1997, Tables 10.1 and 10.2). Control over their own factions not only gave Thai capitalists places in parliament. It has also given them the political power to directly bargain for subsidies and the allocation of rights, for instance in the form of franchises and licenses (Doner and Ramsay 2000). Thus, while Thai capitalists like their counter-parts in the other Asian countries have had to make redistributive transfers, much of these transfers were within 'private' political networks that they controlled.

The number of capitalists going into the political fray in Thailand has also been large, as a result of a long history of accumulation by small-scale immigrant Chinese traders, many of whom became extremely wealthy over a long period of time. This has ensured vigorous political competition between capitalists for the spoils of power, which has prevented the political system from being monopolised by any particular capitalist faction. Instead there has been vigorous competition for entry into markets through political competition between competing factions in the parliament and the bureau-cracy. Though the political costs of this competition have been high in the form of rampant corruption, the long-run economic performance of Thailand has been relatively better than that of its South Asian neighbours because the rights that the capitalist factions were buying through their corruption were on the whole value-enhancing.

How can we explain why this happened? The interesting contrast with the other patterns discussed so far is that, unlike Malaysia, the redistributive flows were neither stable nor uncontested in Thailand. This makes Thailand similar to India in this respect. Both countries have decentralised variants of clientelism. However, the difference is that, in Thailand, *capitalists* were in control of significant chunks of these redistributive coalitions and used their

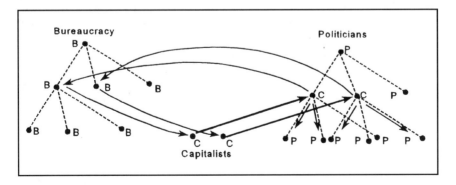

Figure 6.4 Rent flows in Thailand: 1970s and 1980s

political power achieved through this control to politically compete for rents through the political process. Since the size of the political power they could 'buy' depended on the size of the resources they could muster, there was at least some correlation between the potential productivity of the capitalist and their political power, albeit a very loose one.

Capitalist-led rent-seeking proved to be much more damaging in a period of rapid globalisation of financial flows, which happened in the early 1990s. When cheap funds became available in virtually limitless supplies from global markets, the crude balance between the political power of rent-seekers to seek rents and their economic productivity was fatally broken. The drive for liberalisation was motivated by exactly the same processes as the competitive clientelism in the textile industry described by Doner and Ramsay (2000), but it was no longer even roughly value-enhancing. This is because if capital is available in large enough blocks for speculation, the speculator's bets can become self-fulfilling in the short run, regardless of any underlying productivity changes as a result of these investments. Financial and property speculators therefore acquired much greater bargaining power and could drive the rent-seeking process even though it was no longer value-enhancing. Paradoxically, therefore, globalisation may have contributed to the collapse of value-enhancing corruption in Thailand. This means that Thai rent-seeking will have to be much more carefully regulated in the future if its openness to global markets is to be maintained.

Conclusion

The analysis of corruption is important because it offers an interesting window into the political economy of transition and into accumulation processes in developing countries. Drawing the line between 'acceptable' types of accumulation in early capitalism and 'unacceptable' types is never going to be easy. Most processes of primitive accumulation are ugly and politically reprehensible from the standpoint of an advanced capitalist country, where the primitive accumulation stage is lost in history. Developing countries face two pragmatic problems. The first is to distinguish between situations where corruption has impoverishing effects from those where corruption allows rapid growth. The economic (as opposed to moral) problem is not corruption *per se* but the political structures that generate growth-retarding corruption. This analysis suggests that anti-corruption strategies which are concerned with the possible effects of corruption on development have to explicitly identify the underlying political problems.

If corruption is politically generated and if the political structure of societies determines the economic effects of the ensuing corruption, in countries where development is blocked the only long-run solution may be to provoke a sustained public discussion of such arguments so that new political arrangements can eventually be constructed. The relevant political reforms cannot be generalised and certainly have little to do with the promotion of democracy or of civil society, or other such bland objectives (see Khan 1998).

The second and related problem for developmental and progressive policies in developing countries is to think about how the primitive accumulation stage can be made more humanly acceptable for the broader society, which is quite right to regard it as unjust. Here social democratic norms, which may not be immediately achievable, may nevertheless be useful in constructing inclusive political programmes that allow capitalist accumulation to happen while carrying out the maximum possible redistribution to other classes. This is easier said than done, and the experience of Malaysia shows that large-scale redistribution has been successful under very special circumstances. Nevertheless, the challenge even for much more complex redistributive problems faced, say, by India is to construct political movements that can combine acceptable levels of redistribution with capitalist accumulation.

The methods of reform that the conventional approaches have identified – reducing regulation and increasing civil service salaries – are not wrong but are more relevant for addressing residual cases of corruption, which are not driven by systemic forces. We have seen how liberalisation has actually increased corruption in India rather than reduced it. The systemic corruption is ultimately driven by political concerns and gets locked in with economic corruption. Addressing it as a fundamentally economic incentive problem is therefore not likely to work. What is worse, since the state's role in creating new property rights and managing transfers to maximise growth while maintaining political stability is not going to disappear, weakening the state by privatisation and liberalisation may make the problem of constructing political solutions to corruption more difficult. We are already beginning to see this in countries like Pakistan and Bangladesh. Moreover, game theory approaches to corruption, which appear to address the political and institutional aspects of corruption, actually ignore the critical aspects of political and class power that make the effects of corruption dramatically different across countries in the ways we have briefly discussed.

References

Ahluwalia, I.J. (1985) *Industrial Growth in India*, Delhi: Oxford University Press.

Aoki, M., K. Murdock and M. Okuno-Fujiwara (1997) 'Beyond *The East Asian Miracle*: Introducing the market-enhancing view', in Aoki, M., H.K. Kim and M. Okuno-Fujiwara (eds) *The Role of Government in East Asian Economic Development: Comparative Institutional Analysis*, Oxford: Clarendon Press.

Amsden, A. (1989) *Asia's Next Giant: South Korea and Late Industrialisation*, Oxford: Oxford University Press.

Bardhan, P. (1984) *The Political Economy of Development in India*, Oxford: Basil Blackwell.

—— (1997) 'Corruption and development: A review of issues', *Journal of Economic Literature* 35: 1320–46.

Chang, H.-J. (1994) *The Political Economy of Industrial Policy*, London: Macmillan.

Chang, H-J, H.-J. Park and C.G. Yoo (1998) 'Interpreting the Korean crisis: Financial liberalisation, industrial policy and corporate governance', *Cambridge Journal of Economics* 22: 735–46.

Doner, R.F. and A. Ramsay (2000) 'Rent-seeking and economic development in Thailand', in Khan, M.H. and K.S. Jomo (eds) *Rents, Rent-Seeking and Economic Development*, Cambridge: Cambridge University Press.

Harriss-White, B. (1996) 'Liberalisation and corruption: Resolving the paradox (a discussion based on South Indian material), *IDS Bulletin* 27(2): 31–9.

Jomo, K.S. (1986) *A Question of Class: Capital, the State and Uneven Development in Malaya*, Singapore: Oxford University Press.

Jomo, K.S. and C. Edwards (1993) 'Malaysian industrialisation in historical perspective, in Jomo, K.S. (ed.) *Industrialising Malaysia: Policy, Performance, Prospects*, London: Routledge.

Jomo, K.S. and E.T. Gomez (2000) 'The Malaysian development dilemma, in Khan, M.H. and K.S. Jomo (eds) *Rents, Rent-Seeking and Economic Development*, Cambridge: Cambridge University Press.

Jones, L. and I. Sakong (1980) *Government, Business and Entrepreneurship in Economic Development: The Korean Case*, Cambridge: Harvard University Press.

Khan, M.H. (1989) *Clientelism, Corruption and Capitalist Development*, Oxford: Oxford University Press.

—— (1995) 'State failure in weak states: A critique of new institutionalist explanations, in Hunter, J., J. Harriss and C. Lewis (eds) *The New Institutional Economics and Third World Development*, London: Routledge.

—— (1996a) 'A typology of corrupt transactions in developing countries', *IDS Bulletin* 27(2): 12–21.

—— (1996b) 'The efficiency implications of corruption', *Journal of International Development* 8(5): 683–96.

—— (1998) 'Civil society, patron–client networks and the analysis of corruption, in OECD/UNDP: *Corruption and Integrity Improvement Initiatives in Developing Countries*, New York: UNDP, Management Development and Governance Division.

—— (2000a) 'Rent-seeking as process', in Khan, M.H. and K.S. Jomo (eds) *Rents, Rent-Seeking and Economic Development*, Cambridge: Cambridge University Press.

—— (2000b) 'The political economy of industrial policy in Pakistan 1947–71', Department of Economics Working Paper, London: SOAS, University of London.

Kim, J.K. (1994) *Bureaucratic Corruption: The Case of Korea*, Seoul: Cho Myung Press.

Kim, H.-K. and J. Ma (1997) 'The role of government in acquiring technological capability: The case of the petrochemical industry in East Asia', in Aoki, M., H.-K. Kim and M. Okuno-Fujiwara (eds) *The Role of Government in East Asian Economic Development: Comparative Institutional Analysis*, Oxford: Clarendon Press.

Kohli, A. (1994) 'Where do high growth political economies come from? The Japanese lineage of Korea's "Developmental State"', in *World Development* 22 (9): 1269–93.

Kong, T.Y. (1996) 'Corruption and its institutional foundation', *IDS Bulletin* 27(2): 48–55.

Leff, N. (1964) 'Economic development through bureaucratic corruption', *American Behavioral Scientist*, reprinted in Ekpo, M.U. (ed.) (1979) *Bureaucratic Corruption in Sub-Saharan Africa: Towards a Search for Causes and Consequences*, Washington: University of America Press.

Mason, E.S. *et al.* (1980) *The Economic and Social Modernization of the Republic of Korea*, Cambridge: Harvard University Press.

Mauro, P. (1995) 'Corruption and growth', *Quarterly Journal of Economics* 10(3): 681–712.

Phongpaichit, P. and C. Baker (1997) *Thailand: Economy and Politics*, Oxford: Oxford University Press, Bangkok: Asia Books.

Qian, Y. and B.R. Weingast (1997) 'Institutions, state activism and economic development: A comparison of state-owned and township-village enterprise in China', in Aoki, M., H.K. Kim and M. Okuno-Fujiwara (eds) *The Role of Government in East Asian Economic Development: Comparative Institutional Analysis*, Oxford: Clarendon Press.

Rock, M.T. (2000) 'Thailand's old bureaucratic polity and its new semi-democracy, in Khan, M.H. and K.S. Jomo (eds) *Rents, Rent-Seeking and Economic Development*, Cambridge: Cambridge University Press.

Roy, R. (1996) 'State failure in India: Political-fiscal implications of the black economy', *IDS Bulletin* 27(2): 22–30.

Rudolph, L.I. and S.H. Rudolph (1987) *In Pursuit of Lakshmi: The Political Economy of the Indian State*, Chicago: University of Chicago Press.

Shleifer, A. and R.W. Vishny (1993) 'Corruption', *Quarterly Journal of Economics*, 108(3): 599–617.

Sidel, J.T. (1996) 'Siam and its twin? Democratisation and bossism in contemporary Thailand and the Philippines, *IDS Bulletin* 27(2): 56–63.

Wade, R. (1985) 'The market for public office: Why the Indian state is not better at development', *World Development* 13(4): 467–97.

—— (1989) 'Politics and graft: Recruitment, appointment, and promotions to public office in India, in Ward, P.M. (ed.) *Corruption, Development and Inequality: Soft Touch or Hard Graft?*, London: Routledge.

—— (1992) 'The system of administrative and political corruption: Canal irrigation in South India, *Journal of Development Studies* 18(3): 287–328.

Woo-Cumings, M. (1997) 'The political economy of growth in East Asia: A perspective on the state, market and ideology, in Aoki, M., H.-K. Kim and M. Okuno-Fujiwara (eds) *The Role of Government in East Asian Economic Development: Comparative Institutional Analysis*, Oxford: Clarendon Press.

World Bank (1994) *World Development Report 1994*, Oxford: Oxford University Press.

World Bank (1997) *World Development Report 1997*, Oxford: Oxford University Press.

7 The social capital of the World Bank[1]

Ben Fine

Introduction

The notion of social capital has shot to prominence, with a rise in five years from nowhere to a volley of survey articles and special journal issues. Books dedicated to case studies have been published, general volumes are in press and journals have provided for a number of edited collections. Last, but not least, late 1998 marked the opening of a dedicated website to the topic by the World Bank, http://worldbank.org/poverty/scapital. It is surely no accident that the rise of social capital and of the post-Washington consensus should so neatly coincide. For a number of reasons, social capital is the dream concept for the new consensus. First, it incorporates all of the results of the information-theoretic economics – it can be seen as the non-market response to market imperfections. Second, it allows the formal results of the new economics to be expressed in non-economic terms. Thus, social capital can be understood as institutions or as customs that are recognised to matter for development. Third, by the same token, economics can be open to inter-disciplinary endeavour, and vice versa, for 'capital' is 'social'. Fourth, all of this can be seen favourably from the perspective of non-economists – that they are 'civilising' the economists and being taken seriously by them. Last, social capital is such a chaotic and all-embracing notion, that it can mean whatever you want it to, thereby granting extraordinary analytical discretion and power to the hands of those who use it. Woolcock (1998), for example, points to seven or more different areas of application – economic development, (dys)functional families, performance in schooling, community life, (work) organisation, democracy and governance, and collective action.

Not surprisingly, then, social capital has had a number of lives of its own both before (and independent of how) it was taken up by the World Bank. These derived from different traditions. On the one hand, in the work of Bourdieu, who might be uncomfortably located within the Marxist tradition, social capital is broadly understood as the cultural or non-economic counterpart to an exploitative notion of economic capital. It is attached to the processes of stratification by which classes demarcate themselves and reproduce and consolidate advantage – as in the practices by which high culture and education are formed and become the preserve of a dominant class. Crucially, social capital for Bourdieu is highly contextual and irreducibly bound up with the totality of other economic and social practices. On the other hand, mainstream economist Gary Becker (1996) has generalised his highly popularised notion of human capital to that of personal capital (to include all individual experience and not only that around skills), and personal capital has been extended to social capital to incorporate the influence of all personal social interactions. Chicago sociologist James Coleman, who was rational-choice counterpart as well as colleague to Becker, stands at the other extreme to Bourdieu. Coleman's definition of social capital is primarily functional – any social arrangements that allow individuals more readily to achieve their goals. His initial focus was upon educational attainment and the (negative) impact upon this of, more or less, dysfunctional families: the better one's social capital in terms of family background, the better one does at school. Such an approach has inspired a wealth of empirical studies on large data sets in which performance (at school or otherwise) is set against a range of other characteristics (household or otherwise).[2]

Whatever their relative merits, the approaches of Becker/Coleman and Bourdieu are incompatible with one another.[3] Bourdieu deploys the concept critically both in terms of its content and in its implications. Not surprisingly, then, he has increasingly dropped out of the picture, as social capital has tended to be used as an all-embracing umbrella under which to gather anything that might be developmental other than physical and personal resources. In contrast, Coleman has been a source of inspiration for promoting social capital. From such humble beginnings, social capital has blossomed, not least because it has been heavily cultivated by the World Bank, drawing freely but selectively upon the gene bank of suitably modified social theory.

Many have welcomed the emergence of social capital as a progressive acknowledgement of the importance of relating the economic to the social and for its rejection of the *laissez-faire* economism attached to the neo-liberal Washington consensus (even if it offers a pale version of the McNamara stance towards the role of the state in development). Whatever the validity of these sentiments in practice, they can scarcely claim to command the intellectual high ground – justifying analysis on the basis of its influence rather than its veracity. In addition, the concept of social capital carries a considerable downside of its own, especially when married to the post-Washington consensus. It fails to address properly either capital or the social; it tends to set aside issues of power and conflict; it compartmentalises capital into its economic and social components; and it places emphasis on civil society at the expense of state and politics.

In short, social capital is the ideal complement to the economic analysis of the post-Washington consensus. It is the non-market counterpart to market imperfections, whether deliberately designed as such or not. The economics of the post-Washington consensus and the theory of social capital taken together have a gargantuan appetite with the potential to swallow up development studies, and to marginalise alternatives genuinely based on class analysis and political economy.

In the second section, two specific economic applications of social capital are considered: overall economic growth and individual poverty. This is because both countries and individuals are deemed to do well according to their levels of social capital. The next section casts its net wider by offering an overview of the World Bank's social capital website, revealing how social capital is being deployed as an explanatory panacea for both theory and policy. The concluding remarks reveal how such deeply problematic theory supports the evolving post-Washington consensus and the World Bank's putative roles both as knowledge bank and more state-friendly purveyor of aid and policy advice.

Growth and poverty

According to the World Bank's own definition:[4]

> The traditional composition of natural capital, physical or produced capital, and human capital needs to be broadened to include social capital. Social capital refers to the internal social and cultural coherence of society, the norms and values that govern interactions among people and the institutions in which they are embedded. Social capital is the glue that holds societies together and without which there can be no economic growth or human well-being. Without social capital, society at large will collapse, and today's world presents some very sad examples of this.

Thus, social capital fills out everything that is not already taken care of in terms of standard economic analysis.[5] Consequently, for Grootaert (1997), it is the *missing link* in explaining economic development. This represents an acknowledgement of what is missing from neo-classical economics: the social has been taken out by methodological individualism and it can now be put back in again. Further, from an empirical point of view, any aspect of economic performance that is not explained by traditional means can be understood to be due to social capital.

Consider economic growth, for example. Traditionally, mainstream economics has relied upon the estimation of what is termed total-factor productivity to measure the contributions to economic growth. This involves a method of calculating the increase in output due to increase in inputs, such as capital and labour. In effect, if inputs rise by 2 per cent and outputs by 5 per cent, then there is what is termed a residual 3 per cent contribution to growth that remains unexplained. It has been put down to technical progress, for example, and as such is dubbed the change in total-factor (or input) productivity.

Two crucial points need to be made about this empirical approach to growth. First, it has long been known to be fundamentally flawed as a result of what is known as the Cambridge critique of capital theory. Essentially, the model's measurements are only legitimate in a world of just one good for both consumption and production, which can hardly be considered plausible. Without this assumption, measured changes in productivity may reflect changes in prices or income distribution rather than genuine changes in productivity.[6] Second, quite apart from the realism of the assumptions on which it is based (and these include perfect competition and full employment of all resources, as well as the requirement of a single good), the residual or total factor productivity is appropriately dubbed 'unexplained'. It is the extent of our ignorance in understanding the contributions to growth. In order to fill out an explanation, attempts were initially made to include previously omitted inputs in the calculations, especially those that increased disproportionately. Thus, the inclusion of human capital – that labour inputs were becoming more skilled – added to the empirical explanation or, more exactly, reduced the extent of the unexplained residual.

Until the last decade or so, despite its deficiencies, measurement of total-factor productivity had remained the main means by which economists have assessed growth, whether of individual economies or sectors of the economy. Now, however, it has primarily given way to what is known as endogenous or new growth theory.[7] A further problem with the old, exogenous growth theory was that it implied that per capita growth rates would converge across countries given relatively free flow of capital and technology. As this appears to be refuted by the empirical evidence, with the persistence of the undeveloped world, theories have been sought to explain why growth rates differ, especially through differences in rates of productivity increase. Simplifying enormously, an answer has been found in theories of productivity increase in which market imperfections are translated into differences in growth rates and not just into differences in the level of output around which growth rates converge. The literature, theoretical and empirical, has itself witnessed explosive growth with a thousand or more academic contributions since the mid-1980s. It has done so because there is a wide range of market imperfections upon which the theory can be based – around technology, saving, education, finance, economies of scale, externalities, intergenerational transfers, level of inequality, etc., and even non-economic variables such as political regime.

Typically, empirical work has been based upon what are termed Barro-type regressions, in which country or other cross-sectional growth rates are estimated on initial levels of output, increases in factor inputs as before and any number of variables that might reflect market imperfections. Such efforts are bedevilled by a range of theoretical and empirical problems. The Barro-type regressions do not really test the theory. This is because, as soon as even one variable is included in an endogenous growth model, the dynamics can become horrendously complicated, with multiple equilibria and complex paths of adjustment to or around them. Any particular observation of growth might reflect movement towards, away or around one or more growth paths. The Barro-type regressions cannot disentangle such effects. In addition, many of the variables thrown into the regression will themselves be related to one another and should be theorised as such. This is, however, impossible because the models become technically too complicated. In a nutshell, complex causal factors and relations to growth outcomes, and growth dynamics themselves, have been illegitimately reduced to multiple regressions to test convergence by simply adding independent variables to suit.

What is the relevance of all of this to the economic approach to social capital? The answer is straightforward. There is a close overlap between the new growth theory and the economic approach to social capital. Both are based on market imperfections and incorporate non-economic variables. The difference is that growth theory tends to be more firmly rooted within the discipline of economics, while social capital theory wanders outside more. Even so, it follows that the weaknesses in the empirical methods attached to the new growth theory carry over to social capital. Those that claim to have explained differences in growth rates in terms of differences in social capital must be treated with considerable scepticism. Their theoretical and empirical methods will inevitably have failed to take account of the complicated dynamics and estimation problems associated with such an exercise.[8]

None the less, the economic approach to social capital is not confined to the study of its impact on growth. This is because it affects both economy-wide and individual performance, as suggested by Narayan and Pritchett (1997). Their study of income differences in Tanzanian villages is based upon a Participatory Poverty Assessment (PPA) of 6,000 people in eighty-seven villages. Data are collected on associations – membership of a burial society, for example – and cultural attitudes such as compassion, altruism, respect and tolerance. These are the elements of social capital and are perceived to be a potential source of higher income for individuals who possess it but, even more importantly, for inhabitants of villages that possess it irrespective of its individual incidence within the village. If the village has a well-supported burial society, everyone benefits – even those who do not belong.

PPAs are the World Bank's way of undertaking surveys so that the poor can supposedly define for themselves what are the key factors in identifying who are the poor and what causes their poverty. This is to be welcomed in principle. However, there is one glaring contradiction in the relationship between researcher and the poor in this respect. It is impossible for the researcher not to bring analytical preconceptions to the sample survey, and also to its interpretation. I suspect that none of the poor, in Tanzania or elsewhere, has ever identified the condition to be a consequence of inadequate social capital. Popular participation in this case must conform to its presuppositions.

In the event, the study is quite measured in its conclusions. It suggests that there are five mechanisms by which social capital can increase income: horizontal connections inducing more efficient government through better monitoring; co-operation for local problem solving; diffusion of innovations; less imperfect information and lower transactions costs; and informal insurance. It is accepted that these may only affect the level of income and not the growth rate (indicating the absence of any formal model relating social capital to income). However, the study only focuses on social capital that is embodied in individuals, leaving aside affiliation to national associations, more general institutional capacity and cultural attitudes. In addition, some care is taken to establish that the relationship between social capital and income does not run in the opposite direction, (which would occur if those who are richer choose to consume more social capital or associational goods). This is done by choosing an instrumental variable to test for the effect of social capital on income, which requires a variable to be chosen that is correlated to social capital but not to income. The choice made is levels of trust external to the village.

Despite its cautions, the headline for the study, which can blaze publicity for social capital, is dramatic. In the preface, Serageldin (1997, p. vii) claims that:

> This study provides quantifiable evidence that village-level social capital – membership in groups with particular characteristics – significantly affects household welfare. In one telling statistic the study finds that one standard increase in village-level social capital increases household income per person by 20 to 30 percent. By comparison, a one standard deviation in schooling – nearly three additional years of education per person – increases incomes by only 4.8 percent.

There are, however, a number of problems with these conclusions which are liable to be characteristic of other studies irrespective of their individual merits, quality of data, etc. First, the results are derived from cross-section analysis alone, by comparing villages at one point in time rather than examining the experience of a village over time. To understand why this might be a problem, consider the following hypothetical circumstances. Suppose that the distribution of income across Tanzanian villages is given as a distribution, but that the allocation of winners and losers in terms of higher and lower income does indeed depend upon a corresponding distribution of social capital across the villages. The statistical results reported above will follow. *Ceteris paribus*, a village that increases its social capital will also increase its income. However, by assumption, as the distribution of income is given, this can only be at the expense of some other village. In other words, villages will be jockeying for advantage by laying out more and more resources on social capital without any net gain by assumption of zero sum. Villages high in social capital may only prosper at the expense of those without.

Second, the point in the last paragraph is essentially about the need for a systemic analysis of the role of social capital. In a way, for estimation purposes, this is recognised by the use of the instrumental variable and the presumption that it is independent of income. But is this valid? The problem is that nearly all the variables are related to one another either in simple or in complex ways. This can only be disentangled by a more inclusive analysis, both in terms of exploring the relationships between the variables that are present, as well as incorporating the variables that are absent (above village level).

Third, social capital is a peculiar variable and it is inappropriate to incorporate it in a standard way into statistical analysis. At very low levels of social capital – when the first two individuals get together to form the first association – there can only be negligible impact. At very high levels of social capital, the same problem prevails. One more club or member will add nothing. Indeed, it seems reasonable to argue that in terms of the number of individual social interactions, the level of social capital or its impact will take the form of a tilted S-shape – limited to begin with and rising rapidly before tailing off.[9] It follows that the relationships being estimated are not linear, that standard deviations are not likely to be constant and that the dramatic impact expected of social capital is unlikely to materialise at the bottom of the distribution if aimed at poverty alleviation (quite apart from any systemic effects discussed in the previous paragraph).

Fourth, following on more or less immediately from the previous point, social capital is liable to be subject to threshold effects – both in its creation and in its impact. This is highly conducive to multiple equilibria, especially poverty traps. Consequently, the statistics may be measuring a correlation between income and social capital created by high and low equilibria. As a result, raising social capital by one standard deviation will not have the proportionate effect for the poor of raising it by ten standard deviations. Bringing many of the previous points together, it becomes necessary to explain the distribution of high and low equilibria as well as the mechanisms by which villages become allocated to them. Significantly, it is often claimed that social capital is marked by a long gestation period in building it up but that it can be destroyed relatively rapidly as it relies on trust, and so on. Is it not plausible that random events or shocks, such as poor harvest or disease, might have generated both the distribution of income and the distribution of social capital through assignment to different equilibria? They would be correlated but not causally related.

In short, projecting to the urban context, such studies seem to be sophisticated ways of saying that if only ghettos could capture the features of other neighbourhoods, they need no longer be ghettos, indeed that there need no longer be any ghettos at all. More generally, the price of a house in a neighbourhood could be higher if only all house prices were higher in that neighbourhood. Exploration of such propositions is not without worth. They tell us about the ways in which gentrification can take place. However, they do remain of limited value until they are placed in a wider setting, not least how the housing system as a whole functions. Further, the weaknesses discussed above can be addressed to a greater or lesser extent on a piecemeal basis. Taken together, however, they are liable to be intractable. It is certainly more important to address the social and historical specificities of the case studies involved whether, say, of Tanzania as a whole or of individual villages, than it is to refine the estimation techniques in view of model specification, multicollinearity, omitted variables, multiple equilibria, cross-section as representative of time series and the like.

Surfers beware the undercurrents

Growth and poverty are just two applications of social capital in providing a missing explanatory link and policy panacea. More broadly, the World Bank's social capital website has primarily been organised around two themes.[10] One is to specify sources of social capital – families, communities, civil society, public sector, ethnicity and gender; the other theme is by topic – crime and violence, economics, trade and migration, education, environment, finance, health, nutrition and population, information technology, poverty and economic development, urban development, water supply and sanitation. Each of these topics is subdivided with a page or two of text, usually including one or more key readings and propositions. That social capital may have a downside is also explicitly recognised in a minority of these accounts. So social capital can be good or bad depending on how it is used. For example, the possibility of pressure towards use of child labour is seen as a consequence of globalisation in the section on economics, trade and migration, but it does not warrant mention in the section on the family (which does, however, view familial obligations as a potential obstacle to freedom of action).

More generally, the World Bank's social-capital web pages share the following characteristics. First, they tend to be simplistic and reductionist. Thus, the entry under conflict begins by suggesting that 'conflict is the struggle over scarce resources arising over competing goals between two or more parties'. The family is seen as the 'first building block in the generation of social capital for the larger society'. Ethnicity is seen in terms of diversity and difference for which inner organisation and bridging spin-offs have to be set against the potential for conflict. The crucial point is that each of the areas covered under each of these last two themes has long, contested and rich intellectual traditions. These are effectively sacrificed in order to import social capital as an organising concept. It is particularly disturbing, in the context of social capital as elsewhere in World Bank literature, how ethnicity has become reduced to a range of stereotypes, either as clever mutually trusting entrepreneurs or, as groups, engaging in conflict with one another.

Second, social capital tends to be seen in terms of two broad effects, each with a positive and a negative side. Intrinsically, it is good but it can also be bad if it is improperly used or is exclusive. Extrinsically, it can complement the market but it can also obstruct it. Essentially, social capital is nepotism – you have to use the ones you know but at least you know them! Thus, ethnic entrepreneurs benefit from their close-knit relations of trust but if they breach norms for sound commercial reasons, such as doing business outside the community, they may be punished. Such an analytical framework, of course, has the benefits of a dual either/or content – social capital is generally good but can be bad; it can complement but might substitute for the market – so more or less any outcome can be explained, and policy advice is equally flexible in the extent of bucking the market.

Third, while rarely embracing explicitly socially reactionary positions, the two previous characteristics are highly conducive to romanticised views of the objects of study. The entry under 'Social capital can prevent crime and violence' effectively condones disorder by warmly acknowledging that 'social capital is a crucial security system. It is not uncommon to witness a parading mass of cheering people who have apprehended a thief. In some cases, they will beat him or her before turning the culprit over to the authorities.' In general, the family and civil society are perceived as positive influences but they can be negative where corruption and clientelism are concerned. Even more important, though, is what is excluded. The public sector is about good governance based on collaboration with, and decentralisation to, the private sector and civil society. Otherwise politics, trade unions, big business organisations, etc. might just as well not exist.

Fourth, there is nothing in analytical or policy terms to rock World Bank thinking and practice, especially in light of the post-Washington consensus. There is even a hint of critique of stabilisation and structural adjustment:

> Macroeconomists are recognizing that while open trade can yield many economic benefits to nations, those benefits are not evenly distributed among the populace. The danger is that growth which benefits only a small minority of the population increases inequality and can lead to social disintegration .... This in turn ultimately affects the standard of living in a society.
>
>   http://www.worldbank.org/poverty/scapital/topic/econ2.htm

Taken together, however, it is not so much the limited and biased content of these entries that is significant as the scope of intended coverage. The vast bulk of social theory and policy is being incorporated under the umbrella of social capital. This assessment is heavily confirmed by consideration of the database of abstracts of articles that are attached to the website. These are now numbered in the hundreds and cover a bewildering array of topics. At time of writing, two-thirds of the articles make no reference to social capital at all! Many predate its emergence. A number of the abstracts, written for the World Bank through the University of Michigan without original authors' approval of the texts, contain phrases such as 'social capital is not discussed in this article *per se'*. I select two abstracts to illustrate the gargantuan appetite of the social capital database in terms of its subject matter. One, from the *Annual Review of Sociology* of fifteen years ago, Roy (1984), claims that the works of E.P. Thompson, Barrington Moore and Charles Tilly 'contain ample evidence of social capital, although this term was not in use at the time'. I suspect that each would disagree with the first of these assertions and agree with the second! The second abstract is from the *Sociological Quarterly*, Berger (1995). It is an account of the life histories of two Polish and Jewish brothers who survived the Holocaust and, presumably, drew upon and developed their social capital by doing so. In short, across these two abstracts alone, social capital encompasses class action and historical change as well as social agency and structure in the very specialised context of Holocaust survivor research!

The website indicates that the notion of social capital is being used to cover anything that is not traditionally economic. This leaves it definitionally and analytically in a state of chaos, and, yet, 'social capital' neatly complements the economics of the post-Washington consensus, allowing it complacently to incorporate the social and the economic. Such considerations are borne out by examination of a number of satellites attached to the World Bank's website.[11] One of these is the series of Social Capital Initiative Working Papers. The first two cover the twelve successful proposals for funding under the initiative, World Bank (1998). These are extremely diverse and add little of novelty in the analytical and policy arenas, other than to impose social capital, often uncomfortably, as an organising concept. Indeed, the proposals are marked by a degree of unanimity in being unable to define social capital satisfactorily and needing to operationalise it during the course of their research.[12]

A second satellite is the E-mail Discussion Group on Social Capital. Like any Internet discussion forum it contains much that is of very poor quality, but it does also include some gems. The overall impression is one of confusion and ambiguity around what social capital is and how it should be measured. As is accepted by the moderator, Michael Woolcock, in the first posting:[13]

> While social capital conforms imperfectly to standard economic forms of capital such as real estate, it nonetheless serves as a very useful *metaphor* for facilitating discussions across disciplinary, sectoral, and regional lines. The idea of 'human capital' (education and training) suffers from similar problems, but from shaky beginnings in the early 1960s has become enormously helpful in terms of getting these substantive issues taken into consideration at the highest levels of theory, research and policy. One hopes that social capital, though inherently less concrete, will come to occupy a similar place in 'mainstream' discussions somewhere down the line.

In the second issue of the newsletter, Voth comments that the ideas underlying social capital have long been known to sociology but that the current usage is oversimplifying social theory by generalising its application. As Woolcock responds:

> Several critics, not without justification, have voiced their concern that collapsing an entire discipline into a single variable (especially one with such economic overtones) is a travesty, but there are others that are pleased that mainstream sociological ideas are finally being given their due at the highest levels. For them, the term 'social capital' is as much good marketing as it is pragmatic theory! I tend to side with those in the latter camp, while endorsing ... that serious students should commit themselves to mastering the broader literature.

In short, analytically, integrity can be traded off with influence at the highest levels whatever that might be.

In the eighth issue, without moderator response, Legge accepts that social capital is a metaphor but he adds:

> Clearly the metaphor has rhetorical value and this seems to be the main reason for its recent ascendancy ... even here the question of usefulness needs to be asked. Opponents of the neo-liberal hegemony seek to use the term 'social capital' as a way of exercising leverage in policy debates dominated by neo-liberal frameworks .... There is a discussion to be had here about the politics of the emergence, migration and use of this term.

This issue will be taken up in the concluding remarks. Before that, consider the notion of social capital as metaphor. It is an attractive description not least because metaphors abound when it comes to social capital. Societies are understood in terms of whether they do or do not have the equivalent of bowling clubs, as organised around sticks, carrots and hugs, or as cars being driven in Rome as opposed to Helsinki (Raiser 1997).[14] Of course, some of the metaphors have been derived to a greater or lesser extent from analytical discourse, as with externalities, trust and networks. Others are self-referential in the way in which gender and ethnicity are understood, for example. In this respect, the biggest metaphor of all is that of 'social' 'capital', neither term of which tends to be adequately understood. It must be wondered how a collection of metaphors can be the missing key to development.

However, one metaphor that I wish to pursue, and it is popular more generally in the context of development and change, is that of health.[15] Societies without social capital are sick and will not develop unless they obtain more of it and use it appropriately. In other terms, as has been recognised occasionally, this is tantamount to social engineering, not least because policy is designed to encourage certain types of association, those which internalise externalities appropriately, and to discourage others that do not.

Further, to an extent that is not proportionately represented in the literature, health practitioners themselves have rapidly begun to use the metaphor of social capital to explain morbidity.[16] Individuals or various social strata are differentially ill because of their lack of social capital. This idea, however, reflects well-established evidence that individual ill-health is heavily conditioned by both absolute and relative standards of living. Inequality is, for example, bad for the health of the poor because of relative deprivation.[17]

Thus, elements of social deprivation tend to be correlated with and reinforce one another, with detrimental effects on health. The latter is not simply a matter of access to medical care but also dependent on more general capabilities and capacities, including sociability for psychological well-being. Inequalities in health are not eroded with absolute rises in living standards if income inequalities widen. Cross-sectional studies can be a poor basis for causal conclusions and policy, since, if the poor are targeted to emulate the rich, they do not do so in standards of health as the rich become richer. Failure to recognise these points leads to inefficiencies, since more may be lost in dealing medically with ill health and its consequences than is gained even by those benefiting from inequality. These points can be qualified and refined by reference in greater detail to the types of social deprivation concerned, how they come about and the sorts of illnesses to which they lead. Yet the whole of this paragraph has been written without reference to social capital. Why is it needed?

Concluding remarks

If social capital is a metaphor for health and vice versa then we are caught in an infinite regress. In any case, social capital as a metaphor is itself an inappropriate metaphor. This is because it is more akin to a religion. It is the missing link; it is ephemeral but its effects can be seen everywhere; it has its sects, disciples, followers and high priests; it has its downside and a struggle between good and evil; there is the prospect of a promised land; harmony and trust must prevail over conflict, it is based more on belief than it is upon reason, although those beliefs evolve around, and are represented and interpreted in, increasingly complex scriptures; and so on.

But what place does social capital occupy in the Catholic post-Washington displacement of the Lutheran Washington consensus? Let me begin by confessing two errors of judgement or, more exactly, prediction. I have suggested (Fine 1999c, p. 11) that because mainstream economists depend heavily upon formal models, the vague notions attached to social capital would restrict its use to market imperfections and social interaction as individual connections. This is correct, but I was also of the view, less explicitly stated, that such considerations would discourage Stiglitz himself, as leading post-Washington pioneer, from employing the term. This, in a sense, was an acknowledgement of his intellectual integrity and continuing reliance upon his own instincts as a mathematical economist. I have been proven wrong within little more than a year. In his Prebisch Lecture, Stiglitz (1998) devotes a section to social capital that is indistinguishable in use from the vague informalities that are so bountiful elsewhere. Subsequently, each of his major papers allows for at least a passing reference to social capital. This has four disturbing implications.

First, whatever the merits of Stiglitz's information-theoretic economics, he has headed a critique of the Washington consensus from an independent, analytical perspective. His adoption of social capital is just one piece of evidence, among much more, that he is being co-opted to be more diplomatic and less wide-ranging in pursuing the implications of his challenge to the old consensus.

Second, as is evident in Stiglitz's Prebisch Lecture and other World Bank publications that draw upon the post-Washington consensus, the colonisation of the non-economic by the economists is a severe setback to development studies, with key topics, such as industrialisation, gender and ethnicity, being heavily stripped of their empirical and intellectual traditions. As in the World Development Report on knowledge, for example, the procedure is one of economic reductionism to the information-theoretic, who knows what, and otherwise leaving the non-reducible, such as the nature of knowledge itself other than supposedly objective information, in a state of chaotic and fragmentary disorganisation.[18]

Third, and as a corollary, the form taken in the post-Washington consensus by the economic colonisation of the social sciences is extremely one-sided. There is an appropriation of the social by the economic but not vice versa. In other words, while economic analysis and economists have been granted a broader remit, the relationship is not reciprocated. This perhaps explains the general disappointment with Stiglitz's policy perspectives, many of which remain little changed from those of the Washington consensus. On the other hand, the non-economists within the Bank can delude themselves that they are being taken more seriously as the economists encroach upon their territory.[19]

Fourth, during the 1980s, as the deleterious effects of the Washington consensus were recognised in both the economic and social arenas, adjustment with a human face represented the World Bank's response to the negative consequences of its policies for poverty, gender, the environment, etc. These factors were incorporated, however fully, centrally and genuinely, into the portfolio of policy objectives. With the post-Washington consensus embracing social capital, a further step is taken in that these factors become incorporated analytically, albeit on a limited basis. Social objectives increasingly become an instrument as well as a target in the hands of the economists.[20] In addition, as Budlender and Dube (1998) have recognised, social capital forms part of a broader initiative to humanise the World Bank, incorporating the care economy, national accounts from a gender perspective, intra-household resource allocation and sustainability, and so on.

This all leads to my second error – the presumption that social capital would provide the conceptually limited basis on which the post-Washington consensus would both address issues around the developmental state and sidestep the existing literature. As is evident from the work of Peter Evans,[21] such an assessment is correct in the wider debate around social capital. However, despite the inclusion of one of his pieces as a website key reading, both the economic and the state are being excluded from the World Bank's treatment of social capital. In other words, economists are allowed, under the rubric of social capital, to address issues from which they have previously been excluded but non-economists do not address either the economic or the state. This in sharp contrast to the hopes expressed by Woolcock (1998, p. 186) for social capital:

> The challenge for development theorists and policy-makers alike is to identify the mechanisms that will create, nurture, and sustain the types and combinations of social relationships conducive to building dynamic participatory societies, sustainable equitable economies, and *accountable developmental states* [emphasis added].

What is the evidence for this assessment of exclusion of the developmental state from the orbit of social capital? It is glaringly obvious from the structure and content of the World Bank's social-capital website. The programme is situated inside the Division for Environmentally and Socially Sustainable Development. From the perspective of non-economists, social capital has been allowed an almost unlimited free rein as long as it only breaches the borders of the economy and the state. The economists' perspective is unambiguously laid out by Collier (1998), staking out a protected traditional territory that belongs to economics, which then both defines what is non-economic, civil society and how it should be understood – an unintended externality that is not otherwise internalised by selective interactions between government, firm or household:

> Putnam has an excellent reason to chose [*sic*] a form of social interaction in which the internalisation of an externality was indeed incidental to the purpose of association. This is because in civil society the vast majority of social interactions which internalise externalities are like this. There are three major exceptions: social interactions which are obviously purpose-designed for internalising externalities. The first of these is government, which can be regarded as an arrangement for overcoming many of the problems of collective action .... The second is the firm: within the firm resources are allocated partly by non-market processes and this permits internalisation of externalities. The third is the household: within the household resources are allocated by non-market processes which internalise externalities. However, it is generally sensible to work with a concept of civil social capital which excludes the activities of government, the internal organisation of the firm, and the

internal organisation of the household, partly because we already have a huge corpus of work on them, and partly because they are so different from other social interactions. I will refer to the social interactions which exclude the organisation of government and the internal organisation of the firm and the household as 'civil society'. Civil society thus includes the interaction of households, the interaction of firms, and the interaction between households and firms.

This is, of course, a remarkably speculative understanding of civil society, let alone the household, firm and government, based on an uncritical extension of neo-classical economics without reference to a vast literature on the meanings of these terms and whether it is analytically appropriate to construct society and social interaction in this fashion. There is also a presumption of independence between the various issues that are split off for separate consideration.

Where, however, does this leave the concept of social capital? There are those who argue that it, as part of the post-Washington consensus more generally, opens up a more progressive analytical and policy agenda, despite the conceptual shortcomings, many of which are recognised. Such seems to be the position adopted by Woolcock, now within the World Bank, but it is an extremely common position more generally. However, as was raised in the E-mail Discussion Group on Social Capital, the emergence and evolution of social capital is highly intellectually politicised. A case could be made that it provides a framework for combating economism in the social sciences more generally. I doubt such an outcome will come to fruition unless at the expense of a proper economic analysis within social theory. The prospects for engaging successfully with the World Bank on an agreed analytical terrain of social capital are even more bleak, with co-option rather than criticism the most likely result. Just as economics is colonising the social sciences, so the post-Washington consensus incorporates the dissent against its neo-liberal predecessor, and social capital colonises social theory. Social scientists are struggling for status within the World Bank and believe they have won some through engaging with economists over social capital.[22] Whatever the realism of their sense of achievement, that is not the basis on which to revitalise development studies in the wake of the Washington consensus.

The metaphors of 'missing link' and 'social glue' symbolise perfectly the compromise and limited terrain of engagement between economists and social scientists within the World Bank. Both agree that the economics has failed so that they need to supplement the economic with the social. This is the concession of the economists, even if the *modus vivendi* of the non-economists. Thus, economists seek to incorporate the social; non-economists to have it taken seriously. Nor is this simply an intellectual exercise in coming to terms with one another. There is a tacit understanding over policy. Economists despair that their economic engineering, otherwise known as structural adjustment and stabilisation, has faltered because of lack of attention to the social; the non-economists hold out the prospect of social engineering to complement economic policy and interventions.[23] Consequently, the paucity of the World Bank's *economic* analysis remains unchallenged, not least because it has opened what is perceived to be an opportunity for non-economists. The latter are scarcely going to offend in light of the door that has been opened to them, although it has arguably been opened by the push from the other side as opposed to their pull. Analytically, it is not the glue and missing link that need to be critically addressed but the economics of the post-Washington consensus itself. Independent economists and non-economists need not enter the highly loaded analytical terrain being established around social capital in the context of the post-Washington consensus. To do so would be to consolidate and legitimise the knowledge bank of the World Bank, whether as hired mercenaries or unpaid foot soldiers in other people's battles.

Notes

1 This chapter draws in part on Fine (1999e). It was completed while in receipt of a Research Fellowship from the UK Economic and Social Research Council (ESRC) under award number R000271046 to study 'The New Revolution in Economics and Its Impact upon Social Sciences'. Thanks to the many who have given comments and support on work on social capital. Note, at times, page references are not given for citations as material has been used as downloaded from the internet. This is so even where published versions might now exist.

2 Robert Putnam has inspired much work on social capital, and drawn devastating criticism in equal measure, not least for views such as that of (US) social capital as created by bowling clubs and destroyed by television-watching. For a critical overview, see Fine (1999a).

3 As revealed rather than resolved by their joint conference: Bourdieu and Coleman (eds) (1991).

4 This comes from the common foreword to each of the Social Capital Initiative Working Papers.

5 As Woolcock (1998, p. 196) observes, just as 'if all behavior is, by definition, utility-maximizing, then the assumption is rendered non-falsifiable … so too an indiscriminate application of social capital over-explains collective action'.

6 For an account in the wider context of the associated theoretical deficiencies of neo-classical growth theory, see Harcourt (1972 and 1976) and Fine (1980, Chapter 5).

7 For a full account of what follows, see Fine (1999b).

8 For explicit use of social capital in growth regressions, see, for example, Knack and Keefer (1997) and Temple (1999). It should be added that, even if the mathematical and statistical issues involved could be resolved on the basis of available data, it is a moot point whether a general theory of growth and social capital is appropriate as opposed to a country-by-country case-specific study of how the various factors interact with one another.

9 Note, in this context, the problem is equivalently one of how we measure social capital or what functional form we use to model its effects. For a fuller discussion, see Fine (1999f).

10 A third theme is by geographical area – Africa, East Asia and the Pacific, Latin America and the Caribbean, Middle East and North Africa, Europe and Central Asia, South Asia, OECD Nations, Global – but these lead directly to the

database of abstracts and do not have dedicated pages on the Web. None the less, the implication is that social capital has full scope of applicability, geographically as well as historically and conceptually!

11 Apart from the two discussed, there is the social-capital newsletter, *Nexus*. See also the website, http://www.inform.umd.edu/iris/soccap.html, for the IRIS Center at the University of Maryland, which works with the World Bank on social capital.

12 For Grootaert and van Bastelaer (1998):

> The Social Capital Initiative aims to contribute to both the conceptual understanding of social capital and its measure. Although there is a significant and rapidly growing literature on social capital and its impact ... it has not yet provided an integrated and generally accepted conceptual and analytical framework.

13 Woolcock's (1998) own metaphor, occupying the first few pages of his article, begins with the difference in standards between airports in Madras and Singapore!

14 Note that most of the metaphors are drawn from Western experience prior to being imposed on developing countries, a regressive feature of social capital in the field of development studies.

15 As a missing link, social capital corresponds to the doctor's diagnosis as idiopathic – we do not know. In the future, as in the past, given the record of stabilisation and structural adjustment, the diagnosis in the light of failed policies based on social capital may change to iatrogenic – we caused it.

16 See, however, Baum (1997) and Kawachi *et al.* (1997).

17 See, for example, Wilkinson (1996), but also Muntaner and Lynch (1999) for a critique.

18 See Mehta (1999).

19 For a detailed discussion, see Fine (1999d).

20 Thereby, as Hildyard (1998) and others have suggested, opening up for the Washington institutions more powerful levers for intervention for otherwise unchanged policies.

21 See edited collection; Evans (1996).

22 For an account of the evolving position of social theory within the World Bank, and the attempts of social scientists to gain a foothold against the economists, see Francis (1999) and Fine (1999d).

23 See Francis (1999) for the role of World Bank social scientists as social engineers.

References

Baum, F. (1997) 'Public health and civil society: Understanding and valuing the connection', *Australian and New Zealand Journal of Public Health* 21(7): 673–5.

Becker, G. (1996) *Accounting for Tastes*, Cambridge, MA: Harvard University Press.

Berger, R. (1995) 'Agency, structure, and Jewish survival of the Holocaust: A life history study', *Sociological Quarterly* 36(1): 15–36.

Bourdieu, P. and J. Coleman (eds) (1991) *Social Change for a Changing Society*, Boulder: Westview Press.

Budlender, D. and N. Dube (1998) 'Starting with what we have – basing development activities on local realities: A critical review of recent experience', Community Agency for Social Enquiry, South Africa, mimeo.

Collier, P. (1998) 'Social capital and poverty', World Bank, Social Capital Initiative, Working Paper, no 4.

Cooke, B. and U. Kothari (eds) (1999) *Participation, the New Tyranny*, London: Zed Books.

Evans, P. (1996) 'Introduction: Development strategies across the public–private divide', *World Development* 24(6): 1033–7.

Field, M. (1995) 'The health crisis in the former Soviet Union: A report from the "post-war" zone', *Social Science and Medicine* 41(11): 1469–78.

Fine, B. (1980) *Economic Theory and Ideology*, London: Edward Arnold.

—— (1998) 'Neither Washington nor post-Washington consensus: An introduction', mimeo.

—— (1999a) 'From Becker to Bourdieu: Economics confronts the social sciences', *International Papers in Political Economy* 5(3): 1–49.

—— (1999b) 'Endogenous growth theory: A critical assessment', *Cambridge Journal of Economics*, forthcoming, a shortened and amended version of identically titled, SOAS Working Paper, No. 80, February 1998, pp. 1–49.

—— (1999c) 'The developmental state is dead – long live social capital?', *Development and Change* 30(1): 1–19.

Fine, B. (2001) *Social Capital versus Social Theory: Political Economy and Social Science at the Turn of the Millennium*, London: Routledge.

Francis, P. (1999) 'A "social development" paradigm', in Cooke and Kothari (eds) (1999).

Grootaert, C. (1997) 'Social capital: The missing link?', Chapter 6 in World Bank (1997), reproduced as World Bank, Social Capital Initiative, Working Paper, no. 3.

Grootaert, C. and T. van Bastelaer (1998) 'Expected contributions from the social capital initiative', IRIS website.

Harcourt, G. (1972) *Some Cambridge Controversies in the Theory of Capital*, Cambridge, UK: Cambridge University Press.

—— (1976) 'The Cambridge controversies: Old ways and new horizons – or dead end', *Oxford Economic Papers* 28(1): 25–65.

Hildyard, N. (1998) *The World Bank and the State: A Recipe for Change?*, London: Bretton Woods Project.

Kawachi, I., B. P. Kennedy, K. Lochner and D. Prothrow-Stith (1997) 'Social capital, income inequality, and mortality', *American Journal of Public Health* 87(9): 1491–506.

Knack, S. and P. Keefer (1997) 'Does social capital have an economic payoff? A cross-country investigation', *Quarterly Journal of Economics* 62(4): 1251–88.

Mehta, L. (1999) 'The World Bank and knowledge: Critical reflections on the *World Development Report* (1998–99)', mimeo.

Muntaner, C. and J. Lynch (1999) 'Income inequality, social cohesion, and class relations: A critique of Wilkinson's neo-Durkheimian research program', *International Journal of Health Services* 29(1): 59–81.

Narayan, D. (1997) *Voices of the Poor: Poverty and Social Capital in Tanzania*, Washington: World Bank.

Narayan, D. and L. Pritchett (1997) 'Cents and sociability: Household income and social capital in rural Tanzania', Policy Research Working Paper, no. 1796, World Bank.

Raiser, M. (1997) 'Informal institutions, social capital and economic transition: Reflections on a neglected dimension', European Bank for Reconstruction and Development, Working Paper, no. 25.

Rose, R. (1998) 'Getting things done in an anti-modern society: Social capital networks in Russia', World Bank, Social Capital Initiative, Working Paper, no. 6.

Roy, W. (1984) 'Class conflict and social change in historical perspective', *Annual Review of Sociology* 10: 483–506.

Sender, J. (1998) 'Analysis of sub-Saharan Africa's economic performance; limitations of the current consensus', Professorial Inaugural Lecture, SOAS, mimeo.

Serageldin, I. (1997) 'Preface', to Narayan (1997).

Stiglitz, J. (1998) 'Towards a new paradigm for development: Strategies, policies and processes', Prebisch Lecture, UNCTAD, Geneva.

Temple, J. (1998) 'Initial conditions, social capital, and growth in Africa', *Journal of African Economics* 7(3): 309–67.

Wilkinson, R. (1996) *Unhealthy Societies: The Afflictions of Inequality*, London: Routledge.

Woolcock, M. (1998) 'Social capital and economic development: Toward a theoretical synthesis and policy framework', *Theory and Society* 27(2): 151–208.

World Bank (1998) 'The initiative on defining, monitoring and measuring social capital: Text of proposals approved for funding', World Bank, Social Capital Initiative, Working Paper, no. 2.

8 Education and the post-Washington consensus[1]

Ben Fine and Pauline Rose

Introduction

As the post-Washington consensus has sought to displace the Washington consensus by emphasising the significance of market imperfections, one longstanding area of World Bank thinking and funding has shone out like a beacon in contradicting exclusive reliance upon market forces – education. This is hardly surprising given the widely accepted notion that education forms an exception in the weight of market externalities and imperfections that would lead to its under-provision. In addition, in both developed and developing countries, education has increasingly been seen as a panacea for solving problems of economic and social advance. Emphasis on human capital and endogenous growth has marked many of the explanations over the past decade for differing economic performance. Not surprisingly, the watershed literature bridging the transition from Washington to post-Washington consensus has even witnessed a strengthening commitment to education.

That the World Bank has adopted a view reflecting the beneficence of education is evident from its review of 1995, *Priorities and Strategies for Education*. It argues that increases in the educational level of the labour force can promote economic growth, not least in the long-run through technological change, which occurs faster when workers are more highly educated. Education is anticipated to increase individual productivity by the acquisition of skills and attitudes, and to enhance the accumulation of knowledge more generally. Furthermore, 'the creation of human capital is the creation and distribution of new wealth' (World Bank 1995, p. 27), which contributes to the reduction of both absolute and relative poverty, although time lags are likely. Through the acquisition of skills, attitudes and knowledge, education increases the productivity of the labour of the poor and their access to jobs in both the formal and informal sectors, as long as there is no discrimination. Moreover, education of women in particular is believed to result in lower fertility and maternal mortality, and improved child health.

We begin in the second section with a critical assessment of human capital theory, which has dominated World Bank thinking on education from before the emergence of the Washington consensus, and which is equally uncritically accepted by its putative successor. We suggest that human capital theory offers no insights on education as such from an analytical point of view, simply construing it as a chosen stream of (potential) costs and benefits. It leaves education, let alone the education system, as an unopened 'black box'. However, by leaving education out of its analytical framework, it allows any number of factors affecting educational provision to be arbitrarily brought back in to promote and qualify theoretical, empirical and policy work. Unfortunately, irrespective and independent of the World Bank's stance, the notion of human capital theory has itself been increasingly and widely accepted uncritically. Accordingly, its weaknesses need to be exposed in posing alternatives to a consensus that goes far beyond (post-) Washington.

The next section reviews the World Bank approach to education in the light of what can only be deemed its obsessive attachment to human capital theory. As observed, this devotion has not changed with the adoption of the post-Washington consensus with its generalised appeal to market imperfections, since the new consensus incorporates a continuity with the old's specific rationale for support to education in light of its underprovision by imperfect or absent markets. As will be seen, the virtues of education have, if anything, been perceived to be even stronger through the prism of the post-Washington consensus, especially as represented by Joseph Stiglitz. Accordingly, the post-Washington consensus has failed to make a distinctive analytical mark on the issues surrounding education and development. The broader scope of market imperfections embraced by the post-Washington consensus has the effect of intensifying the already irresolvable contradictions within the human capital approach. The more that market imperfections are acknowledged, the more transparent becomes the need to understand education systemically both in itself and in its relationship to development. This is illustrated by reference to Stiglitz's informal pronouncements on the virtues of education and, in the fourth section, by consideration of the World Bank's commitment to female education.

Our own approach to education is outlined in the fifth section. The post-Washington consensus, whatever its analytical weaknesses, locates educational provision within a framework of multiple market imperfections with consequential spillover effects from one market (and non-market) to another – from schooling to fertility, employment and so on. This undermines the case for a human capital approach and argues for it to be replaced by systemic analysis. The latter must eschew a general approach and allow due regard to the social and historical context of educational provision within particular countries. We, therefore, suggest that education should be understood as a 'system of provision', which is located within economic and social relations more generally.

Education as a black box

The burden of this section is to demonstrate that human capital theory is fundamentally flawed, even though confidence in it has strengthened with the dullness of critique that has accompanied the passage of time and use. The almost universal acceptance of human capital theory is due in part to the increasing conservatism of the economics profession as radical alternatives to the mainstream have weakened, to the uncritical spread and use of the notion of human capital in other social science disciplines, to the weakness with which the critique of human capital theory has been pursued, and, not least, the influence of the World Bank itself in promoting reliance upon it. Further, as will be emphasised in this and following sections, the literature on human capital, whether emanating from the World Bank or not, has paradoxically prospered by exploiting its own weaknesses. In a nutshell, from an analytical point of view, human capital theory takes a starting point that essentially sets education aside. Consequently, however unsatisfactorily, education can be brought back in again in pursuit of analytical refinement or in the greater complexity of empirical or case studies.

Human capital theory is the consequence of the ready acceptance of education as a special application of orthodox economic analysis, where human capital is merely the accumulated capacity to be more productive. The advantage of the human capital approach is in its being able to tread well-worn analytical paths for theoretical, empirical and policy purposes. It is complemented by the immediate derivation of analytical results. At the micro-level, the notion of human capital allows wage differentials to be addressed; from wage differentials, rates of return to investment in human capital can be calculated; at the macro-level, the contribution of human capital to growth can be assessed; and policy implications can be drawn in terms of private or public investment in the various tiers of education according to their anticipated rewards. Human capital theory, then, sits firmly within neo-classical economics, drawing upon its various analytical parables.

At its core, the theory is simply an assessment of a stream of costs and benefits, whether borne or accruing to individuals or to the economy as a whole. It follows that it essentially begins without any understanding of the educational process. On the one hand, the 'black box' of how education is provided remains firmly shut other than in the labelling of financial costs and benefits.[2] On the other hand, the theory has no historical or social specificity. The rise of human capital theory within the World Bank, for example, grew out of the more specific application of cost–benefit analysis to calculation of rates of return (Jones 1992). As such, it has nothing to do with education. Exactly the same methodology could be applied to any factor with an economic effect. Indeed, for Becker (1996), human capital is just one component of 'personal capital', a notion that is deployed exactly for any more general purpose.[3] As Baumol and Becker (1996, p. 4) put it:[4]

> The educational production can be described as a listing of the set of variables that are assumed to be the prime determinants of the amount of human capital the student acquires as the result of schooling.

Human capital theory has not always been uncontroversial.[5] Indeed, much of the criticism that it has received can be understood as a critique, explicit or otherwise, of the failure to address the specific nature of education and its emphasis on calculus of costs and benefits. Blaug (1987), for example, refers to a second generation of revisionist scholars in the field who were sceptical in the 1970s, although they quickly gave way to a third generation with no apparent inherited doubts about what they are doing and who overwhelmingly prevail today. Becker (1993, p. xix), the second Nobel Prize winner in economics for contributions to human capital theory in 1992, following Schultz in 1979, proudly observes that human capital has entered the discourse of presidential campaigning – 'a dozen years ago, this terminology would have been inconceivable'. Becker's main concern over the acceptability of the approach centres on the aversion to the notion of education as comparable to an accumulated physical asset with productive potential.

In this respect, in converting, in the 1970s, from a 'True Believer' in human capital theory, and a leading practitioner himself, Blaug (1987) emphasises the influence of Bowles and Gintis (1976). They are perceived to have revealed that the social relations governing schooling have very little to do with a technical relation between inputs and outputs. Rather, Bowles and Gintis understand schools by analogy with mini-factories in which the social relations, of dominance, hierarchy, respect for authority, punctuality, etc., are replicated. This is in order to socialise future workers into accepting the positions that they are expected to occupy. Irrespective of the extent to which Blaug has correctly interpreted Bowles and Gintis, and whether, as he suggests, they merely rediscover Durkheim, he does correctly conclude (1987, p. 132):

> The moment we argue that the chief contribution of education to economic growth is to complement the socialisation function of families ... we necessarily jettison the concepts of any precise quantitative relationship between the growth of the economy and the growth of the education system ... (and question) whether the entire exercise is not perhaps misconceived in its very foundations.

However, understood in these terms, the educational process has still not been significantly opened up by the radical alternative offered by Bowles and Gintis. Rather, a particular (empty) neo-classical theory of education as production of human capital has been replaced by an alternative (more substantive) theory of production, which has itself then equally been projected on to education (understood as a factory for social relations in which we learn to accept and are allocated to our previously given economic positions).

Not surprisingly, the insights offered by Bowles and Gintis and other critics of human capital theory have rarely been taken up by the mainstream.

Rather than addressing directly the specific economic and social relations surrounding schooling, attention has been focused upon refining the production function for human capital: what are its inputs, what are its outputs and what is the relationship between them. Such preoccupations are relatively rare for normal production functions. Data on inputs and outputs are taken from economic statistics, and production functions estimated with technological progress or other factors traditionally allowed to account for any differences in productivity over time or place. The problem for the estimation of human capital production functions has been that the simplest expectations have been confounded since higher output has not always been associated with higher input. Schools with more resources, with lower pupil–teacher ratios, etc. do not necessarily perform better on measures of educational performance.[6]

Paradoxically, it is this simplest of empirical refutations of the approach that has led it to be both refined and to take account, however satisfactorily, of the specific content of schooling itself. This is because, in practice, human capital theory does recognise some of its deficiencies, albeit obliquely, in moving forward from its cost–benefit starting point. Especially in the context of education, analysis is based on a triple structure comprising pre-schooling, schooling and post-schooling, with corresponding attention, respectively, to the inputs to the production of human capital, the production of human capital and human capital as an input itself. It is convenient to begin with the second of these, although we will soon move into consideration of the others. Observe first, that unlike the commercial enterprise, most schools do not have inputs and outputs that can be measured exclusively and simply in terms of costs and revenue. Consequently, once this is recognised and non-priced inputs and outputs are incorporated as they must be, then, the floodgates are opened for any number of factors to count as inputs and outputs. Essentially, any factor that affects educational performance can be understood as an input, whether it be familial background, innate ability, school ethos and environment, gender, race, etc.[7] Similarly, any outcome can be understood as an output, from what you know to whom you know. For theoretical and empirical purposes, it becomes essential to explain the simultaneous interaction between all of the variables.

Thus, in investigating education or schooling as a production function, the black box is being opened up in a most peculiar fashion, which both exploits the weaknesses of the approach and consolidates them, not least because of its individualistic and economistic starting points. Put another way, as more factors are introduced to refine estimates of education production functions, the credibility of the whole exercise is forced to walk an analytical tightrope. This is because, while added variables might add some token realism and educational specificity, the absence of, and need for, systemic analysis of education becomes increasingly apparent for two separate but closely related reasons. First, the more factors that are included into the analysis – ranging from socio-economic characteristics of individuals through school, locational and other higher-level variables – the more education is seen to be part and parcel of society and social functioning as a whole, and not appropriately reducible to a function specifying educational outputs as a consequence of educational inputs. Second, it is also apparent that the various educational inputs that are used to explain educational outputs are far from independent of one another. Each of the variables in the inputs and outputs is connected to the others. They are mutually determining.

The latter point is illustrated in a limited way by the literature that seeks to correct sample selection bias in estimating human capital production functions. Possibly those who stay in school longer have more innate ability or parents who have provided them with a more favourable environment, even by moving children to live closer to schools that are considered to be better for whatever reason. This would bias estimates of the production function if not taken into account by estimation procedures. This is a creeping, piecemeal recognition of the social and systemic nature of educational provision. On a grander scale, it has now become commonplace to attach educational performance to a range of other socio-economic factors, such as health, fertility, nutrition and household income.[8] It is apparent that the education production function has become an implicit proxy for the workings of a major part of the social fabric, hardly to be captured by a set of inputs and outputs measured as costs and benefits.

So far, the discussion has focused primarily upon the education production function for human capital and, consequently, on pre-schooling conditions as these make up educational factor inputs. Now consider the use of human capital as an input into production or the economy more generally. Leaving aside all the previously discussed problems in getting to this point, how does human capital affect economic outcomes? Consider the role in wage determination. It is standard to include human capital as an independent variable in a wage rate regression, in which all other variables have also been included that might affect labour market outcomes. Otherwise, there will be bias in the estimates. However, once again, the implication is that a full understanding of how the labour market functions and grinds out outcomes is essential in order to isolate the effects of human capital, and to be able to calculate rates of return to human capital.[9] In principle, it is necessary to incorporate a whole range of variables such as race, gender, location, sector, occupation, level of trade unionism, capital intensity and degree of monopoly. These variables also mutually condition one another so that a sophisticated understanding of the economy will be necessary in order to assess the effect of human capital on wage determination. In practice, we are more likely to find that the labour market is treated as if working perfectly competitively, with little or no interaction between labour market variables. Much the same is true of growth accounting, which includes the effects of human capital. Whether in the old growth theory, in which human capital is just one more factor to add to those contributing to output, or for the new endogenous growth theory in which, in one way or another, human capital is perceived as a source of productivity increase, the outcome is much the same and paradoxical. Far simpler models are used to understand the relationship between education and growth (or education and other variables such as wages or fertility), than would be used to understand these in the absence of education. It is as if growth theory or whatever can be simplified when adding the effect of education. In particular, estimates of the impact of human capital, both on wages and growth generally, presume the economy is at full employment and perfectly competitive. Otherwise, estimates will be conflating its effects with those of excess capacity and price distortions.

Similar considerations apply to another aspect of the use of human capital theory.[10] In general, the individual returns to human capital are calculated by attempting to compare wage rates, with and without it, while correcting for other factors. However, this takes no account of unemployment. On the one hand, for the individual, this might be expected to understate the returns since the chances of getting a job and of getting better pay are enhanced with more human capital.[11] However, the same cannot be true for the economic system as a whole, particularly if stretched to the limit. If everybody got a Ph.D. in nuclear physics, returns and employment prospects from doing so would drop very quickly. More generally, at the extreme, more human capital might not generate higher incomes, and only generate a competitive race in credentials necessary to obtain the available jobs. The worth of extrapolating from the existing calculation of human capital returns is highly questionable for two reasons, as is illustrated by critical reference to the study of South Africa by Schultz (1998). He observes very high rates of returns to black males for higher education in 1993. However, as is well known by anyone familiar with the South African transition, this reflects a number of factors, not least the wish of all employers to enhance their public image. Such factors will not extend into the indefinite future, let alone to indefinite numbers of black males. By the same token, partly reflecting a problem of data but also a failure to contextualise the relationship between education and the economy, Schultz's use of data from Africa for 1970 to 1985, as the basis for calculating rates of return to human capital, renders his results somewhat limited for projecting returns for the next millennium.

In short, the more human capital theory becomes more realistic and specific to education, the more it undermines its own analytical starting point – that education can be understood in terms of the incidence, usually individual, of costs and benefits. The more social factors are introduced to explain how education is produced to create human capital or to examine its effects in terms of returns, the more education is revealed to be linked to social relations, processes and structures. However, instead of the latter being taken as an alternative analytical starting point, human capital has, paradoxically, been allowed to exploit its weaknesses to develop a vibrant research programme in which education itself and social factors are brought back in to refine the human capital calculations that they invalidate. Just throw in a few more variables and more sophisticated modelling to get the required results, but do not question the broader socio-economic determinants and role of education itself.

Bringing education back in and the post-Washington consensus

Thus, the development of human capital theory from its ideal origins does open the black box of education but in entirely unsatisfactory, and yet, unlimited, ways. The latter fall into three overlapping types for which we briefly offer leading and representative illustrations. One approach to bringing education back in is abstract and offers general speculation about what matters. Laroche *et al.* (1997), for example, point to eight aspects that distinguish human capital from other goods or activities: it comprises innate and acquired abilities; it is non-tradable; it is not always purposefully chosen, as with the young; it accrues through both formal and informal means; it has qualitative and quantitative aspects; it can be general and specific; it is not always fully used; and it is subject to externalities.[12] These distinguishing features raise problems, and research and policy agendas, for human capital around property rights, decision-making, how it is accumulated and how it depreciates, quite apart from measurement problems for national statistics.

An alternative way of bringing education back in, rather than theorising about casual descriptive characteristics, is by refining the simpler versions of the perfectly competitive model that lies at the core of human capital theory. As Mincer (1997) argues, in a typical example, this can lead to consideration of intertemporal optimising over a lifetime as far as investment in human capital is concerned; a technique that is becoming standard.[13] On the other hand, Griliches (1997), for example, is more concerned with whether wages reflect marginal products or not in view of screening or other types of labour market imperfections (considerations that led Blaug to become a sceptic), with these needing to be integrated with the influence of other factors such as innate ability and family background. He concludes that all corresponding decisions need to be modelled simultaneously, an impossible ambition if all socio-economic factors that interact with education are taken into account.

The third mode of reinstating education to the analysis is to create theory directly around one or other empirically observed aspect, which is hypothesised as affecting educational outcomes. This will be illustrated in detail in the next section by reference to gender, following a brief account of the World Bank's educational research and funding, which has thrown up a mixed bag of factors for bringing education back in where, for human capital theory, it would otherwise be absent. This is because it is crucial to recognise that human capital theory has not only served as an analytical fudge (taking education out and bringing it back in) for the World Bank as for so many others, but it has also provided an unlimited rationale for funding education in practice by deploying education to accrue high returns, to alleviate poverty, to reduce fertility, to favour women and so on. The World Bank not only wants to make (or deny) loans, it seeks to justify them. Human capital has shown itself to be a flexible friend in this respect.[14]

The World Bank is important in setting educational priorities and policy-making, given its position as a self-declared leader in the education sector in terms of its intellectual and financial role – which governments and donors follow (either by force or by choice).[15] Despite substantial policy shifts, even reversals, as discussed below, the World Bank's approach to education has remained heavily dependent for its justification upon the application of human capital theory. As observed by Jones (1997a, p. 117), the World Bank's intellectual position towards education has remained unchanged over time:

> What has changed is the bank's perception of its own role, the most dramatic changes being corrections of earlier arbitrariness rather than any shift in fundamentals ... the bank's rationale has barely changed in 35 years, a celebration of the elegance of human capital theory.

The latest World Bank Education Sector Strategy indicates a continued uncritical adherence to the importance of human capital-theory (World Bank 1999b, p. 6):

> The rise of human capital theory since the 1960s, and its widespread acceptance now after thorough debate, has provided conceptual under-pinnings and statistical evidence. Estimates by Nobel-laureate economists have shown that education is one of the best investments, outstripping the returns from many investments in physical capital.

Indeed, this economic approach to education has been endowed with the aura of an article of faith, as is apparent from debate in the *International Journal of Educational Development*, vol. 16, no. 3, over the World Bank's 1995 *Priorities and Strategies for Education*. In his special-issue editorial, Watson (1996, p. 213) suggests that:

> By stressing economic indicators and labour market outcomes, the diversity, complexity and richness of the education process is largely ignored ... overgeneralising a mass of different and country specific evidence, the Bank presents its case as if it has the answers to the world's educational problems: as the authors in this issue are at pains to point out this is quite patently not the case.

However, the variety of criticisms offered by Lauglo (1996), Bennell (1996) and Samoff (1996) are treated with nothing short of contempt by the

World Bank's leading representatives, even if writing in individual capacities, as if their critics need to learn elementary lessons and be a little more worldly and practical. For Burnett and Patrinos (1996) and Psacharopoulos (1996), human capital theory is undisputed, Burnett and Patrinos (1996, p. 273):

> Lauglo's claim that rates of return are controversial we believe, could be due to a confusion between rates of return and human capital theory. The latter is no longer considered controversial.

However, the relationship between theory, policy and practice is unclear; to an extent, it is scarcely penetrable. Human capital has been the only constant of late, a loyal servant over the past two decades. Shifts in policy and financing are evident, gradually moving from an emphasis on vocational education and training and general secondary education in the 1960s towards primary education from the 1970s. The initial antipathy towards primary education was based on the notion, or 'bizarre rationale' according to Jones (1992), that it would make unlimited demands as far as finance was concerned, and self-provision should be relied upon because of the high demand for it. The shift towards primary education can be charted in part in terms of the move from manpower planning to cost–benefit analysis in the early 1980s, although the demise of manpower planning was already evident before this (Jones 1992). From the late 1980s until mid-1990, primary education was a central component of the Bank's poverty-reduction strategy, following severe criticisms of the negative effects of World Bank condition-alities in structural-adjustment loans on the social sectors (see, for example, Cornia *et al.* 1987), thereby allowing an image to be presented of being more attuned to welfare, poverty alleviation, gender issues and popular and community participation. As Ilon (1996, p. 414) observes:[16]

> A careful examination of World Bank educational policies reveals a discernible movement from human capital focused education lending towards educational policies which emphasise stabilisation. Such stabili-sation policies are often promoted under the labels of 'poverty alleviation', 'community empowerment' or 'democracy'.

She does, however, suggest that the new focus has been integrated into the more traditional human capital dialogues. This is evident in recent Bank literature (Burnett and Patrinos 1996, p. 276):

> Since we accept human capital theory and the outcomes approach, then our focus naturally becomes poverty reduction .... Or in other words, empowering the poor by improving their productivity ... is the World Bank's goal in education.

More recently, there are indications of a renewed emphasis on technical and higher education. This is evident, for example, in the 1998/99 World Development Report on *Knowledge for Education*, which proposes that basic education 'should not monopolize a nation's attention as it becomes a player in global markets' (World Bank 1999b, p. 42). Rather, it is proposed that higher levels of education deserve increased attention because of the need to adapt to and apply new information-based technologies.[17]

The Bank's positions have been supported by a wide range of research, which has expanded considerably since the first policy statement in the 1970s. According to the authors of the 1995 *Review*, for example, their acceptance of the human capital perspective relies upon the latest research in top economics journals (Burnett and Patrinos 1996, p. 273). Significantly, the authors focus their attention on the economics, without mentioning education journals in which critiques of Bank policy statements can frequently be found.[18] Moreover, a closer examination of the research on which the statements are based indicates that most of this is undertaken or inspired by World Bank authors or consultants with little reference to critics (Lauglo 1996).[19] Criticisms of previous policy statements are also not alluded to, nor are the lessons learnt. Each document, therefore, stands in isolation.

For the time being, though, human capital theory continues to be seen as the motivation for investing in education, with rates of return analysis still deemed to be playing a central role in determining priorities in education, as highlighted in the 1995 *Review*. Despite criticisms of the approach, the most recent World Bank (1999b) *Education Sector Strategy* continues to rely on evidence on rates of return to justify investment in education, albeit with reference in the vernacular in vogue to issues such as globalisation and democratisation. In fact, the role of rates of return in shaping World Bank educational priorities has increased rather than decreased. Bennell (1996, p. 235) notes that the 1980 policy paper refers to rate of returns to education only once, whereas the 1995 *Review* refers to it over thirty times, 'in order to substantiate, support and qualify a number of key statements about different types of educational investments and the appropriate roles of the public and private sectors'. It could be argued that rates of return analysis is used for internal-advocacy purposes within the Bank, which staff do not necessarily believe themselves. This view is not supported by public pronouncements of Bank staff who believe that human capital theory is no longer considered controversial and are defensive about its reliance on rates of return to education as a diagnostic tool (Burnett and Patrinos 1996, p. 273). This would tend to support Jones's (1997a, p. 368) view that there has not been a real shift in the Bank's position. This is because, despite attempts to broaden the scope of benefits of education to poverty reduction, the tension between bankers and pedagogues remains unresolved.

The emphasis on rates of return to education is not surprising given that the Bank is regulated by the rules of a bank that has to find economic

justification for its loans (Burnett and Patrinos 1996, p. 274). However, as Jones (1992, p. 227) points out, the limitations of its contribution need to be understood in this light:

> Research needs to be driven by operational requirements and must reflect organisational values, aspirations and objectives. What becomes an issue is when researchers working in such contexts deny the institutional parameters that shape and dictate their work, and claim their research to be objective, untrammelled by institutional requirements.

Human capital fits the bill. Furthermore, the narrow focus on economic aspects risks neglecting important features of education. As Lauglo (1996, p. 223) notes:

> The moral and social impact of education is not faced in the *Review* – neither the problems which schools might generate, nor the potential they may have for remedying the social dislocations of modernization and restoring social cohesion.

The processes of teaching and learning, which transform inputs into outputs, remain outside the scope of the Bank's approach to education, leaving the Black Box firmly shut.

Educational financing is one area in which the World Bank has played an important role in influencing policy. Unusually, relative to other programmes under the Washington consensus, the Bank has persistently perceived a role for the state in both the provision and financing of education. Based on arguments of externalities, imperfect capital and labour markets, principal/agent problems and uncertainty of the expected future benefits, there has traditionally been acceptance by the World Bank for the role of the state in providing and financing educational services. Furthermore, since the early 1980s, imperfect information has been used as an explanation for divergence between individual and social returns, where individuals may not be aware of the private let alone the potential social benefits of the service, or be able to finance it. Thus, state involvement in education provision and financing has been seen as a second-best solution.

The extent to which governments should subsidise the education sector has, however, been debated. Mixed signals were sent out by the Bank during the 1980s due to conflict between its economic agenda and the priorities set within the education department. On the one hand, education was seen as a priority for development. On the other hand, conditions of structural-adjustment loans emphasised cuts in government public expenditure and increased reliance on the market. While conditions were not directly imposed on cutting public expenditure in social sectors, in practice these often suffered (Stewart 1994). Simultaneous with concern about public-sector spending, economists affiliated to the World Bank developed an economic model illustrating that, where there is excess demand for education, charging user fees at all levels of education would be advantageous from both an efficiency and equity perspective (Psacharopoulos *et al.* 1986). While the economic framework remains unchallenged by the World Bank, it no longer advocates charging user fees at the primary level in the 1990s. This shift does not appear to be based on an admission of the lessons learnt from the application of increasing user fees in the 1980s (Tilak 1997, p. 72):

> It is interesting to note that, while the earlier international declarations and conventions sought to assure free and compulsory education for all, the term 'free' began to be used more sparingly in the 1980s. Organizations like the World Bank favoured, in the earlier years, the introduction of fees in primary education, simultaneously opposed and supported the same later, and subsequently distanced itself from the practice.

Indeed, World Bank documents advocating fees, which were heavily cited in the 1980s, are no longer referred to in Bank papers in the 1990s. The emphasis has, subsequently, switched from individual payments to community participation (World Bank 1995). The theoretical underpinnings of this development are, however, unclear. What has been clear is that human capital theory can be deployed to support either or neither position in policy and in practice.

What intellectual contribution has been made to the economics of education in the post-Washington consensus era? By way of representative response, it will be shown that the emphasis that has been given to its developmental role during the Washington consensus has been perpetuated and reinforced by Stiglitz. Education continues to be seen as central to the development process. It is a recurring feature in his speeches, in which its role is extended to be not only an instrument required to achieve development but it is also seen as a 'broader objective'. In terms of an instrument of development (Stiglitz 1998a, p. 10) notes that:

> Trying to get government better focused on the fundamentals – economic policies, basic education, health, roads, law and order, environmental protection – is a vital step ... the choice is not whether the state should or should not be involved. Instead it is often a matter of how it gets involved. More importantly, we should not see the state and markets as substitutes ... I would like to argue that the government should see itself as a complement to markets, undertaking those actions that make markets fulfil their functions better.

The justification for a focus on education, and the need for government intervention in it, continues to be based on the notion of human capital and its relationship with growth, as evident from the example of East Asian economies (Stiglitz 1998a, p. 11):

> The role of human capital in economic growth has long been appreci-
> ated .... The East Asian economies, for instance, emphasized the role of
> government in providing universal education, which was a necessary
> part of their transformation from agrarian to rapidly industrializing
> economies .... Left to itself, the market will tend to underprovide
> human capital. It is very difficult to borrow against the prospects of
> future earnings when the human capital itself is not collaterizable ....
> The government plays an important role in providing public education
> and using other methods to make education more affordable.

Although Stiglitz recognises trade-offs between some of the goals of
development, education is seen as an area where there are complementarities
with other goals. He proposes that promoting human capital can advance
economic development, equality, participation and democracy. East Asia is
again drawn upon, this time as an example of universal education creating a
more egalitarian society, facilitating the political stability that is considered
to be a precondition for successful long-term development (Stiglitz 1998a).

Stiglitz's broadened set of objectives includes democratic development
that places emphasis on ownership and participation (Stiglitz 1998b). This
recent emphasis on participation within the World Bank is considered to
have implications for education. According to Stiglitz (1997, p. 6), development strategies from the 1960s to the 1980s saw development as a technical
problem requiring technical solutions; they did not reach deep down into
society, nor did they believe that a participatory approach was necessary.
Participation is seen as a means of improving educational outcomes, and
education can improve participation. On the one hand, 'in some cases –
particularly as in education and health, where individual involvement is an
essential part of the production process – participation can improve other
outcomes (for instance, the amount of learning that occurs)' (Stiglitz 1997,
p. 5). On the other hand, 'for participation to be fully meaningful, it should
be based on knowledge; hence the crucial role of education', (Stiglitz 1997,
p. 22).

Education is, therefore, given top priority by Stiglitz (1997, p. 31) in
promoting development:

> Among the most important [priority] is *education*, because without
> education a country cannot develop, cannot attract and build modern
> industries, cannot adopt new growing technologies as rapidly in the
> rural sector. But most fundamentally, if development represents the
> transformation of society, education is what enables people to learn, to
> accept and help engender this transformation. Education is the core of
> development.

The views of Stiglitz expressed above highlight what he considers to
be new in his approach to education – namely, its importance as both an

instrument as well as an objective of development; the complementarity between states and markets in education provision; and the importance of participation in both educational provision and outcomes. Stiglitz accepts that a focus on health and education, and away from measures of GDP, is far from revolutionary. However, he considers the difference in his outlook is that he has tried 'to argue that the whole is greater than the sum of the parts, and that successful development must focus on the whole – the trans-formation of society' (Stiglitz (1998b, p. 42). It is also evident that the basis for his support for education remains firmly within the human capital paradigm, for which notions such as 'development' and 'transformation' can only serve as rhetoric.

None the less, these contributions of Stiglitz are hardly controversial, remaining uninformed by the depth of literature on development, and education's role within it. These observations are confirmed by reference to what is often his own preferred terrain of illustration as well as of debate more generally – the East Asian NICs. The post-Washington consensus allows both for (limited) industrial policy in view of one set of market imperfections and for publicly supported education in view of another set. What is rare is an account of their interaction, other than through ubiqui-tous production functions. This is a deficiency both in terms of assessing how the educational and industrial systems are compatible with one another and mutually reinforcing, and, possibly even more importantly, why both sets of interventions are the consequence of the same economic, social, polit-ical and cultural conditions. It is surely no accident that the human capital and market imperfections approaches are compartmentalised from one another and mutually incapable of addressing issues of development and transformation.

Bringing gender back in

Economic arguments used by the World Bank to justify a focus on female education provide a good illustration of the problems associated with the human capital perspective. It neglects the broader historical, social and polit-ical context in which gender relations are constructed and, yet, tacks on associated variables in a piecemeal fashion in order to obtain rates of return and efficiency. Emphasis on economic-efficiency arguments in favour of investment in female education is highlighted, for example, in a paper by Lawrence Summers (1994, p. 20), a former chief economist at the World Bank:

> In making an economic argument for investing in female education, I have tried to steer clear of the moral and cultural aspects unavoidably involved in any gender-related question. Partially this reflects my comparative advantage as an economist, but it also reflects a conviction that helping women be better mothers to their children is desirable whatever one's view of the proper role of women in society.

Stiglitz (1996, p. 167–8) relies on these arguments put forward by his predecessor. In particular, he considers the importance of female education to be one of the lessons from East Asia:

> The emphasis on female education led to reduced fertility, thus mitigating the adverse effects of population pressure felt in so many developing countries, and it directly increased the supply of educated labor. Most studies suggest that a worker's wage performance is more directly related to non-school factors, such as home background, than to education in school. Education of women can be thought of as a round-about but high-return way of enhancing labor force productivity.

Here, female education is not considered important for enhancing women's own position in the labour force, but for influencing the productivity of their offspring. In a subsequent paper, Stiglitz (1998b, p. 24) does consider the increased labour force opportunities for educated women. However, he focuses on the effect that their increased wages will have on the family. He, therefore, perceives that women will maintain their role in the household while playing an increased role in the workforce, without considering the implications of this on their workload. As Stromquist (1998, p. 36) points out:

> When the defense for attention to women is based on the principle of efficiency, such an argument downplays the fact that women are productive but exploited under current conditions. The call for 'utilizing women's resources in development' often translates into giving them double and triple working duties.

Expectations of the benefits of female education not only assume that women are not otherwise productive, but also do not challenge the traditional gender division of labour within the household and society. Women who are not in a position to afford childcare and who are expected to play an increased role in the productive sphere could only do so by increasing their own work burden, or by keeping girls out of school to substitute for them in the home.

As in the education sector more generally, the justification for incorporating gender into Bank policy and project work on education continues to be heavily based on rates of returns to education, as evident from the GenderNet website of the World Bank:

> Studies have shown that the economic rate of return of investing in girls' education is at least as high, and usually higher than the return on investing in boys education. When the social returns on girls' education (improved health and education levels of children, lower population growth rates etc.) are considered the case for girls' education is even stronger.
> (http://www.worldbank.org/gender/how/lending.htm)

The recent evidence on rates of return to female education is not, however, as clear cut as suggested.[20] Furthermore, problems of measuring rates of return mentioned previously also apply to gender comparisons. For example, there will probably be selectivity bias since calculations of rates of return are based on the observed wages of women who are working in the labour market. These women often account for a very small proportion of the female population, and those who have access to employment opportunities are likely to exhibit particular characteristics that cannot be generalised. There is, therefore, a problem that educated females included in the sample are not selected randomly. In addition, the calculations assume perfectly competitive labour markets whereas in practice there are many forms of imperfections including, in many countries, gender discrimination in employment opportunities.[21] As employment opportunities expand for women, those currently in the labour market, and the wages and conditions that they experience, are not liable to be representative of outcomes for substantially increased female labour market participation. Moreover, the process is not even incremental with substantial structural change ultimately involved in socio-economic conditions, as is evident from the experience of developed countries (Fine 1992).

Further justification is given to investment in female education by virtue of the anticipated additional social benefits, in terms of reduced fertility, improved child health and so on. However, the externalities associated with girls' education are difficult to value in monetary terms and, therefore, estimation of returns is problematic. In addition, they are not uncontested, as much of the literature might imply. Schultz (1995, p. 48) himself points out, for example, that it is difficult to determine causality in the relationships between market labour force commitment, decline in fertility and the educational attainment of women. More importantly, the arguments for female education do not address whether and how women's control over resources and decision making within the household is improved as a result of increased education. Schooling can, in fact, reinforce the subordinate position of women and may not be sufficient to ensure empowerment. For example, despite massive increases in women's formal schooling, in many countries men continue to dominate in economic and political life (Swainson 1998 and Longwe 1998). Studies, particularly in South Asia, have questioned the validity of the posited direct relationship between female education and fertility decline (Jejeebhoy 1995, Jeffrey and Basu 1996 and Kumar and Vlassoff 1997, for example). The relationship between female education and fertility decline is found to be highly variable and context-specific, with reference to both the level of development as well as the nature of gender relations in the society. The results of these studies suggest that autonomy is crucial to women's control over their fertility, and that the relation between education and autonomy is mediated by the cultural relations of patriarchy (Heward 1997). Weaknesses detected in the relationship should not be used to suggest that priority to female education is misguided, as suggested by Knodel and Jones (1996). Rather, it highlights the need to ensure that the quality and type of schooling received by boys and girls requires attention. Where schooling, either intentionally or unintentionally, ignores the economic and social relations within and around education, the desired outcomes are not likely to be attained.

It is undeniable that World Bank efforts have been successful in raising the profile of gender disparities in education and have provided justification for investment targeted towards girls. However, their reliance on economic arguments is inadequate and misleading. As Baden and Goetz (1997, p. 10) note:

> Tenuous evidence on the relationships between female education and fertility decline, or female education and productivity, can easily be challenged, weakening the justification for addressing gender issues, with a danger that resources will be withdrawn.

Such a fear is not without foundation.[22] Rates of return to human capital are an extremely fragile basis on which to justify investment in female education, quite apart from providing little or no guidance on how to succeed in achieving parity in educational provision and more generally.

Thus, an improved understanding is required to ensure that female education continues to receive attention regardless of fads in interpretation and calculation of economic returns to education. As Stromquist (1994) notes, studies that do not attempt to construct a theoretical understanding of how women's inferior condition emerges and is maintained in society recommend actions as if there were no societal constraints on their attainment. Without a fuller analysis, it is not certain that the desired goals (for example, lower fertility and increased labour productivity) would be attained. Even if they were, the incidence of gender inequality could continue to be reproduced, as is so sharply evident in the developed world. To be effective, analysis of constraints and formulation of interventions has to be situated within the economic, political and social environment that shapes the nature of gender relations in education and society more broadly.

Education as a system of provision[23]

The purpose of this section is to provide an insight into the perspective from which we have critically assessed the World Bank approach to education in general, and female education in particular. In brief, we posit the need to understand educational provision in terms of highly country-specific socio-economic systems rather than as a more or less efficiently co-ordinated stream of costs and benefits attached to education and training. In other words, we need to construct an appropriate understanding of national education systems. This might be thought to be uncontroversial, especially to those not wedded to mainstream economics and economic reductionism.

However, recent developments across the social sciences, with the exception of economics, have been marked by 'structural adjustment' to two sequentially ordered forms of analytical shock therapy, postmodernism and globalisation. Consequently, in the broader education literature to be found outside the orbit of the World Bank, as Green (1997, p. 3) parodies:

> The whole logic of both postmodernism and globalization theory is the national education system *per se* is now defunct, at once irrelevant, anachronistic and impossible. Governments no longer have the power to determine their national systems. They increasingly cede control to regional and international organizations on the one hand ... and to consumers on the other .... Governments can no longer use education to promote social cohesion and to transmit national cultures and should not attempt to do so .... As the national state becomes a marginal force in the new world order so education becomes an individualized consumer good delivered in a global market and accessed through satellite and cable links. National education ceases to exist.

Here, however, a remarkable paradox reveals itself. While it has proved oblivious to the intellectual fashions that have shaken the world of the other social sciences, economics can legitimately claim, in the case of education, to have been far ahead of the field in embracing the thrust suggested by postmodernism and globalisation. It is generalised, homogenising and explicitly individualistic in its approach. Even if antediluvian in its technique, human capital theory has inadvertently and unconsciously led the field in positing that national education systems have ceased to exist or, indeed, in denying that they have ever existed. All we have ever experienced are individual decisions to invest in and deploy human capital, albeit in circumstances (of market imperfections) not chosen by ourselves.

Such an approach embodies, in a less than subtle way, a further feature remarked by Green (1997, p. 4) in the putative demise in national education systems. While the history and understanding of the emergence of public education is strongly associated with goals of social integration and cohesion, and the formation of nation-states (which might be thought to be important in the context of development), these concerns have been displaced by the notion of education as more or less exclusively concerned with national competitiveness – although individuals, of course, may be otherwise motivated by, and manipulated to, other goals such as lower fertility and even education for its own sake. Once again, it is blindingly obvious that human capital got there first and is now way out in front, not least in the new theories of endogenous growth, where human capital is especially prominent in explaining why growth and productivity rates differ.[24]

The absent analytical prince in this theatrical account attached to human capital theory is how education is understood as a system. Across the literature, the notion is more used than elaborated. Most common is a descriptive account in terms of hierarchical configurations of qualifications and institutions. More circumspect is the remarkably thin set of literature that seeks to locate the educational system in its broader socio-economic context. This, however, tends to be done through a historical and comparative method.[25] How and why did national education systems emerge, and how and why did they evolve differently. Such studies are an important antidote to economism and reductionism, especially in demonstrating that non-economics factors have always been paramount. Green (1990), for example, considers factors such as democratisation, progress and reform, urbanisation, proletarianisation, shifting structures of family life, crime, vagrancy, immigration, social unrest and control, institutional traditions, state policy and class alliances, militarisation, and nationalism.

The weakness of these accounts complements their strengths. In avoiding an approach to education as an imperfect market, the economic also tends to be neglected, an unfortunate feature in view of the appropriation of the economics of education by the human capitalists. An exception is to be found in the work of Ashton and Green (1996) that, significantly, is less concerned with education as schooling and more with skill formation and use, necessarily imparting consideration of employment and productivity.[26] They address the relationship between the economy and education and training, focusing on factors such as an evolving system of profitable accumulation, diversity across the economic system, the relative autonomy of the education and training system, the significance of the nation-state, and the contradictory tensions across all aspects of the economy and the education and training system.

They also address the conditions necessary for the successful attainment of a high skill strategy. These include elite state and employer commitment to skill formation and innovative use of productive system; heavy reliance on the educational system for language, science, maths and IT provision; regulation and accountability of training at the workplace; workers' commitment to the education and training system; and integration of training on and off the job. Further, such conditions can (fail to) arise through a variety of country-specific institutional forms – how industrial relations interact with technology choice, for example – and hence education and training systems. In the case of gender and education, how these specifically interact with the broader socio-economic system is of crucial importance and is hardly reducible to a more or less refined human capital approach.

Without the space to go into details, we would press the implications of such an approach further, and perceive education, as well as training and skills, as attached to a 'system or provision'[27] with the following elements. First, education is, indeed, provided through a series of economic and other activities from the building of schools, to the setting of curricula, and to the functioning of labour markets for teachers. Second, educational provision is situated not only sequentially in terms of pre-school, school and post-school environments, it is also potentially interactive with the full panoply of economic, social, political and cultural relations. Third, both the intrinsic educational process and its extrinsic context and impact are heavily embroiled in social structures, relations and processes, and their associated conflicts, which are themselves attached to underlying economic and political interests. Finally, as a result, the formation and evolution of education systems is historically contingent. While there are systematic factors in place, their interaction cannot be predetermined. In other words, national educational systems need to be allowed to define themselves and be understood as such in the light of underlying economic and political interests. They should not be forced within a framework or typology of pre-determined systems, let alone a system-less human capital theory.

By comparison, human capital theory simply sets these issues aside other than as the outcome of aggregated individual choice based on unchanging preferences across generations. Interestingly, the post-Washington consensus is, in principle, capable of accepting and analysing the presence of socio-economic systems. It does so, for example, in case of differing financial systems, as outlined elsewhere in this volume. Analytically, however, this depends upon reducing such systems to the historically evolved non-market, collective, institutional and customary responses to market and informational imperfections. The reductionism attached to such flimsy principles is incapable of doing justice to the rich complexity of educational systems and, not surprisingly, to our knowledge, no attempt has been made to understand education as a system in these terms (even though the need for state intervention is acknowledged on this basis). In effect, the failure of the post-Washington consensus to understand education systemically is a sharp reflection of an approach to education in terms of market failures. So pervasive are the market imperfections and their mutual spillovers in such an account that the education system as such and its socio-economic determinants increasingly appear as the necessary analytical starting points, rather than some generalised notion of market failure.

It has, thus, become so unusual, especially for economists, to address education in systemic terms that it is worthwhile justifying the approach by appeal to a particularly prominent issue even for the orthodoxy. Recent literature has emphasised the relationship between education, particularly schooling, and fertility decline, with the relationship usually crudely modelled and estimated. But stand back a moment. Are we to understand (reduced) fertility decisions as the aggregated outcome of individual choices? Consider the experience of the now developed economies – without taking them as a model of modernisation for the developing countries to emulate, even if this were possible. Little more than a century ago, they went through what is known as the demographic transition, which has attracted an enormous literature and numerous debates. These have focused on the sequencing, variety and interaction of factors such as industrialisation, urbanisation, proletarianisation, welfarism and labourism, consumerism, household formation and culture, stratification by class, quite apart from educational provision in the round and with respect to contraception.[28] The vast majority of this literature, from considerably different methodologies and vantage points, is systemic and historical in content, and necessarily so given the extraordinary transition in economic, social, political and cultural life that it attempts to confront. It is hardly surprising that this literature should run in parallel with human capital theory, which, for both Washington and post-Washington consensus, is incapable of adequately incorporating the issues involved.

Conclusion

The general theme of our chapter is that the human capital approach to education, to which the World Bank is and has long been obsessively attached, is characterised by a paradox in which education is first taken out of the analysis and then brought back in. The latter, however, has the effect of undermining the paradigm itself, since the more issues are reincorporated the more the need is potentially raised for account of socio-economic processes, structures and relations, and how they fit together to reproduce or transform society and initiate and promote development. The only other possibility is to remain firmly committed to some form of rational-choice analysis, enriched by the information-theoretic results associated with the post-Washington consensus.

While this might provide a soft analytical landing for the most fanatical of mainstream neo-classical economists, it is not liable to be an option for the less extreme within economics and social theory more generally. However, it is also worth emphasising a further result and point of departure from the human capital approach to education in theory and to World Bank policies in practice. This is to recognise that any educational system, as the outcome of historically and socially evolved socio-economic practices, is inevitably specific to the particular country within which it is located. Accordingly, this must be reflected in our research and policy, and not in the form of remorseless calculation of rates of return to education and corresponding allocation of finance where these are high enough (and subject to manipulation to make them so). Further, education as panacea for development and for the World Bank's image as humane and female- and child-friendly must not be allowed to dull the senses to the continuing poverty of their analytical and policy perspectives.

Notes

1   Thanks to many for comments on an earlier version. Use has been made of an unpublished mimeo, Agbodza and Fine (1996). This chapter was completed whilst Fine was in receipt of a Research Fellowship from the UK Economic and Social Research Council (ESRC) under award number R000271046 to study 'The New Revolution in Economics and Its Impact upon Social Sciences'.

2 See also Blaug (1987) and Samoff (1996) for their discussions of schooling as a black box.

3 For a critique, see Fine (1998b).

4 In extending the notion of human to social capital, Coleman (1988, p. S100) is particularly clear about what is going on:

> Probably the most important and original development in the economics of education in the past 30 years has been the idea that the concept of physical capital ... can be extended to include human capital as well. Just as physical capital is created by changes in materials to form tools that facilitate production, human capital is created by changes in persons that bring about skills and capabilities that make them able to act in new ways.

Note that a dual distortion is involved – in how capital is understood in the first instance as physical, prior to its being applied to education.

5 We leave aside the devastating theoretical and empirical implications of the Cambridge critique for human capital theory; however, see contribution on social capital in this volume.

6 For a review of the literature, see Card and Krueger (1996). See also Hanushek (1995) and Kremer (1995).

7 Of course, this creates resonances with one branch of social-capital theory, especially that associated with Coleman, in which educational outcomes are a consequence of familial background etc.

8 See, for example, the African Development Report (1998, p. 122), in which each of these factors are shown to be connected to each of the others, with household income also perceived as mutually conditioning accelerated economic growth.

9 For a full account, see Fine (1998a, Chapter 3) and, in the context of the dual problem of measuring labour market discrimination against women, while netting out differences in human capital, see Fine (1992). See also Preston (1997) for a careful review of the explanatory power of human capital theory for Australia.

10 For a discussion of many of the issues, see Bennell (1996).

11 See also Chiswick (1997, p. 5) on the questionable assumptions that those in schooling bear the private costs of being so as well as foregoing employment.

12 See also OECD (1998, pp. 31–2, 74 and 86–7) for the range of elements involved in the stock, the returns and the costs and benefits of human capital, respectively.

13 For him, this militates against learning later in life, as returns in the form of higher wages will only extend over a shorter remaining lifetime. This is presumed to explain why wages over a life-cycle rise from a low level before peaking and falling (in parallel with levels of human capital, which need to be renewed).

14 See Jones (1992) for an account of how education came to be a favoured target for World Bank loans and, having become so, has become internalised as part of a loan culture with considerable momentum.

15 Psacharopoulos (1981, p. 141) stated that the 1980 Bank Policy Paper deserves the full attention of the academic community as it represents the major explicit statement on applied educational policy in LDCs and, therefore, suggested that 'It might not be an exaggeration to treat this Paper as a modern Bible on educational development'. Furthermore, the 1995 World Bank (1995, p. 145) *Review* reports that it is the largest single source of external finance for education in developing countries, accounting for about a quarter of all external support.

16 See also Puiggros (1997).

17 It appears as if adult literacy is liable to continue to be neglected since it is very difficult to deploy as a general rationale for making loans. See Jones (1992 and 1997a). However, we do not cover this issue here.
18 For example, complete issues of journals have been dedicated to criticism of World Bank policy papers including *Prospects* 1980 and 1981; *Comparative Education* 1981; *Canadian and International Education* 1983; *Comparative Education Review* 1989; as well as *International Journal of Educational Development* 1996.
19 See Jones (1992, pp. 226–7) on the World Bank's research in the era of its commitment to human capital theory.
20 See, for example, Kingdon (1998) and Appleton *et al.* (1995).
21 For example, Kingdon (1998) shows that wage differentials between men and women in her sample are determined more by labour market discrimination than by differences in educational attainment.
22 See, for example, Knodel and Jones (1996).
23 The approach outlined in this section has been applied to schooling (and health, electrification and housing) in the context of South Africa (MERG 1993).
24 For a critical exposition, see Fine (1999).
25 Archer (1979) is the classic reference. For a review of approaches, see Green (1990).
26 See also Ashton *et al.* (1999) and Green *et al.* (1999).
27 See Fine and Leopold (1993).
28 For an approach to the transition in these terms in the context of Britain and female labour markets, see Fine (1992).

References

African Development Bank (ADB) (1998) *African Development Report: Human Capital Development*, New York: Oxford University Press for the African Development Bank.
Agbodza, C. and B. Fine (1996) 'The genealogy of human capital theory: One step forward, two steps back', mimeo.
Appleton, S., J. Hoddinott, P. Krishnan and K. Max (1995) *Gender Differences in the Returns to Schooling in Three African Countries*, Milano: Economics Energy Environment.
Archer, M. (1979) *Social Origins of Educational Systems*, London: Sage Publications.
Ashton, D. and F. Green (1996) *Education, Training and the Global Economy*, Cheltenham: Edward Elgar.
Ashton, D., F. Green, D. James and J. Sung (1999) *Education and Training for Development in East Asia: The Political Economy of Skill Formation in Newly Industrialised Economies*, London: Routledge.
Baden, S. and A. Goetz (1997) 'Who needs sex when you can have gender? Conflicting discourses on gender at Beijing', *Feminist Review* 56: 3–25.
Baumol, W. and W. Becker (1996) 'The economist's approach', in Becker and Baumol (eds) (1996).
Becker, G. (1993) *Human Capital: A Theoretical and Empirical Analysis with Special Reference to Education*, Chicago: University of Chicago Press.
—— (1996) *Accounting for Tastes*, Cambridge, MA: Harvard University Press.
Becker, W. and W. Baumol (eds) (1996) *Assessing Educational Practices: The Contribution of Economics*, Cambridge, MA: The MIT Press.
Bennell, P. (1996) 'Using and abusing rates of return: A critique of the World Bank's 1995 *Education Sector Review*', *International Journal of Educational Development* 16(3): 235–48.

Blaug, M. (1987) *The Economics of Education and the Education of an Economist*, New York: New York University Press.

Bloch, M., J. A. Beoku-Betts and B. R. Tabachnik (eds) (1998) *Women and Education in Sub-Saharan Africa: Power, Opportunities and Constraints*, Colorado: Lynne Rienner Publishers.

Bowles, S. and H. Gintis (1976) *Schooling in Capitalist America: Educational Reform and the Contradictions of Economic Life*, London: Routledge and Kegan Paul.

Burnett, N. and H. Patrinos (1996) 'Response to critiques of priorities and strategies for education: A World Bank review', *International Journal of Educational Development* 16(3): 273–6.

Card, D. and A. Krueger (1996) 'The Economic Return to School Quality', in Becker and Baumol (eds) (1996).

Carnoy, M. (1999) 'Globalisation and educational restructuring', mimeo.

Carrier, J. and D. Miller (eds) (1998) *Virtualism: The New Political Economy*, London: Berg.

Chiswick, B. (1997) 'Interpreting the coefficient of schooling in the human capital earnings function', World Bank, Human Development Department, Policy Research Working Paper, no. 1790.

Colclough C. (ed.) (1997) *Marketising Education and Health in Developing Countries: Miracle or Mirage?*, Oxford: Clarendon Press.

Coleman, J. (1988) 'Social capital in the creation of human capital', *American Journal of Sociology* 94, Supplement, S95–S120, reproduced in Swedberg (ed. (1996).

Cornia, G., R. Jolly and F. Stewart (1987) *Adjustment with a Human Face*, Oxford: Clarendon Press.

Fine, B. (1992) *Women's Employment and the Capitalist Family*, London: Routledge.

—— (1998a) *Labour Market Theory: A Constructive Reassessment*, London: Routledge.

—— (1998b) 'The triumph of economics: Or "rationality" can be dangerous to your reasoning', in Carrier and Miller (eds) (1998).

Fine, B. (2000a) 'Endogenous Growth Theory: A Critical Assessment', *Cambridge Journal of Economics* 24(2): 245–65, a shortened and amended version of identically titled, SOAS Working Paper, No. 80, February 1998.

Fine, B. and E. Leopold (1993) *The World of Consumption*, London: Routledge.

Green, A. (1990) *Education and State Formation: The Rise of Education Systems in England, France and the USA*, London: Macmillan.

—— (1997) *Education, Globalisation and the National State*, London: Macmillan.

Green, F., D. Ashton, D. James and J. Sung (1999) 'The role of the state in skill formation: Evidence from the Republic of Korea, Singapore and Taiwan', *Oxford Review of Economic Policy* 15(1): 82–96.

Griliches, Z. (1997) 'Education, human capital, and growth: A personal perspective', *Journal of Labor Economics* 15(1), Part 2: S330–S344.

Hanushek, E. (1995) 'Interpreting recent research on schooling in developing countries', *World Bank Research Observer* 10(2), August: 227–46.

Heward, C. (1997) 'The women of Husseinabad and the men in Washington: The rhetoric and reality of "Educating the Girl Child"', paper presented at the Oxford Conference on Education and Development, Oxford.

Ilon, L. (1996) 'The changing role of the World Bank: Education policy as global welfare', *Policy and Politics* 24(4): 413–24.

Jeffrey, R. and A. Basu (1996) *Girls' Schooling, Women's Autonomy and Fertility Change in South Asia*, New Delhi: Sage.

Jejeebhoy, S. (1995) *Women's Education, Autonomy and Reproductive Behaviour: Experience from Developing Countries*, Oxford: Oxford University Press.

Jones, P. (1992) *World Bank Financing of Education: Lending, Learning and Development*, London: Routledge.

—— (1997a) 'The World Bank and the literacy question: Orthodoxy, heresy and ideology', *International Review of Education* 43(4): 367–375.

—— (1997b) 'On World Bank education financing', *Comparative Education*, 33(1): 117–29.

Kingdon, G. (1998) 'Does the labour market explain lower female schooling in India?', *Journal of Development Studies* 35(1): 39–65.

Knodel, J. and G. Jones (1996) 'Post-Cairo population policy: Does promoting girls' schooling miss the mark', *Population and Development Review* 22(4): 683–702.

Kremer, M. (1995) 'Research on schooling: What we know and what we don't: A comment on Hanushek', *World Bank Research Observer* 10(2), August: 247–54.

Kumar, A. and C. Vlassoff (1997) 'Gender relations and education of girls in two Indian communities: Implications for decisions about childbearing', *Reproductive Health Matters*, 10: 139–50.

Laroche, M., M. Mérette and G. Ruggeri (1997) 'On the concept and dimensions of human capital in a knowledge-based economy context', University of New Brunswick, Department of Finance, Working Paper, no. 89-01.

Lauglo, J. (1996) 'Banking on education and the uses of research: A critique of World Bank priorities and strategies for education', *International Journal of Educational Development* 16(3): 221–33.

Longwe, S. (1998) 'Education for women's empowerment or schooling for women's subordination?', *Gender and Development*, 6(2): 19–26.

MERG (Macroeconomic Research Group) (1993) *Making Democracy Work: A Framework for Macroeconomic Policy in South Africa*, Cape Town: CDS.

Mincer, J. (1997) 'The production of human capital and the life cycle of earnings: Variations on a theme', *Journal of Labor Economics* 15(1), Part 2: S26–S47.

OECD (1998) *Human Capital Investment – an International Comparison*, Paris: OECD.

Prendergast, R. and F. Stewart (eds) (1994) *Market Forces and World Development*, London: Macmillan Press.

Preston, A. (1997) 'Where are we now with human capital theory in Australia?', *Economic Record* 73(220): 51–78.

Psacharopoulos, G. (1981) 'The World Bank in the world of education: Some policy changes and some remnants', *Comparative Education* 17(2): 141–5.

—— (1996) 'Designing educational policy: A mini-primer on values, theories and tools', *International Journal of Educational Development*, 16(3): 277–9.

Psacharopoulos, G., J.-P. Tan and E. Jimenez (1986) *Financing Education in Developing Countries*, Washington, DC: World Bank.

Puiggros, A. (1997) 'World Bank education policy: Market liberalism meets ideological conservatism', *International Journal of Health Services* 27(2): 217–26.

Samoff, J. (1996) 'Which priorities and strategies for education?', *International Journal of Educational Development* 16(3): 249–71.

Schultz, T.P. (1995) *Investment in Women's Human Capital*, Chicago: University of Chicago Press.

—— (1998) 'The formation of human capital and the economic development of Africa: Returns to health and schooling investments', African Development Bank, Economic Research Papers, no. 37.

Stewart, F. (1994) 'Education and adjustment: The experience of the 1980s and lessons for the 1990s', in Prendergast and Stewart (eds) (1994).

Stiglitz, J. (1996) 'Some lessons from the East Asian miracle', *World Bank Research Observer* 11(2): 151–77.

—— (1997) 'An agenda for development for the twenty-first century', Ninth Annual Bank Conference on Development Economics, Washington DC: World Bank.

—— (1998a) 'More instruments and broader goals: Moving toward the post-Washington consensus', the 1998 WIDER Annual Lecture, Helsinki: WIDER.

—— (1998b) 'Towards a new paradigm for development: Strategies, policies and processes', the 1998 Prebisch Lecture, Geneva: UNCTAD.

Stromquist, N. (1994) 'Gender and basic education in international development cooperation', UNICEF Staff Working Papers no. 13, New York: UNICEF.

—— (1998) 'Agents in women's education: Some trends in the African context', in Bloch *et al.* (eds) (1998).

Summers, L. (1994) 'Investing in all the people: Educating women in developing countries', EDI Seminar Paper, no. 45, Washington DC: World Bank.

Swainson, N. (1998) 'Background paper on gender and education', mimeo, Oxfam.

Swedberg, R. (ed) (1996) *Economic Sociology*, Cheltenham: Edward Elgar.

Tilak, J. (1997) 'Lessons from cost recovery in education', in Colclough (ed.) (1997).

Watson, K. (1996) 'Editorial', *International Journal of Educational Development* 16(3): 213–14.

World Bank (1995) *Priorities and Strategies for Education: A World Bank Review*, Washington, DC: World Bank.

—— (1999a) *Education Sector Strategy*, Washington, DC: World Bank.

—— (1999b) *World Development Report. Knowledge for Development*, Washington, DC: World Bank.

9 The post-Washington consensus and lending operations in agriculture

New rhetoric and old operational realities

Jonathan Pincus

Introduction

Many observers of the World Bank have commented on the disjuncture between the World Bank's rhetoric and the reality of lending operations. 'Schizophrenia' is a favoured characterisation (Rich 1994, 182; Kapur *et al.* 1997, 125; Winters 1997; Gavin and Rodrik 1995, p. 331), although Gustav Ranis prefers a metaphor that goes literally to the heart of the organisation, positing 'two separate circulatory systems [in the Bank] with relatively little real capillary action between them':

> One, encompassing the President's office, the Bank's research wings, and, usually, the chief economist in each of the operating regions, is concerned with generating, or at least propagating, innovative ideas and analyses .... The other encompasses the operating departments, where the continuous flow of project and programme lending approvals is what matters, where the frequent arrival of 'new direction' ideas is met with a jaundiced eye and the well-worn bureaucratic response that 'we are already doing it', and where it is generally recognised that the bottom line chances for recognition and promotion are largely tied to being polite but getting on with the lending.
>
> (Ranis 1997, p. 79)

The perception that inconsistency (or a 'development gap' in the Bank's terminology) persists between the World Bank's rhetoric and the design and implementation of projects has important implications for the institution's perception of itself as a *development agency* rather than solely, or even primarily, a development bank. Since its founding, the Bank has stated consistently that the ideas and expertise that it brings to poor countries are more important than its financial contribution (IBRD 1948, 17; Mason and Asher 1973, 331; Wolfensohn 1999). This is in part a defensive argument put forward as an answer to the fungibility problem and, in later years, to evidence of the tenuous links between loan conditionality and policy change (Stiglitz 1999, p. 580; Mosely *et al.* 1995; Killick 1998). The Bank has also found it necessary in the 1990s to focus increasingly on non-financial justifications for its existence as private-sector flows have come to dominate capital transfers to developing countries (Gilbert *et al.* 1999, p. 607). However, more positively, it also reflects the Bank's self-image as a leading generator, repository and disseminator of knowledge relating to the development process, and the importance that the leadership attaches to closing the 'knowledge gap' between rich and poor countries (World Bank 1998a; 1998b).

The Bank's aspiration to reinvent itself as a 'Knowledge Bank', and more specifically as an 'honest broker' (Stiglitz 1999, p. 590), providing objective market and technical information to governments and investors alike, hinges crucially on the proposition that its activities as an intellectual actor and as a project lender are consistent and mutually reinforcing. The idea of a 'comprehensive development framework' – now the centrepiece of Wolfensohn's efforts to re-emphasise the Bank's technical and motivational roles – assumes that the experiences gained from past projects will inform the country's development strategy just as the strategy shapes the selection, design and implementation of new projects (Wolfensohn 1999). To the extent that changing ideas about development feed into lending operations, and, conversely, project experiences inform development theorising, the Bank is uniquely placed to 'bundle' these disparate activities within one conceptual framework (Gilbert *et al.* 1999, p. 615). If, however, as Ranis suggests, the gap between rhetoric and reality is structural rather than incidental, the Bank will find it increasingly difficult to justify combining responsibility for these various functions within one institution.

Recent years have seen the publication of numerous studies examining the extent to which Bank operations have lived up to the institution's rhetoric with regards to poverty alleviation, environmental sustainability and other aspects of its core development mission (for example, Ayres 1983; Kapur *et al.*, 1997; Caufield 1996; Rich 1994). This chapter takes up the more specific question of the institutional obstacles that exist within the Bank to achieving greater convergence between theory and practice. Based on examples taken from the agricultural sector in general and Indonesia's agricultural portfolio in particular, the chapter focuses on a set of operational imperatives that influence project selection, design and implementation. Although these operational imperatives do not determine the Bank's lending strategy, they do make some strategies more feasible than others. More specifically, I will argue that the Bank's evolving agricultural development strategy has – at least since the McNamara presidency – failed to take sufficient account of the institution's strengths and weaknesses as a lending institution. As a result, the Bank's rhetoric has outpaced its capacity to deliver in operational terms. The problem has become more acute in recent years, as the Wolfensohn Bank's rhetorical emphasis on participation, knowledge and institution building has not been matched by a convincing effort to address the Bank's operational limitations in these areas.

The remainder of the chapter is divided into four parts. First, we briefly describe a set of four operational imperatives that have exerted a powerful influence on the content and impact of the World Bank's lending programme. The following section reviews the evolution of the Bank's approach to rural development since the 1960s, and gauges the extent to which operational imperatives have shaped these strategies. We then move on the specific case of the agriculture portfolio in Indonesia, taking a closer look at two projects from the 1990s that have attempted to live up to the Bank's new rural-sector rhetoric. The final section concludes and briefly discusses the implications of the analysis for the World Bank ambitions as a development agency.

Operational imperatives

The idea that operational imperatives constrain the way the World Bank goes about its business is not new. Indeed, internal Bank documents – particularly studies produced by the Bank's Operations Evaluations Department (OED) – offer some of the sharpest insights into the nature of these constraints and strategies to overcome them. At times the issue has leapt to the top of the agenda – for example following the release of the controversial Wapenhans report on portfolio management – only to retreat into relative obscurity (Wapenhans *et al.* 1992).

This section reviews four key operational imperatives: the Bank's status as a preferred creditor, pressure to lend, centralisation and institutional capture. Although this is not an exhaustive list, these closely interrelated imperatives together add up to a powerful force for conservatism within the Bank's operational divisions. They have also proven to be highly resistant to organisational restructuring or changes in the style and operational priorities of upper management. As we shall see in the next section, these four imperatives have played a particularly important role in the evolution of the Bank's agricultural portfolio.

The Bank as a preferred creditor

The World Bank's original mandate was to provide foreign exchange for specific projects for which private financing was unavailable, and for which a government guarantee could be obtained (IBRD 1948, p. 14). In its early years the Bank favoured large-scale investments in infrastructure such as ports, power and communications, while steering clear of so-called 'social-overhead' projects like health, sanitation and education. Social lending was considered undesirable on several grounds: first, the projects were not obviously self-liquidating; second, the foreign-exchange component was typically small; and, finally, avoiding 'soft' projects was thought to reassure the financial markets and hence improve the Bank's credit rating (Mason and Asher 1973, p. 154).[1]

Over the years the Bank has relaxed these criteria to allow for a larger and more diversified lending programme and in response to changing external conditions. The project focus, weakened by structural-adjustment lending in the 1980s, is now largely defunct; in FY 1999 adjustment (non-project) lending accounted for more than half of new commitments for the first time in the Bank's history. Social lending now makes up more than one-third of the Bank's project portfolio, and local cost financing is now well established. As of June 1999, local expenditures accounted for 42 per cent of cumulative IBRD and IDA disbursements (World Bank 1999a).

The one facet of the original mandate that has remained intact is the requirement of recipient governments to guarantee all IBRD and IDA loans.[2] This provision is viewed as essential to the Bank's credit rating and hence the institution's ability to raise finance at reasonable cost.[3] In operational terms, the guarantee assigns ultimate responsibility for the end use and repayment of Bank loans to the host government. This essentially defines the Bank as a public-sector lending institution; governments were and remain the Bank's primary clients.

The function of providing government loans was broadly consistent with the Bank's early role of financing investments in public goods, usually large infrastructure projects. It is less suited to many of the institution's contemporary concerns, for example policy reform, institution building and governance. As we shall see in the next section, agricultural-sector loans are a good example of the failure of loan conditionality to induce policy change. The Bank's own work on aid effectiveness blames bad government policies and weak institutions for poor loan performance, and recommends making loans only to governments with good policies (as defined by the Bank) already in place (World Bank 1998b). However, if this conclusion were pursued to its logical limits, the Bank would quickly deplete its own client base; the Bank cannot both focus on the poor and restrict itself to countries with strong public-sector institutions and ready made neo-liberal policies.

One strategy that the Bank has pursued to broaden its constituency base is to increase the role of non-government organisations in the identification, design, implementation and evaluation of projects. NGO participation rates as reported in successive annual reports have increased from 20 per cent of projects in FY 1989 to slightly more than half of all projects in FY 1999, with even higher rates in agriculture and social-sector projects. Critics point out that quantitative measures do not tell us much about the depth or quality of NGO involvement, and that the Bank tends to use these organisations as low-cost service providers rather than active participants in the entire project cycle (Covey 1998, p. 89). Certainly there remains scope for improving the quality of projects through greater public participation, a theme that has been picked up enthusiastically by the Bank in recent years.[4]

However, the extent to which NGOs are able to move into a real decision-making role is limited by the Bank's status as a lender to governments; it is ultimately governments that must repay the loans, and for obvious reasons they jealously guard their right to determine how the funds are used.

Another important implication of the government guarantee is that the World Bank does not have a simple, market-based measure of project success or failure. The Bank enjoys preferred creditor status, meaning that borrowing countries continue servicing their Bank loans even if they are in default on commercial loans. Unlike commercial banks, therefore, the World Bank does not measure the quality of its portfolio based on the share of non-performing loans. Project and programme loans, however risky, and whatever the final outcome, are typically repaid in full. The Bank must therefore rely on ex-post evaluations as a guide to the success or failure of projects. However, the Operations Evaluation Department – although often a source of objective, informed criticism of Bank activities – is widely recognised as marginalised within the Bank and largely ineffective (Rich 1994, p. 171).[5]

Pressure to lend

By the early 1960s the Bank was already faced with the twin problems of high earnings from its portfolio and a shortage of 'bankable' projects (Mason and Asher 1973, p. 418). The response at the time consisted of expanding lending operations and staff, taking on riskier projects and eventually including the kinds of 'social-overhead' projects that had earlier been ruled out as inappropriate to the Bank. This process accelerated under Robert McNamara, who dramatically increased lending and set aggressive annual targets. The primary gauge of operational success became the volume of new lending, and career advancement of operations staff became closely tied to the amount of money that they could move.

By the 1990s this phenomenon had a name: 'pressure to lend'. In response to concerns over the trend decline in quality of the Bank's loan portfolio (see Table 9.1), Lewis Preston set up a portfolio-management task force chaired by Bank Vice-President Willi Wapenhans. The resulting Wapenhans report, as it has since become known, drew attention to the declining share of successful projects in the portfolio, particularly in agriculture, and identified the main cause as weaknesses in the project appraisals process resulting from pressure on operations staff to meet lending targets (Wapenhans *et al.*1992).

Pressure to lend has three immediate consequences, all of which have a negative impact on project quality. First, once a project idea has the backing of the recipient government, operations staff tend to hurry through the design stage in an effort to get the project appraised at the earliest possible date. Not enough time is spent gathering information about past projects or other related activities, or consulting with potential project beneficiaries. Second, once projects have been designed, operations staff do not so much

Table 9.1 Project performance, 1974–99

Sector and region	Per cent satisfactory				
	1974–80	1981–9	1990–3	1994–7	1998–9
Region					
Sub-Saharan Africa	79	58	54	55	61
East Asia and Pacific	92	78	80	84	81
Europe and Central Asia	86	77	73	72	83
Latin America and Caribbean	85	62	64	78	81
Middle East and North Africa	89	78	70	66	69
South Asia	89	73	73	67	66
All regions	85	68	66	68	72
Selected sectors					
Agriculture	75	58	59	69	62
Environment	–	–	–	56	80
Finance	83	72	57	59	74
Human resources	86	74	78	70	73
Industry	83	61	58	51	40
Programme and Policy	100	64	71	83	65
Technical assistance/public-sector management	100	56	56	88	80
Telecommunications	97	83	64	82	100
Transport	87	73	74	76	93
Urban	100	80	77	60	85
Water and sanitation	100	71	69	55	48

Source: OED, *Annual Review of Evaluation Results* – various years.

appraise them as *promote* them within their departments and ultimately to the executive board.[6] Finally, staff have little incentive to supervise ongoing projects, and instead concentrate on pouring new projects into the pipeline. Unfortunately, the decline in the quality of supervision has come in tandem with greater project complexity associated with the Bank's increasing use of conditionality and the trend towards more diversity in the lending portfolio (Rich 1994, p. 255).

The combination of greater complexity and weaker supervision has meant that borrowers are able to disregard their obligations under loan agreements with little fear of detection or penalty. Wapenhans decried the 'evidence of gross non-compliance', suggesting that borrowers had fulfilled less than one-fourth of the legal and financial covenants in existing loan agreements (Wapenhans *et al.* 1992, p. 8). This problem is greatly compounded by centralisation and institutional capture as discussed below.

Centralisation

This operational imperative at first glance appears out of place in the context of the Wolfensohn Bank given the current rhetorical emphasis on decentralisation, participation and 'empowerment'. As a bank, however, the present management has inherited procedures and practices from a time when the institution was geared towards financing large-scale infrastructure projects with minimal supervision needs (or at least minimal supervision by the task manager on site) and consisting of a few large disbursements. Mason and Asher's description of the problem in the early 1970s remains apposite:

> Once an agency is launched as a centralised institution, it tends to remain so. Key staff members develop a vested interest in the functions they perform and resist sharing them with field personnel. It becomes much more difficult to decide which functions can be decentralised. The dispatch of an almost infinite number of visiting missions to conduct surveys, prepare economic reports, inspect projects and evaluate progress seems more normal than establishing a finite number of resident missions. And if in the process an embryonic 'foreign service' is developed but service within it is not made essential to advancement on the career ladder, time so spent can easily become a handicap. Out of sight and without authority, the field personnel are also often out of mind when higher-level, more responsible jobs become available at headquarters.
>
> (Mason and Asher 1973, p. 73).

From its earliest days, power was heavily concentrated in headquarters, and despite numerous reorganisations the basic pattern has not changed. The focus on headquarters, and the relative powerlessness of resident mission staff, has also made the Bank an exceptionally inward-looking organisation. According to the Volker Commission, the average operations staff person spends only seven per cent of his or her time on recipient country contacts (cited in Ranis 1997, p. 78). In practice this means that shared conceptions (or misconceptions) are rarely tested against field reality, and are thus extremely difficult to dislodge.

Centralisation also complicates the implementation of small-scale, human resource-oriented projects owing to the time and effort required to satisfy the Bank's accounting system and disburse money to the field. Again, this was less of a problem when loans were used to fund capital-intensive projects, since most of the funds in these projects were released on the basis of large, integrated contracts for equipment, construction and so forth. Task managers speak wistfully of the times when they could pay for several years' contracting work with one cheque (carried by hand from the central bank to the finance ministry and then to the project) and supervise the work in an afternoon. Things are no longer so simple. Projects like micro-credit and community-based resource managment require processing thousands of small disbursements that must be reconciled against expenditures by the host government and, eventually, the Bank. As we shall see in the case of one project in Indonesia, the system can easily become overloaded, affecting the level and timeliness of the flow of funds, and thus project quality.

Institutional capture

Pressure to lend, centralisation and the Bank's limited client base create the ideal conditions for institutional capture. By capture we mean the process by which Bank operations staff come to identify their interests with the interests of their clients in the recipient country government. As Kapur *et al.* note, 'much lending takes on the character of a habitual transaction, with few immediate expectations beyond a capital transfer and desire to sustain a long relationship' (1997, p. 270). The developmental impact of ongoing projects takes a backseat to the next project idea. This future orientation means that task managers are often unwilling to draw too much attention to non-compliance for fear of losing the government's commitment to take on the next round of projects.

The incentive structure for capture is straightforward. Task managers, who typically operate in one sector in several countries or one large country, quickly develop working relationships with government officials in the relevant ministries. These officials, who implement projects under the supervision of the task manager, are also responsible – or are closely connected to the people responsible – for the approval of the *next* proposed Bank project for the sector. Given that the task manager wants the project (pressure to lend) and the government needs the loan, it does not take long for an understanding to develop in which the shortcomings of existing projects are overlooked in exchange for a smooth path for new projects in the pipeline.

The resulting co-operative mechanisms help to explain the lengths to which operations staff will go to oblige their counterparts in borrowing country governments. For example, the Morse commission investigating the Narmada dam controversy was stunned to find that 'the Bank is more concerned to accommodate the pressures emanating from its borrowers than to guarantee implementation of its policies' (quoted in Rich 1994, p. 253). Evidence of the impact of the project on local people was ignored, distorted and hidden by both the Indian government and the Bank in an attempt to protect both parties and to avoid a disruption in the flow of projects and funds.

The World Bank's approach to agricultural development

The World Bank's thinking on agricultural development has passed through a number of distinct phases since the 1940s. A general outline of these changes is presented in Table 9.2, which sets out the Bank's institutional priorities, the public documents most closely associated with these priorities and one or more 'showcase' or paradigmatic agricultural projects for each period.[7] Shifts in policy have come in response to internal changes in top management and to external factors including pressure from member countries and non-governmental advocacy groups. This section will trace the evolution of these policies. As we shall see, there has been a consistent trend since the 1960s towards more complex projects and a more diverse rural portfolio, which for the most part has meant greater demands on operations staff in the areas of design and supervision. These ambitions have proved difficult to realise in practice, not least because of the institutional limits imposed by the operational imperatives described in the previous section.

After a brief period in which European reconstruction dominated the agenda, the Bank sought to establish a role for itself in the developing world. As noted above, the original focus was on public goods, particularly large, foreign-exchange-intensive infrastructure projects. Aside from irrigation projects, and some small loans for agricultural machinery, the Bank largely stayed away from the agricultural sector: through 1961 agriculture accounted for only three per cent of World Bank lending (Kapur *et al.* 1997, p. 109). This relative neglect of agriculture on the operations side did not reflect, as is often supposed, an anti-agriculture bias within the Bank or among the prominent development economists of the day.[8] Rather, the Bank felt that its comparative advantage lay elsewhere given the small foreign-exchange component of agricultural credit, extension and research projects (Kapur *et al.* 1997, p. 262). Moreover, the fact that agricultural decision-making was often in the hands of millions of small farmers suggested that the productivity of capital investment in agriculture was dependent on the prior adoption of appropriate policies (World Bank 1972, p. 36). For this reason it was felt that more rapid progress could be made in other sectors, such as energy, transport and industry.[9]

Agriculture's operational profile was given a boost during the presidency

Table 9.2 World Bank and agricultural development

Period	World Bank priorities	Strategic statement	Showcase agricultural project
Early Bank (1947–59)	Infrastructure (power) European reconstruction Latin America	IBRD 1948	Irrigation Agricultural machinery
Woods Bank (1959–68)	Food production Economic analysis India	Woods 1964	Agricultural credit Livestock development
McNamara Bank (1968–81)	Poverty reduction Income distribution Small farmers	Chenery, *et al.*,1974 McNamara 1981: 231–64 (Nairobi speech).	Integrated Rural Development Projects (IRDP) T & V extension
Washington consensus Bank (1981–91)	Trade liberalisation Price liberalisation Privatisation	World Bank 1981 Schiff and Valdes 1992	Sectoral Adjustment Lending (AGSECAL)
Post-Washington consensus Bank (1992–)	Comprehensive development framework 'Knowledge bank' environment Participation Institution-building Governance	McCalla and Ayres 1997 World Bank 1998a Wolfensohn 1999	Community-based resource management Microfinance

of George Woods (1963–8). Under Woods, agricultural lending increased to 12 per cent of the Bank's portfolio. More significant than the increased volume of lending, however, was the acceptance of non-traditional projects explicitly oriented towards crop production, such as agricultural credit, extension and smallholder development schemes. Woods also oversaw the Bank's moves into non-project lending (in the form of balance of payments support for the purchase of necessary inputs and capital goods in India) and investment in primary education.[10] The move towards riskier projects was driven by a combination of factors, notably surplus earnings from existing loans and a perceived shortage of 'bankable' projects in financially solvent countries (Kapur *et al.* 1997, p. 175). The appearance of the International Development Agency (IDA) in 1960, set up in part to address these problems and to enable the Bank to refocus its efforts on poorer countries, provided an important vehicle for the new initiatives. Woods also expanded the economics staff and elevated economic analysis to a more central and strategic role from its traditional function as servant to the operations divisions (Kraske *et al*. 1996, p. 134). With these innovations, Woods set the stage for the transformation of the Bank under Robert McNamara.

One area of particularly rapid expansion during the Woods presidency was agricultural credit. The share of credit projects in the Bank's agriculture portfolio rose sharply from five per cent during the period FY 1948–63 to 41 per cent in FY 1964–8. Agricultural credit – channelled through development banks, commercial banks, co-operatives and project authorities – was the most obvious mechanism through which the Bank could provide support for the dissemination of Green Revolution technologies to the small farmers of Asia and Africa. The success of the new high-yielding wheat and rice varieties had reinforced the need for investments in irrigation and drainage, while also creating demand for a range of new interventions, including seed multiplication, fertiliser production, distribution of inputs, storage and processing capacity. Access to credit would provide the funds farmers needed for higher current and capital expenditures at the farm level (World Bank 1972, p. 42). The approach recognised the decentralised nature of agricultural decision-making, but attempted to deliver assistance through the centralised vehicles (banks and agriculture ministries) most accessible to the Bank.

All of this changed during the presidency of Robert McNamara from 1968 to 1981. McNamara's mission was to release the Bank from its self-imposed conservatism and to transform it from a financial intermediary into a development agency. Within six months of taking office he had announced his intentions to double the volume of lending, to be achieved through expanded efforts in Africa and Latin America, and more intensive activity in agriculture and education (McNamara 1981, p. 6). Lending to agriculture was expected to quadruple by 1973, a target that was not immediately met, but which was easily surpassed in McNamara's second term.[11] Overall, lending under McNamara grew from US$2.6 to 12.9 billion in real terms and the number of Bank staff more than tripled.[12]

McNamara stressed that his intention was to change the Bank fundamentally and development assistance more broadly, not just to deliver 'more of the same' (McNamara 1981, p.8). To be sure, the early McNamara Bank was not short of ideas on how to refocus the Bank on poverty alleviation. However, as Kapur, Lewis and Webb show in their encyclopaedic history of the Bank, successive initiatives meant to signal the end of 'trickle-down economics' were constrained by the real world of operational imperatives. Population control, singled out in the President's first major address, met with immediate resistance in borrower countries (Kapur *et al*. 1997, p. 236). Executive directors remained sceptical of housing, health and nutrition projects that were viewed as tackling effects rather than causes (Kapur *et al*. 1997, p. 254). Employment generation spoke directly to the relief of poverty but was difficult to translate into self-liquidating development projects, and in any case the Bank in the early 1970s still resisted moves to increase local-cost funding (Kapur *et al*. 1997, p. 416). Although lending for primary education – a priority carried over from Woods's Bank – grew rapidly during the early McNamara years, it never amounted to more than four per cent of the institution's total portfolio. Water and sewerage projects, particularly in urban areas, gained acceptance but their expansion was hindered by persistent implementation problems attributed to weak management in recipient countries (Kapur *et al.* 1997, 258).[13]

After several false starts, McNamara had decided by 1973 to focus on small farmers as offering the clearest expression of the Bank's commitment to the theme of growth with equity (Chenery *et al.* 1974). In a landmark speech to the board of governors delivered in Nairobi, McNamara set out his vision of development and the future role of the Bank. The problem, he concluded, was that 'growth is not equitably reaching the poor ... and the poor are not significantly contributing to growth' (McNamara 1981, p. 242). Since most of the poor live in rural areas, the key to resolving these related problems was to increase the productivity of small-scale farming. Fortunately, recent economic studies had shown that output per hectare was typically higher on small farms, and the dissemination of new technologies could further enhance the productivity of small farm operations.[14] McNamara set a goal of increasing output on small farms at an average annual rate of five per cent by 1985. The Bank, he believed, could achieve this ambitious target through support for six components: land and tenancy reform, better access to credit, assured availability of water, extension and research, improved public services and the development of rural institutions. The last, which he viewed as the 'most critical', marked a radical shift in the Bank's rhetoric: McNamara's call for 'new forms of rural institutions and organization that will give as much attention to promoting the inherent potential and productivity of the poor as is generally given to protecting the power of the privileged' were suggestive of forms of collectivism that ran counter to the Bank's historical emphasis on private initiative and minimal government intervention in markets (McNamara 1981, p. 249).

In practice, however, the Bank's new rural development strategy was far less radical than the rhetoric of the Nairobi speech. The emphasis on productivity-enhancing technologies and cost recovery effectively removed landless agricultural labourers from the target group even though they are the poorest rural dwellers and account for the largest share of the rural population below the poverty line. Although land reform figured prominently in the 1973 Nairobi speech, it never materialised in project form. Faced with mounting pressure to increase lending, Bank operations managers were not prepared to raise contentious issues of asset distribution with their clients in recipient governments (Kapur *et al.* 1997, p. 416).

Pressure to meet McNamara's ambitious lending targets was the driving force behind the design of the new rural development strategy. Area development projects, including crop-specific schemes such as tea and cotton development, quickly emerged as the vehicle of choice for operations staff.[15] These projects – modelled loosely on India's community development schemes and pilot projects in Mexico and Bangladesh supported by the Rockefeller and Ford Foundations – were designed to tackle simultaneously the full range of impediments to increasing smallholder productivity (Donaldson 1991, p. 168). They combined irrigation and other infrastructure with dissemination of seeds, pesticides and fertilisers, credit, livestock, storage facilities, transport and marketing arrangements. Not coincidentally, they also called for larger injections of World Bank funds, which suited the needs of operations staff straining to meet lending targets in the face of the limited absorptive capacity of the poorest recipient countries.[16]

Ultimately the size and complexity of area development projects proved to be a weakness rather than a strength.[17] Recipient governments lacked the managerial capacity to co-ordinate project implementation, and in many locations research and extension systems could not cope with demands for suitable, farm-tested technologies. The creation of autonomous project management agencies helped some projects to meet tight implementation schedules, but worked to undermine institutional development in host government agencies (Donaldson 1991, p. 179). The Bank's own disbursement system could not cope with the vast number of small purchases required, and operations departments lacked the resources for adequate supervision and technical guidance (Cassen 1985, p. 124). As a result these schemes proved a disappointment: OED's review of the period concludes that more than half of all projects achieved a rate of return of less than 10 per cent, the Bank's rule of thumb for economic viability. Moreover, twelve of fifteen projects in Eastern and Southern Africa failed (World Bank 1988, p. 21).

Another intervention designed to reach small farmers was the 'training and visit' (T & V) extension system. T & V was first adopted on a large scale in India and then promoted aggressively in other countries and regions. The idea was to create a national network of field-based agents to transmit technical information from the research system to small farmers on the basis of a calendar of daily visits and weekly training sessions. The Bank favoured the T & V approach in part because it was viewed as an improvement over older, commodity-based systems, but also because it fitted neatly with the Bank's operational imperatives. New extension networks required large-scale investment in buildings, vehicles and technical assistance. Moreover, the centralised nature of the system facilitated project design and supervision, and also suited the needs of the Bank's counterparts in government agriculture ministries (Purcell and Anderson 1997, p. 88). Between 1977 and 1996, the Bank spent $2.1 billion on free-standing extension projects and another $2 billion on extension components of larger projects (Purcell and Anderson 1997, Annex Table 5.3).

Agriculture reached its peak as a share of total lending in the years FY 1976–8 and fell steadily following McNamara's departure in 1981 (see Table 9.3). The change at the top was one factor in agriculture's relative decline. Tom Clausen, the new president, did not attempt to emulate his predecessor's fiery anti-poverty rhetoric, and he was more at ease with the conservative agenda pursued by the newly elected Reagan administration in Washington and the Thatcher government in London (Kraske *et al*. 1996, p. 214). The appointment of Anne Kreuger as chief economist signalled his support for an avowedly neo-liberal research programme, a stance mirrored on the operations side by a heavy reliance on austerity as the preferred adjustment mechanism to the period's massive external shocks. However, most of the operational priorities pursued by the Clausen Bank were for the most part already in place in the last years under McNamara.[18] Agriculture and sub-Saharan Africa remained the focus of new lending initiatives, but these had to be balanced against increased investment in energy and power (intended to help borrowing countries exploit domestic alternatives to imported oil) and structural-adjustment lending. As energy and programme lending increased, agriculture- and rural-sector spending in general lost their earlier predominance; nevertheless, in real dollar terms agricultural operations remained at the high levels established by McNamara throughout the 1980s.

There was, however, a pronounced shift in the allocation of projects within the agricultural sector itself (Table 9.4). The defining agricultural operation from 1984 to1991 was the agricultural sectoral adjustment loan (AGSECAL). AGSECALs made up 17 per cent of agricultural lending during the period, or about six billion dollars. In line with the general reaction against state-led development within the Bank, IMF and among major donors (the USA, UK and Germany), AGSECALs identified government intervention in input and output markets and barriers to international trade as the main cause of poor performance in the agricultural sector, particularly in Africa and Latin America. This stunning reversal in the Bank's approach from the micro-management of the McNamara years was expressed most forcefully, and controversially, in the 1981 Berg Report (World Bank 1981).

AGSECALs called for a combination of reduced or eliminated subsidies, price liberalisation of agricultural inputs and outputs, and reform of trade policy and exchange rates. The main thrust of the new approach was that alignment with international prices for agricultural inputs and outputs would increase efficiency and stimulate agricultural production.[19] Although there was plenty of evidence of price disincentives in African agriculture, the Bank did not set out the case systematically until the publication of a major study on agricultural pricing policy in 1992 (Schiff and Valdes 1992). Nevertheless, the idea of a large and significant supply response to agricultural prices was accepted as an article of faith on the operations side and guided the design of AGSECALs throughout the 1980s.

OED's internal review of AGSECALs, however, could identify only one case in which the intended supply response had materialised (Meerman 1997, p. 58).[20] Later AGSECALs, perhaps with an eye to improving internal evaluation results, sidestepped the issue entirely by omitting all references to the intended output effects of reform. However, OED also failed to detect the missing link between theory and performance; in their view, the reason

Table 9.3 World Bank lending operations by sector, 1976–99 (constant 1982 US dollars, millions and percentage of total)

	Agriculture	DFCs/ financial sector	Education	Energy and power	Industry	Non-project	Population, health, nutrition	Transportation	Urban development	Water supply	Other	Total
1976–8	3,772	1,221	482	1,568	1,016	309	321	1,753	289	497	559	11,788
1979–81	3,715	986	635	2,397	829	724	107	1,734	439	879	541	12,987
1982–4	3,353	1,069	578	2,980	725	1,366	129	2,004	468	619	775	14,065
1985–7	3,765	2596	715	3,555	603	1,398	213	1,894	948	719	784	17,189
1988–90	3,433	1,579	944	2,797	1,491	2,375	538	2,132	1,159	658	875	17,980
1991–3	2,937	940	1,662	2,893	1,044	2,603	1,168	1,739	1,254	888	1,169	18,289
1994–6	2,356	1,418	1,529	2,458	310	2,317	1,129	2,128	938	748	1,474	16,804
1997–9	2,294	2,616	1,532	1,174	749	4,952	1,023	2,485	667	502	1,547	19,539
1976–8	32.0	10.4	4.1	13.3	8.6	2.6	2.7	14.9	2.5	4.2	4.7	100.0
1979–81	28.6	7.6	4.9	18.5	6.4	5.6	0.8	13.4	3.4	6.8	4.2	100.0
1982–4	23.8	7.6	4.1	21.2	5.2	9.7	0.9	14.2	3.3	4.4	5.5	100.0
1985–7	21.9	15.1	4.2	20.7	3.5	8.1	1.2	11.0	5.5	4.2	4.6	100.0
1988–90	19.1	8.8	5.2	15.6	8.3	13.2	3.0	11.9	6.4	3.7	4.9	100.0
1991–3	16.1	5.1	9.1	15.8	5.7	14.2	6.4	9.5	6.8	4.9	6.4	100.0
1994–6	14.0	8.4	9.1	14.6	1.8	13.8	6.7	12.7	5.6	4.5	8.8	100.0
1997–9	11.7	13.4	7.8	6.0	3.8	25.3	5.2	12.7	3.4	2.6	7.9	100.0

Table 9.4 World Bank agricultural operations, 1976–99 (constant 1982 US dollars, millions)

	Agricultural credit	Agricultural sector loan	Agro-industry	Area development	Fisheries	Forestry	Irrigation and drainage	Livestock	Perennial crops	Research and extension	Other
1976–8	602	–	131	862	36	62	1,286	300	290	182	21
1979–81	481	21	192	760	43	166	1,419	160	269	192	13
1982–4	635	168	359	835	15	95	893	28	205	117	3
1985–7	683	676	37	702	36	161	930	127	168	243	–
1988–90	636	590	366	502	12	228	661	133	138	169	–
1991–3	568	576	133	509	32	109	779	17	60	154	–
1994–6	113	467	–	594	2	165	666	45	44	102	156
1997–9	141	309	–	529	37	100	770	–	20	154	234
1976–8	16.0	0.0	3.5	22.8	1.0	1.7	34.1	8.0	7.7	4.8	0.6
1979–81	12.9	0.6	5.2	20.4	1.2	4.5	38.2	4.3	7.2	5.2	0.4
1982–4	18.9	5.0	10.7	24.9	0.5	2.8	26.6	0.8	6.1	3.5	0.1
1985–7	18.1	17.9	1.0	18.7	1.0	4.3	24.7	3.4	4.5	6.5	0.0
1988–90	18.5	17.2	10.7	14.6	0.4	6.6	19.2	3.9	4.0	4.9	0.0
1991–3	19.4	19.6	4.5	17.3	1.1	3.7	26.5	0.6	2.0	5.2	0.0
1994–6	4.8	19.8	0.0	25.2	0.1	7.0	28.2	1.9	1.9	4.3	6.6
1997–9	6.1	13.5	0.0	23.1	1.6	4.3	33.6	0.0	0.9	6.7	10.2

for poor performance was that AGSECALs were not radical enough. According to OED, 'The Bank bought into the public-production-and-control model and sought to make it efficient' rather than focus on privatisation and competitive local markets (Meerman 1997, p. 1). Other, more convincing explanations for the weak supply response, including those based on careful empirical work in Africa, did not figure in the Bank's rhetoric or project design.[21]

By the end of the 1980s the poor performance of AGSECALs posed a major dilemma for operations staff. OED studies revealed that agriculture had consistently performed worse than other sectors since the 1970s (Table 9.1). This was an important factor underlying the shift towards sector reform programmes and away from large-scale area development and crop-specific projects. Until appropriate macro-policies were in place, the argument went, the Bank could do little to promote technological change at the farm level. However, by the early 1990s it was clear that AGSECALs had performed no better than investment projects. Having already undermined the logic of public investment in agriculture, there appeared to be few viable alternatives on the horizon. Agricultural credit programmes had also received low marks from OED (World Bank 1993a), as did the T & V extension system (Purcell and Anderson 1997). Meanwhile, advocacy groups had launched successful international campaigns calling attention to the negative environmental and social impacts of large-scale irrigation and frontier resettlement projects, notably in India, Indonesia and Brazil (Rich 1994).

As a result of these internal and external pressures, the scale of agricultural operations declined sharply in the 1990s. By the end of the decade agriculture lending had dropped 40 per cent in real terms from its mid-1980s peak, and accounted for less than 12 per cent of the Bank's overall portfolio (Table 9.3). The Bank was in clear need of a rethink of its sectoral strategy as a means toward divining a new rationale for agricultural lending.

In 1997 the Bank published a revised agricultural strategy in a report entitled *Rural Development: From Vision to Action*, co-authored by then Director of Rural Development Alex F. McCalla (McCalla and Ayres 1997). *Vision to Action* is a remarkable document in many ways, not least of which is the bluntness of its criticism for past Bank efforts in agriculture. The report contains an incongruent mix of themes drawn from advocacy groups – such as environmental sustainability, gender awareness and the need for more local participation – and items drawn from the traditional Washington consensus agenda like government retrenchment and market liberalisation. Acknowledging the relatively poor performance of rural-sector loans, the authors single out traditional investments such as area development projects, irrigation and agricultural credit as needlessly top-down, ecologically unsound, inefficient and insensitive to the needs of the poor (McCalla and Ayres 1997, p. 33). Crop production, input supply, processing and marketing – to the extent that these are supported by the public sector – are also off the agenda. Underlying the change in focus is a return to the theme of the World Bank as a development agency rather than a development bank. Building on the 'knowledge bank' concept spelled out in the 1998 *World Development Report*, McCalla and Ayres describe the Bank as:

> a knowledge-based institution with a global mandate. It has limited capital transfer capabilities, compared with overall development needs: it fosters development primarily by synthesizing and disseminating knowledge. It is not a technical agency but a user, collaborator, developer, and financier of technical capacities around the world.
>
> (McCalla and Ayres 1997, p. 27)

In the context of rural development, the report argues, the Bank should concentrate on policy, research and extension, reform and privatisation of agricultural services, and participatory resource management, for example social forestry, water users' groups and micro-credit.

Like much of the Bank's recent rhetoric, *Vision to Action* implicitly assigns blame for the poor performance of agricultural projects to recipient country governments (World Bank 1998b).[22] Institutional development and decentralisation – the two *idées fixes* of the report – are equated with government withdrawal from agricultural services. In line with OED's analysis of AGSECALs, sectoral-adjustment programmes are to emphasise privatisation of production, input supply, seed multiplication, research, extension and marketing. Agricultural credit, meanwhile, is to be delivered through non-government organisations as preferred intermediaries. User associations will supplant specialised government agencies – many of which were established by the Bank as part of area development projects – in the development, operation and maintenance of irrigation and drainage schemes. Community development is to be pursued through matching grants to communities, in this case meaning either NGOs or local governments.

The Bank's embrace of a decentralised, community-based approach to agricultural development raises a number of immediate issues. First, and most incongruously, the report uncritically adopts the language of neo-populism, largely redefining power relations in terms of access to government patronage while studiously avoiding discussion of social relations of production in general and class power in particular.[23] Second, and of more direct relevance to the problem at hand, is the question of the Bank's comparative advantage as a development agency. The role of the Bank as a public-sector lender would appear to be limited if the state is to restrict itself to the creation of an 'enabling framework' for decentralisation and community participation. Moreover, as we shall see in the following section, the skills and resources needed for successful participatory development along the lines of the populist model are precisely those which the Bank does not possess: namely, operational flexibility, institutional independence, an intimate knowledge of local economic, political and cultural conditions, and ample staff time for identification, design, public consultation, supervision and evaluation.

In at least one sense, then, the Bank has come full circle after fifty years' experience of rural development. Like the early Bank, the post-Washington consensus Bank is once again stressing its role as a provider of public goods, a desire to supplement rather than replace private investment and a limited role for the state. However, by the 1990s, the definition of public goods has changed in ways that would mystify the Bank's first generation of managers. Physical capital accumulation has been relegated to a supporting role in favour of intangibles such as knowledge, governance and 'social capital'. This represents a high-risk strategy for the agricultural operations divisions; at a time when overall spending on agriculture has declined precipitously in real terms, the Bank has chosen to distance itself from its historical strengths and move headlong into areas in which it has no demonstrable comparative advantage. As we shall see in the case of Indonesia, the future prospects of the Bank's agricultural portfolio hinges on the extent to which the institution can demonstrate that it can acquire these traits, and thus close the gap between rhetoric and operational reality.

The case of Indonesia

Indonesia enjoyed a uniquely intimate relationship with the World Bank during the country's three decades under General Suharto. The USA-trained technocrats in charge of economic policy developed an enduring rapport with senior Bank management based in part on shared values and perspectives, but also on the political importance of these ties for both sides. As the Bank's position in India weakened in the 1960s, Indonesia stood as an example of a populous Asian country that had emerged from economic autarky to embark on a successful, outward-oriented stabilisation programme. Indonesian technocrats, meanwhile, valued the leverage that Bank resources and policy support gave them in their internal clashes with some of the more nationalistic – and often more corrupt – members of Suharto's inner circle. Indonesia was the first country to host a Bank resident mission, and even as the personalities changed the policy dialogue was held at an unusually senior level on both sides (Kapur *et al.* 1997, p. 471).

Lending gathered pace in the 1970s, with particularly fruitful links emerging in the technocrats' strongholds of the finance ministry and the state planning agency (BAPPENAS): financial sector and structural adjustment lending accounted for 21 per cent of the Bank's total portfolio by the 1990s. Such was the Bank's faith in Indonesia's economic team that no policy conditionality was attached to structural-adjustment loans in the 1980s and early 1990s (World Bank 1999b, p. 17). Strong operational relationships were also forged with the agriculture, transport and public works ministries, and with the State Electricity Company (PLN). By the early 1990s IBRD disbursements to Indonesia had reached $25 billion or about 10 per cent of the institution's total lending portfolio.

According to OED, Bank projects in Indonesia have achieved exceptionally high performance ratings across all sectors. Of the 167 loans evaluated between 1968 and 1996, 87 per cent of projects (by lending amount) received a satisfactory rating as compared to the Bank-wide rate of 75 per cent. Remarkably, 100 per cent of power projects, which make up one-fifth of the total portfolio, were judged to be satisfactory. Even the relatively low rate of 75 per cent in agriculture compares favourably with the Bank-wide average of 65 per cent (World Bank 1996, p. 25).

The Bank also took great pride in its policy role in the 'Indonesian miracle', delivering criticism behind closed doors but offering enthusiastic public support for the government. Strong evidence of institutional capture did not go unnoticed within the Bank. For example, in a memorandum to McNamara in 1979 Shahid Husain, then vice president for East Asia, wrote:

> I have a very uneasy feeling about the nature of this relationship. It has been too personal ... I have been appalled to see how little and how restricted the discussion of our economic reports on Indonesia has been ... [T]he discussion that has taken place has been in the nature of nego-tiations on wordings and phrases and much less on objectives and policies.
>
> (Kapur *et al.* 1997, p. 323)

Despite these concerns the situation remained essentially unchanged. Twenty years later, as the Bank attempted to come to grips with its role in Indonesia's economic meltdown, internal documents again raised the issue of capture. A draft country assistance review concluded that:

> The Bank became prisoner of 'group think' whereby questioning Indonesia's success (going against the group's perceptions about Indonesia) was unwelcome. The resistance to warnings that risks were mounting, heard within and outside the Bank, was prevalent at all levels in the Bank. The incentive to take a close look at Indonesia's development model was also reduced because, for many Bank staff, asso-ciation with a 'successful' large country had had a beneficial impact on career opportunities.
>
> (World Bank 1999b, p. 10)

'Group think' manifested itself at every level, from the Bank's continued support for the failed transmigration programme to self-censorship in semi-public (grey-cover) policy documents. When the government objected to a draft poverty assessment report in 1990, for example, the Bank simply changed the numbers (Pincus 1996, p.18 n. 21). In 1992, when Suharto disbanded the Dutch-led Intergovernmental Group on Indonesia in response to the Netherlands' position on the East Timor question, the Bank stepped in to lead the newly formed Consultative Group on Indonesia. Similarly, in 1997 the Bank's resident representative in Jakarta, Dennis de Tray, vehemently denied allegations that up to one-third of World Bank funds were being lost to corruption. Less than a year later it emerged that as he was making these comments an internal Bank memorandum was being prepared that not only substantiated the charges but also confirmed that the Bank possessed detailed information on how the money was being lost (Schwarz 1999, p. 316).

The economic and political uncertainties of the post-Suharto era have left both parties groping for new rules of engagement. Now free to discuss Indonesia's 'critically weak institutions' and the attendant problem of 'endemic corruption', the Bank has placed governance and institution-building at the top of the agenda (World Bank 1999c, p. 1). The new government of Abdurahman Wahid, meanwhile, has adopted a more nation-alistic, and at times openly hostile, stance towards the Bank and IMF in an attempt to distance itself ideologically from the Suharto regime (Shari and Cohn 2000). For now, however, the rhetoric on both sides is tempered by the immediate need to get on with the lending: Indonesia, once again eligible for IDA credits, obtained approvals for new credits worth $2.7 billion in the last fiscal year mostly in the form of quick-disbursing non-project loans.

Indonesia's agriculture portfolio

Indonesia's agricultural loan portfolio has broadly followed the Bank-wide trends reviewed in the previous section (Table 9.5). Irrigation was the logical point of departure for the Bank when it returned to Indonesia in the late 1960s: a 1967 Bank report indicated that 50–60 per cent of irrigation systems were in disrepair and were servicing only a small fraction of their respective command areas (Van der Eng 1996, p. 62). Over the three ensuing five-year plans, the Bank carried out nineteen separate irrigation rehabilitation and construction projects, centred mostly on Java but also contributing to a doubling of technically irrigated area in the outer islands.

Irrigation and drainage have remained the most important subsector through the 1990s, although recent loans have focused on improving management and efficiency of operations rather than new construction.[24] As in other regions, controversy arising from the negative environmental impact of dam construction and botched resettlement programmes has had a chilling effect on lending for new irrigation schemes. By far the most spec-tacular case in Indonesia was the mishandling of resettlement from the reservoir area of the Kedung Ombo dam in Central Java. During the course of the project, funded in part by a $156 million loan, villagers were subject to abuse at the hands of the military, forced to relocate to unsuitable and poorly serviced transmigration sites and denied claims to compensation. The Bank's performance stands as an extreme example of deficient supervision, bureaucratic capture and unresponsiveness to public pressure.[25]

The Bank's second major interest in Indonesian agriculture in the 1970s and 1980s was the government's transmigration programme. Transmigration sought to resettle poor people from the populous islands of Java and Bali to

Table 9.5 World Bank rural-sector projects in Indonesia, 1976–99 (constant 1982 US dollars, millions)

	Agricultural credit	Area development	Fertilisers	Irrigation and drainage	Perennial crops	Research and extension	Other	US $ M
1976–8	14	78	76	150	0	12	–	330
1979–81	–	80	–	116	142	59	–	396
1982–4	–	75	22	64	99	20	5	285
1985–7	43	55	–	117	42	22	18	296
1988–90	–	–	–	72	–	16	51	139
1991–3	63	4	61	110	24	9	–	270
1994–6	–	36	–	59	–	16	36	147
1997–9	–	9	–	75	–	–	2	86
Total	360	1,008	475	2,288	920	462	334	5,847

The figures are given as percentages below.

	Agricultural credit	Area development	Fertilisers	Irrigation and drainage	Perennial crops	Research and extension	Other	US $ M
1976–8	4.3	23.5	22.9	45.6	–	3.7	–	100.0
1979–81	–	20.1	–	29.2	35.9	14.8	–	100.0
1982–4	–	26.2	7.7	22.5	34.7	7.1	1.8	100.0
1985–7	14.4	18.4	–	39.5	14.1	7.5	6.1	100.0
1988–90	–	–	–	52.1	–	11.4	36.6	100.0
1991–3	23.3	1.6	22.5	40.6	8.8	3.2	–	100.0
1994–6	–	24.4	–	40.0	–	11.2	24.4	100.0
1997–9	–	10.9	–	87.1	–	–	2.0	100.0
Total	6.2	17.2	8.1	39.1	15.7	7.9	5.7	100.0

the outer islands of Sumatra, Kalimantan and Irian Jaya (West Papua). The Bank provided loans totalling about $500 million for transmigration up to 1985, and another $1 billion for related smallholder and nucleus estate projects. These area development and crop-specific projects (rubber, coconut, palm oil) shared the integrated rural development approach common to the period, and were plagued by the problems associated with these projects in other countries. Poor site selection, failure to deliver land and services to settlers, cost overruns and poor co-ordination between the agricultural, agro-processing and agricultural service components of the projects reduced their effectiveness and economic viability (World Bank 1986). Transmigration, nucleus estate and swamp reclamation projects almost without exception received unsatisfactory ratings from the OED.

Transmigration was also widely criticised by environmentalists for causing deforestation and destruction of coastal wetlands, charges with which the Bank now concurs (Rich 1994, p. 36).[26] However, transmigration was a high priority for the Suharto government, and despite repeated failures the Bank soldiered on. The focus shifted from the development of new reset-tlements to 'second-stage transmigration' aimed at improving the economic situation of thousands of previous transmigrants and encouraging more sustainable farming practices. In line with the Bank's new approach to agri-culture, these projects sought to decentralise design and implementation and to put greater emphasis on the ecological limits of development in fragile agro-ecosystems.[27] One such project, the 1994 Integrated Swamps Development Project, is reviewed briefly below.

Research and extension was the third investment priority in agriculture. The Bank promoted the T & V system through three free-standing national extension projects beginning in 1976 and supporting investments in the research system and secondary-level agricultural education. The system was also adopted by the area development and nucleus estate projects associated with the transmigration programme. The government accepted the T & V approach enthusiastically, largely because it fit neatly with the *Bimas* (mass guidance) rice intensification programmes already in place. *Bimas* provided farmers with subsidised credit packages consisting of cash, seeds, fertilisers and pesticides. Farmers, organised into groups, communicated with the extension service through 'contact farmers' who met regularly with exten-sion agents, who in turn received new information from subject matter specialists. Although *Bimas* was phased out in the 1980s due to high default rates, the programme had proved an effective means of rapidly dissemi-nating a uniform package of inputs. The centralised extension system was retained, and the number of field-level extension agents rose from 5,200 in 1975 to 36,500 in 1990 (Van der Eng 1996, p. 104).

As in other countries where it was adopted, T & V was too rigid and centralised to involve farmers in the processes of technology generation, testing and learning. Packaged technologies proved ineffective at helping farmers to manage diverse farming systems, and hence made little impact

Table 9.6 World Bank agriculture and rural-sector loans to Indonesia, 1990–9

Sector	Subsector	US $ M	Project title	FY
Agriculture	Forestry	20.0	Second forestry institutions and conservation project	1990
Agriculture	Agricultural credit	125.0	Second BRI/KUPEDES small credit project	1991
Agriculture	Area development	15.5	Yogyakarta upland area development project	1991
Industry	Fertilisers	221.7	Fertiliser restructuring project	1991
Small-scale enterprises	Irrigation and drainage	125.0	Provincial irrigated agricultural development project	1991
Agriculture	Agricultural credit	106.1	Agricultural financing project	1992
Agriculture	Irrigation and drainage	225.0	Irrigation subsector 11 (O. and M.) project	1992
Agriculture	Perennial crops	87.6	Tree crop smallholder development project	1992
Agriculture	Irrigation and drainage	54.0	Groundwater development project	1993
Agriculture	Research and extension	32.0	Integrated pest management training project	1993
Agriculture	Area development	65.0	Integrated swamps development project	1994
Agriculture	Irrigation and drainage	55.0	Dam safety project	1994
Agriculture	Irrigation and drainage	165.7	Java irrigation improvement and water resources management project	1994
Environment	Conservation	56.5	National watershed management and conservation project	1994
Agriculture	Land titling	80.0	Land administration project	1995
Agriculture	Research and extension	63.0	Second agricultural research management project	1995
Agriculture	Area development	19.1	Kerinci-Seblat integrated conservation and development project	1996
Agriculture	Area development	26.8	Sulawesi agricultural area development project	1996
Agriculture	Area development	27.0	Nusa Tenggara agricultural area development project	1996
Agriculture	Area development	16.3	Maluku regional development project	1998
Agriculture	Area development	20.5	Bengkulu regional development project	1998
Environment	Conservation	6.9	Coral reef rehabilitation and management project	1998
Agriculture	Irrigation and drainage	300.0	Water resources sector-adjustment loan	1999

outside of the main rice-growing areas. Even within the major 'rice bowls', command-style extension could not cope effectively with ecological, social and economic heterogeneity (Antholt 1991). Inadequate budgetary support and poor research-extension linkages also weakened the sustainability of the system in Indonesia. According to OED, 'imposing a uniform extension method in a country like Indonesia, with its wide range of production and socio-economic circumstances, was unlikely to be the most cost-effective use of public extension investments' (Purcell and Anderson 1997, p. 76).

By the late 1990s Indonesia's agricultural portfolio was in decline and in search of new direction. The showcase projects of the past three decades – irrigation development, transmigration and agricultural extension – could no longer provide a convincing rationale for continued lending. The latter half of the decade has seen the portfolio pulled in opposite directions: on the one hand towards large, non-project loans reminiscent of the SECALs of the 1980s (for example, in water management and the fertiliser industry), and on the other 'second-stage' area development projects. These changes reflect similar trends in the country-wide portfolio. With regards to the second group of projects, the challenges facing the Bank are to demonstrate that it possesses the operational capacity to implement community-based, decentralised rural development projects, and to convince the government that these projects represent a productive use of loan funds. The two examples discussed below suggest that the Bank still has some way to go to reach these objectives.

Two examples

Integrated Pest Management Training Project

It would be difficult to imagine a project that is more in harmony with the rhetoric of the Wolfensohn Bank than the Integrated Pest Management Training Project (IPMTP). The original idea is simple: indiscriminate use of broad-spectrum insecticides disrupts the ecological balance of flooded rice fields, increasing the risk of pest infestation. Farmers were introduced to chemical pesticides through *Bimas* packages that encouraged them to use the same inputs on every field and in every season regardless of local conditions. Over time the mismatch between input use and local farming conditions proved to be destabilising. Farmers needed to learn how to apply the basic principles of agro-ecology in order to tailor their cultivation practices to the specific conditions in their own fields.

The elimination of pesticide subsidies in the late 1980s set the stage for the large-scale IPM training. After a failed attempt to deliver IPM training through the existing T & V system, the government experimented with a new approach under a USAID-funded grant project implemented by the national planning board (BAPPENAS) with technical assistance provided by the Food and Agriculture Organisation (FAO). The planning agency was chosen as lead agency because of fears that the close links between the chemical companies and the agriculture ministry would scupper the project (Hammig 1998, p. 6). Under the new approach, training was conducted on the basis of season-long 'farmer field schools' consisting of twenty-five to thirty farmers working with an experienced trainer-cum-organiser. Each week during the season, the farmers conduct 'agro-ecosystem analysis' of two fields: one cultivated using the standard package system and another based on agro-ecological principles. Field schools were intended not only as a means of training farmers, but also as an organising tool to help revive the largely moribund farmer groups established under the T & V system. This 'learning by doing' approach proved to be exceptionally successful: from 1989 to 1992 about 200,000 rice farmers attended season-long IPM field schools, and an estimated 30,000 farmers learned IPM through informal field schools set up by trained farmers on their own initiative and using their own resources (Hammig 1998, p. 10). A 1991 survey indicated that these farmers had reduced insecticide use substantially and there was some indication of positive yield effects (World Bank 1993b, p. 4).

IPM fits neatly with the Bank's new priorities for the agriculture sector as expressed in *Vision to Action*. The main objective is to increase productivity and promote environmental sustainability through the dissemination of knowledge; it aims to build local institutional capacity and a vehicle for enhanced local participation; and it called for a radical decentralisation of agricultural decision making from the extension system to farmers. IPMTP, appraised in 1993, was designed to expand the existing project to reach 880,000 farmers over a five-year period. The Bank provided a loan of $32 million to be supplemented by $14 million in government financing and a grant from USAID of $7 million to cover the costs of technical assistance.

Operational imperatives were in evidence from the earliest days of project implementation. Although the project design called for BAPPENAS to maintain administrative control, it quickly became apparent that the key players in the agency had been reshuffled following the 1993 elections, and the new team in BAPPENAS was not committed to the project design. After a lengthy period of bureaucratic skirmishing, the project was transferred to a special project management team in the office of the secretary general of the ministry of agriculture (Hammig 1998, p. 12). This was a risky move, not only because of the continuing links between the agriculture ministry and the chemical companies but also because resentment within BAPPENAS threatened to deprive the project of government budgetary allocations. Government funding had indeed emerged as a major problem by the time of the mid-term review in October 1995: during the first two years of implementation, actual expenditures were only one-third of the levels envisaged in the project design, and the government allocation for the third year was set at two-thirds of the target (World Bank 1995, p. 16).[28] Despite a project extension and increased allocations in subsequent years, the government was forced to cancel $6 million of the original loan.[29]

Project management in the agriculture ministry remained 'weak and ineffective' according to periodic World Bank supervision missions (World Bank 1997, p. 8). The planning and budgeting processes, originally envisioned as decentralised and farmer-responsive, remained opaque and tightly controlled by the centre. An important indicator of the government's lack of commitment to the project was the ministry's repeated refusal to comply with provisions in the loan agreement calling for project activities to be included in the official job descriptions of IPM trainers (World Bank 1997, p. 2).

Another reason for the slow pace of disbursements was the cumbersome process through which Bank loan funds were delivered to field activities. Funds were delivered through the central finance ministry through provincial and district finance offices and then to district-level agricultural service agencies before finally reaching field staff. In view of the vast number of small expenditures involved in training (plastic sheeting, pens, paper, transport costs) the system amounted to, in the words of one member of the technical assistance team, 'trying to buy lunch with a home mortgage'.[30] Not surprisingly, disbursements arrived after the season had already begun, and field operators received only a fraction of the budgeted sums. This had a negative impact on training quality (Braun 1997). Disbursements had not been a problem during the initial USAID project owing to the greater flexibility possible using grant funds. Throughout the course of IPMTP, control over budgets tended to drift upwards within the bureaucracy, and successive Bank supervision missions failed to put corrective measures in place (Hammig 1998, p. 14).

Nevertheless, enthusiasm for IPM at the local level remained high. An independent review of the project documented numerous cases in which village heads and farmers' groups funded their own field schools or follow-up activities. Farmer-trainers assumed a progressively larger role, and the evidence suggests that the quality of farmer-led activities is equal to that of government trainers (Braun 1997).

From the Bank's perspective, the experience of IPMTP was mixed. The institution demonstrated its eagerness to fund an innovative, decentralised training project that amounted to a reversal of the previously dominant T & V strategy. In terms of implementation, however, the Bank was constrained by two important factors. First, the project highlighted the problems associated with using loan funds to finance community-based activities. The Bank and the government's disbursement mechanisms did not allow for local control over planning and failed to deliver resources in sufficient amounts or in a timely manner. Second, the Bank's supervision mechanisms proved inadequate to the task of monitoring a project consisting of tens of thousands of individual activities implemented by hundreds of local authorities. The Bank carried out nine supervision missions by Washington-based staff over a six-year period, for which it awarded itself a 'highly satisfactory' rating (World Bank 2000). However, as noted in the Wapenhans report, arms-length missions of this sort are ineffective in the face of persistent non-compliance with the loan covenants and the project design (Wapenhans *et al.* 1992, p. 20). Despite these problems, the Bank was eager to persevere with plans for similar projects, notably a second integrated pest management project and a decentralised agricultural and forestry project borrowing the farmer field school approach (World Bank 1999c).

Integrated Swamps Development Project

Coastal swamps are fragile ecosystems that can support limited agricultural production given judicious selection of sites and crop mix, careful management of soils and water, and protection of surrounding ecosystems such as forests, estuaries and mangroves. Close attention to water supply and drainage are required to prevent the build-up of soil toxicity. Swamp development is also limited by social and economic factors such as distance to markets, labour availability and farmers' understanding of swamp ecology.

The Integrated Swamps Development Project (ISDP) is an example of the Bank's efforts to rejuvenate traditional area development projects through decentralisation of design and implementation. It will be recalled that area development projects came to the fore during the McNamara years, and in Indonesia these projects were closely associated with the government's transmigration programme. The Bank supported two swamp reclamation projects in the 1980s with loans totalling $87 million.[31] The objective of the projects was to develop swamp lands for the settlement of 14,000 transmigrant families in Sumatra. Both fell short of their goals as set out in the appraisal documents. Swamps I eventually received an unsatisfactory rating from OED, while Swamps II was substantially reprogrammed, with responsibility for implementation transferred from the transmigration ministry to the South Sumatra planning agency (World Bank 1994, p. 7). Poor site selection, labour shortages, absence of support services and pest infestations combined to reduce the estimated economic rates of return of the projects to 6 and 2 per cent, respectively (World Bank 1994, p. 8). By 1992 the Bank was urging the government to cease further expansion on swamps (World Bank 1992, p. 115).

The aim of ISDP, approved in 1994, is to upgrade drainage, flood control and transportation infrastructure, and to provide a range of services including agricultural extension and clean drinking water in an area of 78,000 hectares in Sumatra and Kalimantan. The project is a 'second-stage' area development designed to improve the living standards of previous transmigrants and to learn from the mistakes of the earlier swamps projects. As such it includes a strong community development component, including the strengthening of farmer groups, participatory extension and collaboration with local NGOs on environmental monitoring. Credits provided to farmers to cover one season of inputs were to be repaid into revolving funds controlled by farmer groups.

Beginning in May 1997, the Indonesian NGO Yayasan Duta Awam (YDA) conducted an independent monitoring exercise of project activities in West Kalimantan and Riau province, Sumatra. The evaluation, conducted over a fifteen-month period, was originally intended as part of a broader assessment of pesticide use in agricultural development schemes.[32] YDA discovered that input packages promoted by the project included highly toxic (WHO category IA and IB) pesticides in contravention of World Bank and government guidelines. Use of pesticides, and the incidence of pesticide poisoning, increased in the fifteen villages surveyed. The evaluation also found evidence of the kinds of systematic corruption that had plagued earlier area development projects. Drainage works were improperly sited and poorly constructed, resulting in flooding of fields and villages. Project officials levied unofficial 'fees' on project participants, and farmers were asked to sign blank receipts for inputs that never arrived. The delivery of promised credits was irregular and interest charges were not fully explained to participants.

YDA also noted an absence of consultation mechanisms to involve farmers in project implementation. 'At present', they write, ' "farmers' participation" consists of ISDP paying farmers to clean canals of weeds rather than engaging them in the design, implementation and evaluation of project goals in accord with community goals' (Pesticide Action Network 1999). Subsequent consultation missions carried out by the project met with village headmen but did not involve project participants.

The resident mission in Jakarta responded promptly to these charges by proposing a fact-finding survey with university and NGO input to investigate the situation in the field. The Bank also assured YDA that farmer groups would be involved in the reprogramming of activities and the design of a follow-up project. Some of the defective drainage works were repaired, and some farmers received compensation for irregular fees that they had paid for project services. However, the fact-finding survey was postponed for nearly a year, and ultimately the Bank declined to take part in the mission. The Bank did not respond to YDA requests for the release of the project's financial audits and the creation of an independent body to receive complaints from farmers. Moreover, no action was taken on the pesticide issue, despite the project's clear contravention of the Bank's own operational guidelines.

The immediate problems associated with the implementation of ISDP are unfortunately common in Indonesia, and suggest that the government is not fully committed to community-based, 'second-stage' area development projects. The experience of ISDP also has broader implications for the Bank. As YDA concludes:

> So the obvious question arises: even when field-based participatory monitoring is carried out – by project beneficiaries themselves, with training and guidance from a local NGO, and at no cost to the Bank or

government, and when recommendations are hand-delivered from the field and presented in the capital as well as to the project task manager and other Bank officials, with a commitment from the local people to assist the Bank in correcting its mistakes – why is the Bank still unable to implement mid-course corrections in a timely fashion?

(Pesticide Action Network, 1999)

This demonstrated lack of responsiveness to public pressure is, to say the least, at odds with the Bank's pronouncements on participation, governance and local empowerment. The evidence from both projects reviewed here suggests that task managers still instinctively ally themselves with their clients in the government, and find it difficult to respond to demands for greater openness and accountability. Damage control is the preferred course of action. This behaviour is understandable given the operational imperatives discussed in this chapter, yet it calls into question the Bank's capacity to operate as a development agency rather than a public-sector bank.

Conclusions

The Bank is the world's leading development institution in terms of size, money and policy influence. But strength carries with it costs as well as benefits. The Bank has been constantly buffeted by a wide range of interests and agendas emanating from donors, borrowers, non-government advocacy groups and the private sector. Left- and right-wing populists have found in the Bank an attractive target, often for what the institution symbolises rather than what it actually does.

In response, the Wolfensohn Bank has launched a rhetorical offensive aimed at satisfying all of these competing demands. To its core objectives of poverty reduction and economic growth, the Bank has added governance, participation, decentralisation, gender, knowledge and environmental sustainability. That these are worthy goals is not seriously questioned; rather, the problem facing the Bank is whether the institution has the capacity to deliver on all or even some of them. Although goal proliferation is not a new phenomenon at the Bank, the institution has in recent years shown less self-restraint than in the past when it comes to adding new items to its agenda (Kapur *et al.* 1997, p. 1,216). This approach may succeed in quieting critics for a time, but it also has the effect of lengthening the list of success criteria that the Bank must ultimately meet if it is to retain its special status among the multilateral development institutions.

The Bank's ability to meet this challenge will depend on the extent to which it is able to close the gap between its rhetoric and the reality of lending operations. This is most apparent in agriculture, a sector that has traditionally performed poorly in operational terms but remains vital to the central objectives of poverty alleviation and economic growth. This chapter has shown that the Bank's current rhetorical preoccupation with decentralisation, participation and environmentalism has thrust it into operational domains that are out of step with its managerial capacity and comparative advantage as a lending agency. In short, the Bank increasingly thinks like an NGO but still acts like a public-sector bank. The result of this mismatch is a widening gulf between the institution's ambitions and what it can achieve on the ground.

Correcting this imbalance will require change on both the rhetorical and operational fronts. As a first step in this direction, the Bank must take greater cognisance of its own institutional capacity when formulating economic policy and sectoral strategies. This amounts to more than a shift from *ex ante* to *ex post* conditionality as favoured in the Bank's most recent work on aid effectiveness (World Bank 1998b). The principle of selectivity should apply not only to the worthiness of borrowers, but also to the competence of the Bank to provide analysis and advice in the various fields subsumed under the broad heading of development.

On the operations side, the Bank needs to come to grips with the persistent problems of pressure to lend, centralisation and institutional capture that have stood in the way of efforts to improve project performance. Curiously, despite its professed concern for governance and institution building, the Bank has vigorously resisted attempts to apply institutional analysis to its own operations divisions. However, as long as these perverse incentive structures remain in place, task managers will continue to emphasise quantity over quality, to paper over weaknesses in existing projects and to identify their interests with their clients in borrowing countries. Redressing these problems may in the end result in a smaller Bank, but one with a more focused and hence more durable mission.

Notes

1   In the words of Robert Cavanaugh, the Bank's chief fund-raiser for 1947–59:

> [I]f we go into the social field ... then the bond market would definitely feel that we were not acting prudently from a financial standpoint .... If you start financing schools and hospitals and water works, and so forth, these things don't normally and directly increase the ability of a country to repay a borrowing.
>
> (Kapur *et al.* 1997, pp. 119–20)

2   According to the IBRD *Articles of Agreement*:

> When the member in whose territories the project is located is not itself the borrower, the member or the central bank or some comparable agency of the member which is acceptable to the Bank, fully guarantees the repayment of the principal and the payment of interest and other charges on the loan.

> This provision does not apply to the International Finance Corporation, the Bank's private-sector investment division.

3 The Meltzer Commission report argues that if private lenders were given similar guarantees they would be indifferent to the use of loan proceeds and would therefore be willing to finance social-sector projects. The report therefore questions the need for a public-sector institution to perform this function (Meltzer *et al.* 2000, p. 82).

4 With, inevitably, its own website (http://www.worldbank.org/participation).

5 Catherine Caufield provides the following anecdote as an example of OED's lack of influence on operations: 'Due to a production error, one-third of the paragraphs in a 1990 OED report on a $40 million agricultural project in Indonesia ended in mid-sentence. Two years later no one outside the OED had asked for the full text' (Caufield 1996, p. 255).

6 This is particularly apparent with regards to environmental impact assessments (EIAs). According to the Environmental Defence Fund, out of 158 agricultural projects during the years 1990–5 only five were assessed on the basis of full EIAs (Kleiner 1996).

7 Such a schematic approach of course runs the risk of oversimplifying the Bank's position. There are plenty of examples in each period of intense disagreements over theory and policy within the Bank's management and among the executive directors. As we shall see, the preoccupations of researchers and technical specialists are often at odds with the day-to-day concerns of operations staff charged with responsibility for putting their ideas into practice. The erratic and sometimes contradictory political demands of the US Treasury and Congress, in addition to competing pressures from other major shareholders, have also hindered management's efforts to articulate a coherent strategic vision (Gwin 1997). Nevertheless, the Bank is and has always been a highly centralised institution and it is probably fair to speak of dominant trends or paradigms in the Bank's approach to rural development issues.

8 The Bank's earliest statements on development emphasise raising agricultural productivity (see IBRD 1948). On the views of development economists of the period, see Lewis 1984, p. 128.

9 In a sense the early Bank pursued a policy of *ex ante* conditionality that would return to favour in the late 1990s World Bank 1998b).

10 The Bank's first education loan was made in 1962 but activity in this sector accelerated rapidly during Woods' term.

11 Bank/IDA combined lending for agriculture was US$600 million FY1964–8, $1,906 million for FY 1969–73 and $4,814 million FY 1974–8. All figures are in current dollars calculated from annual reports and exclude non-agricultural rural development projects.

12 Constant 1982 US dollars. The share of agriculture in the total portfolio increased from 18 to 30 per cent from 1970 to 1981.

13 Kapur, Lewis and Webb conclude: 'Each was relevant to poverty, but none met the Bank's need for 'bankable' projects – large-scale, foreign-exchange, mostly hard terms loans that would be acceptable to borrowers and attractive to the Bank's principal shareholders' (Kapur *et al.* 1997, p. 247).

14 He goes on to assert that 'it is, of course, output per hectare which is the relevant measure of agricultural productivity in land-scarce, labour-surplus economies; not output per worker' (McNamara 1981, p. 247). This is a logical *non sequitur* given the inescapable link between low levels of labour productivity and low wages and/or returns to family labour.

15 Irrigation and area development projects accounted for 73 per cent of all rural-development lending for the period FY 1974–86 (World Bank 1988, p. 4).

16 The Bank's own Operations Evaluation Department concluded that:

> [F]rom the point of view of Bank managers, at a time when the Bank's lending was expanding rapidly, area development projects were an effective vehicle for committing funds. As a result, Bank project staff recall feeling that they were under pressure to produce bigger and broader projects
>
> (World Bank 1988, p. 22)

17 Albert Hirschman, for one, reached this conclusion long before the idea of IRDPs became official policy:

> The comprehensive program whose many components are given equal emphasis and are pronounced to be interrelated in effect covers up the ignorance of the experts about the real cure of the malady they have been summoned to examine; if they knew, they would be proposing a far more sharply focused program
>
> (Hirschman 1995, p. 23)

18 Robert Ayres noted in 1983 that the ideological and operational differences between McNamara and Clausen were less pronounced than their rhetoric would suggest: 'While McNamara's Bank had for some a "leftist" image which obscured the real nature of its operations, Clausen's Bank has acquired for others a "rightist" image which likewise obscures what the Bank is really doing' (Ayres 1983, p. 238).

19 This conclusion was recognised in the Bank's review of AGSECALs: 'Supply response, the change in production due to such adjustment, is the acid test of the theory' (Meerman 1997, 31).

20 The successful project was the 1986 Kenyan Agricultural Adjustment Loan.

21 The relationship between output prices and supply response is greatly complicated by factors on both the supply and demand side, including labour constraints, limited access to industrial inputs and incentive goods, shortages of working capital, the continued need for public investment and the weakness of domestic food markets owing to deflationary policies associated with stabilisation and structural-adjustment programmes (see, for example, Moseley *et al.* 1995, Sender and Smith 1990, Berthelmy and Morrison 1987).

22

> Promoting local and community development is one of the most important activities in which the Bank is engaged. Experience has shown that projects are much more likely to reflect people's priorities, reach their goals, and be sustainable when they are designed and executed with a high degree of influence from beneficiaries. Local and community-driven development therefore addresses the failed approaches of the past, which were too centralized and statist to effectively reach poor rural communities.
>
> (McCalla and Ayres 1997, p. 82)

23 This is a general problem for post-Washington consensus writers. Power is discussed in terms of the relationships between central and local government and between local government and 'civil society' (World Bank 2000, p. 122). Civil society itself is treated as an undifferentiated mass, omitting reference to power relations not directly involving government institutions. This is most apparent in the reports produced by the Poverty Group's 'Consultations with the Poor', which reduce 'powerlessness' to the effects of arbitrary or corrupt bureaucracies (see Narayan *et al.* 1999). This fits in neatly with the Bank's agenda of government retrenchment and decentralisation, but fails to address

the real issues of poverty and exploitation (see Ben Fine's chapter on social capital in this volume).

24 Indonesia embarked on its first agricultural-sector loan with a $300 million water resources adjustment project signed in 1999.

25 According to OED's review of events, the task manager disregarded the warnings of the Bank's internal sociology adviser that the resettlement plans were deficient, paid no attention to the processing of compensation and organisation of the transmigration sites and ignored the intervention of the Jakarta-based Legal Aid Foundation (LBH) in 1987. The Bank then compounded the problem by denying the charge of negligence and attempting to shift the blame to the government. The report goes on to say:

> When LBH provided the Bank a copy of its chronology of abuse in September 1987, the task manager considered the informal transmission irregular and did not warrant a response. Even after the Bank's first resettlement expert visited the site in May 1988 (no Bank resettlement expert visited the site during preparation or appraisal), the resident mission was uncomfortable with his observations and felt his report was emotional and exaggerated. In fact, the headquarters division responsible for the project as well as the resident mission were uncomfortable even that his mission had been planned – by AGR [Agriculture and Rural Development Department] and outside the regular supervision routine.
>
> (World Bank 1998c, p. 28)

26 The 1999 draft country assistance review laments the Bank's role in the transmigration programme and the inattention paid to environmental concerns:

> Even though seven Bank loans eventually materialised in support of transmigration, the Bank's financial contribution to the programme was relatively minor, yet its catalytic role in revitalising the program was substantial. Unfortunately, environmental impact concerns were not on the agenda at that time.
>
> (World Bank 1999c, 20)

27 See Table 9.6 for a list of area development projects approved in the 1990s.
28 The author was a member of the mid-term review team.
29 Curiously, the Bank's final evaluation report applauds the government for 'the high priority in its funding in spite of severe budget constraints' (World Bank 2000, p. 8). In fact, funding levels increased after the onset of the financial crisis, and were lowest during the period 1993 to 1997.
30 Field interview, October 1995.
31 Swamps Reclamation Projects I and II, approved in 1981 and 1984, respectively.
32 The exercise was carried out in collaboration with Pesticide Action Network, North America, with financial support from the Rockefeller Brother Fund.

References

Antholt, C.H. (1991) 'Agriculture extension in the 21st century: Lessons from South Asia', in Rivera, W. and D. Gustafsen (eds) *Agriculture Extension: Worldwide International Evolution and Forces for Change*, New York: Elsevier.

Ayres, Robert (1983) *Banking on the Poor: The World Bank and World Poverty*, London: MIT Press.

Berthelmy, J.C. and C. Morrison (1987) 'Manufactured goods supply and cash crops in sub-Saharan Africa', *World Development* 15(10).

Braun, Ann R. (1997) 'An analysis of quality in the Indonesian Integrated Pest Management Training Project: Report of a technical audit conducted for the World Bank', Jakarta, Integrated Pest Management Training Project, mimeo.

Cassen (1985) *Does Aid Work?* Oxford: Clarendon Press.

Caufield, Catherine (1996) *Masters of Illusion: The World Bank and the Poverty of Nations*, London: Pan Books.

Chenery, H.B. *et al.* (1974) *Redistribution With Growth*, Oxford: Oxford University Press for the World Bank.

Covey, Jane G. (1998) 'Is critical co-operation possible? Influencing the World Bank through operational collaboration and policy dialogue', in Fox, Jonathan and L. David Brown (eds) *The Struggle for Accountability: The World Bank, NGOs and Grassroots Movements*, London: MIT Press, pp. 81–120.

Donaldson, Graham (1991) 'Government sponsored rural development: Experience of the World Bank', in C. Peter Timmer (ed.) *Agriculture and the State*, London: Cornell University Press.

Gavin, Michael and Dani Rodrik (1995) 'The World Bank in historical perspective', *American Economic Review* 85(2), Papers and Proceedings of the Hundredth and Seventh annual Meeting of the American Economics Association, May: 329–34.

Gilbert, Christopher, Andrew Powell and David Vines (1999) 'Positioning the World Bank', *Economic Journal* 109, November: 598–633.

Gwin, Catherine (1997) 'US relations with the World Bank, 1945–1992, in Kapur, Devesh, John P. Lewis and Richard Webb (eds) *The World Bank: Its First Half Century*, Washington, DC: Brookings Institution Press, pp. 195–274.

Hammig, Michael (1998) 'USAID and Integrated Pest Management in Indonesia: The Investments and the Payoffs', Jakarta, US Agency for International Development, June, mimeo.

Hirschman, A.O. (1995) *Development Projects Observed*, Washington, DC: The Brookings Institution (reissued, originally published in 1967).

International Bank for Reconstruction and Development (1948) *Annual Report 1947–1948*, Washington, DC.

Kapur, Devesh, John P. Lewis and Richard Webb (1997) *The World Bank: Its First Half Century, Volume 1, History*, Washington, DC: Brookings Institution Press.

Killick, Tony (1998) *Aid and the Political Economy of Policy Change*, London: Routledge.

Kleiner, Mimi (1996) 'What the World Bank knows best: Its agricultural lending fails to help the poor or safeguard the environment', Washington, DC, Environmental Defense Fund, October 22, mimeo.

Kraske, Jochen with William H. Becker, William Diamond and Louis Galambos (1996) *Bankers with a Mission: The Presidents of the World Bank, 1946–1991*, Oxford: Oxford University Press for the World Bank.

Krueger, Anne O., Maurice Schiff and Alberto Valdes (eds) (1991) *The Political Economy of Agricultural Pricing Policy*, London: Johns Hopkins University Press.

Lewis, W. Arthur (1984) 'Development economics in the 1950s', in Meier, Gerald M. and Dudley Seers (eds) *Pioneers in Development*, Oxford: Oxford University Press for the World Bank, pp. 121–37.

Mason, E.S. and R.E. Asher (1973) *The World Bank since Bretton Woods*, Washington, DC: Brookings Institution Press.

McCalla, Alex F. and Wendy S. Ayres (1997) *Rural Development: From Vision to Action*, Washington, DC: World Bank.

McNamara, Robert S. (1981) *The McNamara Years at the World Bank: Major Policy Addresses of Robert S. McNamara, 1968–1981*, London: Johns Hopkins University Press for the World Bank.

Meerman, Jacob (1997) *Reforming Agriculture: The World Bank Goes to Market*, Washington, DC: World Bank, Operations Evaluation Department.

Meltzer, Allan H. *et al.* (2000) *Report of the International Financial Institution Advisory Commission*, March, http://phantom-x.gsia.cmu.edu/IFIAC.

Mosely, Paul, Jane Harrigan and John Toye (1995) *Aid and Power: The World Bank and Policy-Based Lending*, London: Routledge.

Mosely, Paul, Turan Subasat and John Weeks (1995) 'Assessing adjustment in Africa', *World Development* 23(9): 1459–73.

Narayan, Deepa, Robert Chambers, Meera Shah and Patti Petesch (1999) 'Global synthesis: Consultations with the poor', Washington, DC, Poverty Group, World Bank, September 20, mimeo.

OED (annual) *Annual Review of Evaluation Results*, Washington, DC.: World Bank.

Pesticide Action Network (1999) 'Indonesian farmer call for World Bank reform', *PANUPS*, May 17 (http://www.panna.org/resources/panups.html).

Pincus, Jonathan (1996) *Class Power and Agrarian Change*, London: Macmillan.

Purcell, Dennis L. and Jock R. Anderson (1997) *Agricultural Extension and Research: Achievements and Problems in National Systems*, Washington, DC: Operations Evaluation Department, June 1.

Ranis, Gustav (1997) 'The World Bank near the turn of the century', in Culpeper, Roy, Albert Berry and Frances Stewart (eds) *Global Development Fifty Years After Bretton Woods: Essays in Honour of Gerald K. Helleiner*, London: Macmillan in association with North–South Institute, pp. 72–89.

Rich, Bruce (1994) *Mortgaging the Earth: The World Bank, Environmental Impoverishment and the Crisis of Development*, Boston: Beacon Books.

Schiff, Maurice and Alberto Valdes (1992) *The Political Economy of Agricultural Pricing Policy: Volume 4, A Synthesis of the Economics in Developing Countries*, London: Johns Hopkins University Press for the World Bank.

Schwarz, Adam (1999) *A Nation in Waiting: Indonesia's Search for Stability*, London: Allen & Unwin.

Sender, John and Sheila Smith (1990) *Poverty, Class and Gender in Rural Africa: A Tanzanian Case Study*, London: Routledge.

Shari, Michael and Laura Cohn (2000) 'The World Bank: Time to scale back in Indonesia?', *Business Week*, April 17.

Stern, Nicholas (1997) 'The World Bank as "intellectual actor" ', in Kapur, Devesh, John P. Lewis and Richard Webb (eds) *The World Bank: Its First Half Century, Volume 2, Perspectives*, Washington, DC: Brookings Institution Press, pp. 523–610 (with Francisco Ferreira).

Stiglitz, Joseph (1999) 'The World Bank at the millennium', *Economic Journal* 109, November: 577–97.

Van der Eng, Pierre (1996) *Agricultural Growth in Indonesia: Productivity Change and Policy Impact Since 1880*, London: Macmillan.

Wapenhans, W.A. *et al.* (1992) *Report of the Portfolio Management Task Force*, Washington, DC: World Bank, July 1, mimeo.

Winters, Jeffrey A. (1997) 'Down with the World Bank', *Far Eastern Economic Review*, February 13: 29.

Wolfensohn, James D. (1999) 'A proposal for a comprehensive development framework: A discussion draft', Washington, DC: World Bank, January 21, mimeo.

Woods, George (1964) 'Report of the president to the executive directors on proposed Bank/IDA policies in the field of agriculture', Washington, DC: World Bank, January 17.

World Bank (1972) *World Bank Operations: Sectoral Programs and Policies*, London: Johns Hopkins University Press for the World Bank.

—— (1974) *Redistribution with Growth*, Oxford: Oxford University Press for the World Bank.

—— (1981) *Accelerated Development in Sub-Saharan Africa: An Agenda for Action*, Washington, DC.: World Bank.

—— (1986) 'Indonesia: Tree crops sector review', Washington, DC, mimeo.

—— (1988) *Rural Development: World Bank Experience 1965–1986*, Washington, DC, World Bank, Operations Evaluation Department.

—— (1992) *Indonesia: Agricultural Transformation, Challenges and Opportunities*, Washington, DC, World Bank, September 1.

—— (1993a) *A Review of Bank Lending for Agricultural Credit and Rural Finance*, Washington, DC: Operations Evaluation Department, June 29.

—— (1993b) *Staff Appraisal Report: Indonesia, Integrated Pest Management Training Project*, Washington, DC: World Bank, March 5.

—— (1994) *Staff Appraisal Report, Indonesia, Integrated Swamps Development Project*, Washington, DC, World Bank, May 17.

—— (1995) 'Indonesia: Integrated Pest Management Training Project, mid-term review mission, aide memoire', Washington, DC: World Bank, Agriculture Operations Division, East Asia Pacific Region, December 6, mimeo.

—— (1996) *Indonesia in Perspective: A Country Briefing*, Washington, DC: World Bank, Indonesia Discussion Paper Series, Number 5.

—— (1997) 'Indonesia, Integrated Pest Management Training Project, sixth supervision mission, aide memoire', Jakarta: World Bank, Portfolio Management and Implementation Unit, April 2.

—— (1998a) *World Development Report: Knowledge for Development*, Oxford: Oxford University Press for the World Bank.

—— (1998b) *Assessing Aid: What Works, What Doesn't and Why*, Oxford: Oxford University Press for the World Bank.

—— (1998c) *Recent Experience With Involuntary Resettlement: Indonesia – Kedung Ombo*, Washington, DC: Operations Evaluation Department, June 2.

—— (1999a) *The World Bank Annual Report 1999*, Washington, DC: World Bank.

—— (1999b) *Indonesia: Country Assistance Review*, Washington, DC: World Bank, January 6, mimeo.

—— (1999c) *Indonesia: Country Assistance Strategy*, Washington, DC: World Bank, February 16.

—— (2000) 'Indonesia, Integrated Pest Management Training Project, implementation completion report', Washington, DC: World Bank, East Asia and Pacific Region, January 24.

Index